Understanding Latino Delinquency

A book in the series:

Criminal Justice Recent Scholarship
Edited by Marilyn McShane and Frank P. Williams III

Understanding Latino Delinquency

Cynthia Perez McCluskey

LFB Scholarly Publishing LLC
New York

First published 2002 by LFB Scholarly Publishing LLC.
First printing in paperback, 2003.
All rights reserved.

Library of Congress Cataloging-in-Publication Data

McCluskey, Cynthia Perez.
  Understanding latino delinquency : the applicability of strain
theory by ethnicity / Cynthia Perez McCluskey.
      p. cm. -- (Criminal justice recent scholarship)
  Includes bibliographical references and index.
  ISBN 1-931202-21-4 (alk. paper)
  1. Juvenile delinquency--Research--United States. 2. Juvenile
delinquency--United States--Cross-cultural studies. 3. Hispanic
Americans--Ethnic identity. 4. Hispanic Americans--Social
conditions. I. Title. II. Series.
  HV9104 .M328 2001
  364.36'089'68073--dc21

2001004865

ISBN 1-931202-21-4 (casebound)
ISBN 1-59332-003-5 (paperback)

Printed on acid-free 250-year-life paper.
Manufactured in the United States of America.

Table of Contents

Acknowledgments

This work would not have been possible without the generosity of the Rochester Youth Development Study and the Denver Youth Survey. I am especially grateful for the guidance and support provided by Terry Thornberry and David Huizinga throughout this project.

I would also like to express my gratitude to Donald and Rachel Perez who emphasized the value of learning since I can remember, and continually demonstrate the importance of family.

This book is dedicated to my husband, John McCluskey, and my daughter, Liliana, who have taken me on a different journey altogether.

CHAPTER 1
Introduction

In criminology and other fields concerned with the study of human behavior, there are varying schools of thought on the generality of theoretical models. On one hand, there are those who believe that theories of behavior apply universally. For example, learning theory focuses primarily on the situational aspects of behavior and is thought to apply universally, since all individuals are influenced in the same way by their environment. At the other end of the spectrum are those who believe that theoretical perspectives are historically and culturally specific. For example, in the study of Mexican Americans in the United States, Chicano social scientists often argue that researchers should move beyond traditional theories to explain Latino delinquency, because those theories fail to consider the Chicano perspective, and were originally generated for White, European males (Blea, 1988; Mirandé, 1987).

The purpose of the current investigation is to explore the middle ground between these extremes to determine whether one general theory of antisocial behavior, traditional strain theory, is universal in its application to ethnic groups, or whether culturally specific models of behavior can inform a theory that has been offered and accepted as a general explanation of deviant behavior. Utilizing multi-ethnic samples from the Denver Youth Survey and the Rochester Youth Development Study, this study will determine whether the traditional strain theory perspective as proposed by Merton (1938) and elaborated by Cloward and Ohlin (1960), applies to Latinos in the same way it does to other ethnic groups.

This investigation follows a recent line of inquiry in criminology which has attempted to incorporate race and ethnicity into theoretical

1

models. Typically, criminologists include dichotomous 'race' variables in models, which allows them to see whether membership in a particular group can make a difference in predicting outcomes. But understanding *how* membership in certain racial or ethnic groups affects behavior may provide even greater insight. There may be interaction effects between ethnicity and other factors traditionally associated with crime (peers and family, for example) that have not yet been explored. This study addresses this possibility by examining the influence of ethnicity within strain theory.

CRIMINOLOGY AND ETHNICITY
While traditional theories of crime have largely been accepted as general explanations of human behavior, criminologists have been exploring the idea that "race matters," as Cornel West (1994) and others have suggested.[1] Theorists examine differences of gender, race and social class to explain deviant behavior across groups. If one accepts the contention that race impacts behavior and others' perception of that behavior, then one is also likely to give credence to the idea that *ethnicity* is an important consideration in examining inter-group differences. Therefore, this investigation explores the ways in which ethnicity impacts traditional theories of crime, with a primary focus on the application of strain theory to Latino adolescents, a population that has been typically neglected in criminological research.

Although some studies of crime and delinquency include race, the variable is often dichotomized into White and non-White categories. Latinos are not always recognized as a distinctive group, especially in the field of criminology (Flowers, 1988). Given the variation in skin color, some Latinos are categorized as White and others Black; as a result members of this ethnic group have been disjoined. The impact of ethnicity on criminal behavior cannot be fully explored as long as Latinos are divided according to skin color. While shades of coloring may differ, Latinos have cultural ties that bind them together as a unique ethnic group, and as such, they require independent examination. An additional consequence of dichotomizing Latinos is that differences between African American youth and their White counterparts may be obfuscated as long as Latinos are considered part of both racial groups (Flowers, 1988). Other times individuals of Latino origin are categorized strictly as non-White, as some consider Latino involvement in crime to mirror that of

African Americans, and therefore, does not require separate attention (Flowers, 1988; Romero & Stelzner, 1985).

Rather than focusing on broad differences by race, it may be important to take into account the potential impact of group history and culture on relationships within a theoretical model. A group's shared experience might influence certain relationships and could contribute directly or indirectly to criminal behavior. As Flowers suggests, "we must consider the associative significance of historical mistreatment of minorities and their criminality and victimization today" (1988:3). This approach is often neglected when examining minorities and crime. In his theoretical perspective on "gringo justice," Mirandé (1987) suggests that a theory of Chicano crime must consider the colonization of Chicanos. Since racial and economic oppression are assumed to be interwoven, the colonization of Chicanos is "an essential historical fact that cannot be ignored. Just as any theory of black oppression must consider the legacy of slavery, so any perspective on the Chicano must be cognizant of its colonial legacy" (p.222). Blea has also suggested that theoretical perspectives on ethnic groups should be based on that group's experience (1988).

While historical influences on group behavior are difficult to assess, sensitization to the history of Latinos in the United States provides an important contextual framework for understanding the present Latino condition. One might expect that the group's history of oppression has had a lasting impact on culture and might be observed indirectly through an examination of group characteristics and attitudes. For example, one might expect that oppressive treatment from the country's racial majority might influence Latino attitudes toward social institutions. Aside from those factors related to history, Latinos have unique characteristics such as language, religiosity, and specific cultural values that arguably influence the applicability of certain theoretical constructs. To gain a better understanding of criminal behavior across ethnic groups, it is crucial to determine whether traditional theories apply generally to human behavior, or whether examinations of theory should be conducted by ethnicity.

Considering the history and culture of one Latino group, Mirandé (1985) and Blea (1988) suggest that traditional theoretical perspectives of delinquent behavior do not adequately apply to Mexican-Americans, since they are based on White, European immigrant groups. Mirandé argues that Mexican-Americans were initially brought to the United States by conquest and not immigration, and therefore he does not expect traditional theories to apply to Chicanos. In addition, Mirandé argues that some traditional theories serve to reinforce negative stereotypes by commonly depicting Chicanos as "1) controlled and manipulated by traditional culture, 2) docile, passive, present oriented, fatalistic, and lacking in achievement, 3) victimized by faulty socialization which takes place in an authoritarian family system, dominated by the cult of *machismo*, and 4) violent and prone to antisocial and criminal behavior" (1985:2).

Theories which "blame the victim" are most strongly criticized by Chicano social scientists. Explanations of deviant behavior which identify internal defects in Chicano youth or culture as key explanatory variables are thought to reinforce the image of Chicanos as inherently criminal (Mirandé, 1987: 212). By their nature, approaches which "blame the victim" also downplay the economic and political discrimination that has been experienced by Latinos; an important factor which may help to explain Latino delinquency. As a solution to the inadequacies of traditional perspectives, Mirandé and Blea have argued for the development of a Chicano sociology to develop new paradigms and theoretical frameworks consistent with a Chicano world view and responsive to the nuances of the Chicano culture (Mirandé, 1985).

This investigation addresses several of Mirandé's concerns. First, the argument that traditional theories are inappropriate for explaining Latino behavior is considered to be a testable hypothesis. Rather than dismissing traditional theories altogether, it may be important to first objectively assess their utility in explaining Latino delinquency. Although such theories were not originally developed specifically for Latinos, they are general in scope and are likely to include concepts that apply to a variety of ethnic groups. Identifying those concepts requires a test of theoretical models with various ethnic groups, which this study achieves. Analysis of separate ethnic groups would identify strain concepts specifically related to Latinos, and determine the overall utility of strain theory in explaining Latino delinquency. Examination of theories with multiple ethnic samples might also reveal interactions between ethnicity and theoretical constructs. An understanding of historical and cultural influences on delinquent behavior might therefore be understood within the context of traditional theories. Second, the theoretical model that has been chosen for the current analysis, strain theory, also addresses

Mirandé's concern about the inappropriateness of "blaming the victim" theories. Strain theory identifies the social structure as the primary motivation for delinquency, and as such, is not an approach that blames the victim.

TRADITIONAL STRAIN THEORY
In proposing his theory of anomie, Merton was one of the first scholars to articulate the significance of a society's social structure in the production of rule breaking behavior. Historically, the motivation for deviant behavior was thought to be internal. Merton, however, identified two concepts within the social system which provide the foundation for an external source of delinquency, culture goals and institutionalized means of achieving goals. The theory of anomie proposes that the disjunction between common economic success goals and access to the legitimate means of achieving those goals (education, employment) creates the pressure to engage in illegal behavior to achieve success. Further, Merton argues that the disparity between goals and expectations for achievement is negatively related to class. Those within the lower class are faced with the greatest pressure to engage in delinquent methods of goal attainment, since access to legitimate channels of success is most limited.

Despite widespread acceptance of strain theory as an explanation of deviant behavior, concerns about its generalizability can be raised. One pertains to its ability to explain norm violations of various ethnic groups within society. For the most part, strain theory was designed to explain the delinquency of lower class males. Having presented his theory as general explanation of human behavior, Merton argues, at least implicitly, that those who are similarly situated within the social structure should react in similar ways, without regard to ethnicity. In their elaboration of Merton's work, Cloward and Ohlin discuss the influence of race on several elements of opportunity theory.

This attempt to address issues of race is evident in other sociological works of the time. In 1963 for example, Berger argued that in addition to the class system, "there are other stratification systems that are far more rigid and therefore far more determinative of an individual's entire life than that of class. In American society a notable example of this is the racial system, which most sociologists regard as a variety of caste" (p.83). Understanding how race and class systems are interrelated is especially relevant for strain, given its concentration on economic positioning. While Cloward and Ohlin introduce race in their discussion of strain theory, there is still much to be learned about potential influences of ethnicity on the traditional strain model.

In empirical tests of strain and subsequent revisions of the theory, researchers have generally failed to elaborate upon Cloward and Ohlin's ideas. The absence of hypotheses on ethnicity and deviance in both the theoretical development and empirical testing of strain is unfortunate for two reasons. First, the assumption that strain theory is generalizable to all ethnic groups is problematic given the lack of empirical evidence to support such a conclusion. Second, potential interactions between ethnicity and theoretical constructs within the strain model have not been fully explored. Since the impact of ethnicity has not been fully articulated in the strain model, criminologists are currently unaware of the possible impact that history and culture might have on strain. Without examining these concerns, the assumption that strain theory applies universally can be challenged through empirical inquiry.

PURPOSE OF STUDY
To explore this concern, this study examines the potential impact of historical and cultural characteristics of Latino Americans within a Mertonian strain perspective. This ethnic population has quickly become the second largest minority group in the country, and is expected to surpass the African American population by the year 2005 (del Pinal & Singer, 1997; Reddy, 1993).[2] As a growing segment of the United States population, and of the criminal justice system, it is becoming increasingly important to consider the etiology of Latino delinquency. Specifically, this analysis will determine whether strain theory applies similarly to Latinos and other ethnic groups. In assessing the consistency of strain theory, it is important to know whether the same strain variables account for delinquency among all racial/ethnic groups to the same degree; the same strain variables account for delinquency among ethnic groups but to different degrees; or whether modifications to the theory are necessary to develop a more inclusive explanation for delinquency.

While research has been conducted in the past to explain Latino gang involvement, drug use, and violence, it is largely atheoretical (Rebach, 1992). Therefore, an additional goal of this study is to provide a theoretical basis for anticipated differences in the application of strain theory to Latinos. In specifying hypotheses related to Latinos and strain heory, a modified strain model is developed to illustrate the ways in which the theory is expected to apply differently to the ethnic group. The modified strain model, described in detail in Chapter 3, traces anticipated differences in strain theory relationships across ethnic groups and introduces cultural factors into the traditional strain model. While strain theory has been described as one possible theoretical approach for explaining Latino delinquency (Blea, 1988; Moore, 1978; Vigil, 1988), little empirical knowledge has been generated comparing the utility of the theory to explain the delinquency of Latinos to other minority and non-minority youth. Some studies have applied elements of strain to Latino samples (Perez y Gonzalez, 1993; Rodriguez & Recio, 1992; Rodriguez & Weisburd, 1991), but few have compared the applicability of strain to multiple ethnic groups within the same sample.[3] The current investigation allows for such a comparison to be made between two separate Latino groups and their African American and White counterparts.

LATINOS IN THE UNITED STATES
This study employs longitudinal data from the Denver Youth Survey (DYS) and the Rochester Youth Development Study (RYDS) to examine the traditional and modified strain theory models. Study samples allow for the examination of multiple ethnic groups, including Latinos of Mexican and Puerto Rican descent. Latinos in the DYS and the RYDS are treated as members of a collective ethnic group, although they represent two distinct countries of origin. The term Latino is used to refer to people of Latin American descent living in the United States and is often used interchangeably with the term Hispanic (del Pinal & Singer, 1997).[4] The U.S. Latino population is comprised of those from Mexico, Puerto Rico, Cuba, Central America, and South America.

Latinos are considered a distinct ethnic group because of the similarities they share: a common Spanish language, minority group status, and treatment by the mainstream U.S. population as newcomers. In addition, Latinos evidence shared sociodemographic characteristics which differentiate them from other ethnic and racial groups. Latinos are concentrated in certain geographic locations, with a substantial proportion of the population living in urban areas.[5] Overall, the Latino population is youthful, and on average, tends to demonstrate lower levels of educational achievement and income compared to other groups (del Pinal

& Singer, 1997; Marín & Marín, 1991). The experiences of Latinos are described as converging, where urban life, poverty, and discrimination are cited among Latinos of various countries of origin (Moore & Pachon, 1985).

At the same time, Latinos are characterized as an ethnic group that shares traditional values such as familism, which involves a strong attachment to both immediate and extended family. A common value system is thought to bind all Latino groups:

> "The significance ascribed to values such as familialism (the importance of relatives as referents and as providers of emotional support) and to social scripts such as 'simpatía' (the preference for positive interpersonal interactions), are characteristics shared by most Hispanics independent of their national background, birthplace, dominant language, or any other sociodemographic characteristic" (Marín & Marín, 1991:2).

Marín & Marín assert that common cultural values are more likely to distinguish Latinos as members of a clearly identifiable group than demographic characteristics (1991). Latinos are also considered a distinct ethnic group because they are treated as such by the mainstream American population. Within the United States, Latinos are considered a group with common characteristics and common problems (Moore & Pachon, 1985). Generated by the U.S. government, the term Hispanic, in itself, implies group commonalities and a certain degree of homogeneity (Marín & Marín, 1991; Oboler, 1995).

Of all Latino groups, Mexican Americans and Puerto Ricans are most similar in terms of demographic characteristics such as age structure, income, and employment. The two represent the largest Latino sub-groups, with Mexican Americans comprising 64 percent of the total Latino population, and Puerto Ricans comprising 11 percent (del Pinal & Singer, 1997). Both groups also contain a substantial proportion of youth; approximately 40 percent of each are eighteen years old or younger. Mexican American and Puerto Rican families are also most likely to be poor when compared to all other Latinos, with 28 and 36 percent living below poverty, respectively. The unemployment rate is also consistent (del Pinal & Singer, 1997).[6] Given their similarities, both

Latino groups are expected to demonstrate comparable behavioral patterns. In the pages that follow, various criminological studies that include Latino groups are cited; some focus exclusively on the Puerto Rican experience, and others are primarily concerned with Mexican Americans (or Chicanos). Given the similarities across groups and the lack of information on the ethnic group generally, findings from all studies of Latinos are utilized to derive general hypotheses on the larger population. Strain theory findings across groups are examined to determine the extent to which Mexican Americans and Puerto Ricans are similar.

In spite of larger group similarities, researchers acknowledge that Latinos emerge from varying countries of origin; each with its own unique background (del Pinal & Singer, 1997; Marín & Marín, 1991; Oboler, 1995). While they may share common cultural values and treatment as a minority group, the history and experiences of Mexicans and Puerto Ricans in the U.S. are not identical. Scholars have noted differences in immigration status, fertility rates, family structure, and education.

Puerto Ricans are considered United States citizens, regardless of whether they are born on the island of Puerto Rico or the U.S. mainland. Puerto Ricans living in the country are not regarded as international migrants as are those who emigrate from Mexico. As a result, they do not experience the same challenges to their citizenship status as Mexican Americans and other Latino groups. At the same time, the Puerto Rican population in America is not experiencing the same rate of growth as Mexican Americans. The fertility rate of Puerto Ricans is lower than that of Mexican Americans; in 1995, the reported number of births per 1,000 women ages 15 to 44 was 76 and 117, respectively. The increased fertility rate among Mexican Americans affects the overall size and youthfulness of the population (del Pinal & Singer, 1997). Finally, the educational attainment of each group varies. In comparison to Whites and African Americans, Puerto Ricans and Mexican Americans are less likely to graduate high school. When an intragroup comparison is made, it is clear that Mexican Americans are the least likely group to earn a high school diploma (del Pinal & Singer, 1997).[7]

Flowers (1998) has suggested that the examination of multiple Latino groups is necessary for uncovering differences by country of origin. He argues that the uniqueness of each Latino group makes it virtually impossible to examine Latinos as one entity. While Mexican Americans and Puerto Ricans are treated as members of a larger ethnic group in the current analysis, each has its own unique history and experience in the United States. As such, intra-group differences are investigated to determine whether findings are consistent across Latino groups. Common themes might be identified among both populations, and conclusions may be drawn about Latinos generally. Independent examination of those populations allows for the identification of specific relationships within strain theory which differ by country of origin.

SUMMARY OF RESEARCH GOALS
This study assesses the applicability of strain theory across ethnic groups, testing the hypothesis that it is a general explanation of crime. Chapter 2 provides a review of the basic tenets of strain theory as originated by Merton (1938) and developed by Cloward and Ohlin (1960). Next, the literature on Latino culture is examined to uncover the potential impact that ethnicity may have on the model in Chapter 3. Hypotheses related to ethnic variation in strain are presented in a modified strain theory model which will be empirically examined in conjunction with the traditional model. Sampling and methodology of the study are described in detail in Chapter 4. Strain theory concepts are examined across groups for mean differences in Chapter 5, along with an assessment of bivariate relationships by ethnicity. In Chapters 6 and 7, the traditional and modified strain theory models are examined across ethnic groups. The overall explanatory value of models is assessed, as are specific strain relationships to determine whether anticipated differences by ethnicity bear out. In doing so, this inquiry attempts to achieve a better understanding of the necessity of a culturally specific model of strain in explaining criminal behavior among Latinos. A culturally specific version of strain might also be helpful in making the theory, as a whole, a more inclusive theoretical perspective.

CHAPTER 2
Traditional Strain Theory

Robert Merton's theory of anomie and subsequent elaborations by Cloward and Ohlin have significantly contributed to the understanding of crime among lower class youth. The common theme of unequal access to legitimate means has demanded consideration of social structural factors as sources of deviance. At the time Merton presented his theory, causes of deviant behavior were primarily identified at the individual level. Deviance was considered to be generated from biological and psychological deficiencies, thus having little to do with the social structure.[1] Merton's anomie theory suggests that "social structures generate the circumstances in which infringement of social codes constitutes a 'normal' (that is to say, an expectable) response" (Merton, 1957:131). Deviance from conventional norms was assumed by Merton to be an expected response of individuals, given certain social conditions.

Merton identified two primary elements of culture that influence antisocial behavior; culturally defined goals and acceptable means of achieving those goals. Economic success in American culture as one goal in particular that is emphasized throughout society and transcends class lines. The acquisition of money is considered to be a symbol of prestige which is instilled in American culture. Various elements of society reinforce and transmit the American Dream, including the family, the school, and the workplace (Merton, 1968). Means of achieving monetary success, such as education and employment, are morally or institutionally prescribed. A discrepancy between these two social forces can occur when the success goal is accepted by society as a whole, yet access to legitimate means of achieving that goal is limited for a proportion of the

11

population:

> "It is the combination of the cultural emphasis and the social structure which produces intense pressure for deviation...the dominant pressure leads toward the gradual attenuation of legitimate, but by and large, ineffectual, strivings and the increasing use of illegitimate, but more or less effective, expedients." (1968:199)

Merton describes the opportunities for fulling the American Dream as variant by economic position, where access to legitimate means is inversely related to class. Attaining the economic success goal is especially difficult for those within the lower class, where education and employment opportunities are restricted. Specifically, Merton describes limited occupational opportunities among the lower class and the relegation to manual labor and the 'lesser white-collar jobs,' which are characterized by little hope for advancement. Although the American culture goal is wide-ranging, the legitimate avenues toward that goal are not equally distributed throughout society. Instead, accessability of legitimate means is influenced by one's position in the social structure. As a result, the members of the lower class experience 'structural inconsistency,' where, "on the one hand, they are asked to orient their conduct toward the prospect of large wealth... and on the other, they are largely denied effective opportunities to do so institutionally" (Merton, 1968:200).

Deviant behavior is seen as a normal consequence of the discrepancy between the commitment to goals and access to legitimate means, and may be more pervasive among the lower class because of limited legitimate opportunities. Since economic success in American society is a universal aspiration and access to that goal is structured by class, members of the lower class are more likely to experience dissociation between aspirations and legitimate opportunities for achieving success. As a result, the relationship between poverty and crime in America is more pronounced, in comparison to other societies with differential success goals by class.

Given the conditions of the social structure, individuals respond to strain in various ways. Five adaptations to widely accepted goals and limited institutionalized means are described by Merton. Adaptations to anomie are described in terms of one's commitment to culture goals and means, and are illustrated in the following way:

		CULTURE GOALS	INSTITUTIONALIZED MEANS
I.	CONFORMITY	+	+
II.	INNOVATION	+	-
III.	RITUALISM	-	+
IV.	RETREATISM	-	-
V.	REBELLION	±	±

Table taken from Merton (1938:676)

Conformity, the most common mode of adaptation, is characterized by a sustained commitment to both goals and legitimate means. *Innovation* results when commitment to success goals is maintained without acceptance of institutionalized means. Access to means is limited, yet success remains a primary goal, resulting in an increased pressure to engage in innovative techniques, including criminal behavior, for goal attainment. *Ritualism* involves a compromise of goals while maintaining commitment to legitimate means. Adherence to conventional methods of goal attainment remains strict, although the goals have been scaled down. *Retreatism*, on the other hand, is characterized by substance abuse and other forms of escapism. An inevitable conflict arises from failure to achieve success through legitimate means, and if accompanied by an inability to utilize illegitimate means because of internalized objection, the retreatist abandons both goals and means and attempts to escape. The fifth and least common adaptation, *rebellion*, results in the substitution of a new set of goals and norms to replace the prevailing social structure. It differs from other adaptations in that it seeks to reinvent the social structure, rather than work within it.

The mode of adaptation one adopts is not constant, according to Merton. Individuals may shift from one adaptation to another as social activities change. In addition, responses to anomic pressure are related to one's position within the social structure. As Merton describes, "class strata are not only differentially subject to anomie, but are differentially subject to one or another type of response to it" (1968:217). Highest levels of strain are experienced by those of the lower class, primarily because there exist fewer opportunities for legitimate success in such a community. The absence of legitimate opportunity among the lower class is met with increased pressure to achieve economic success through illegitimate means, or an innovative adaptation to achieve success.

OPPORTUNITY THEORY

In 1960, Cloward and Ohlin presented their elaboration on the basic elements of strain theory by giving a detailed account of the causal process that results in deviant behavior.[2] Like Merton's theory of anomie, opportunity theory attempts to explain the delinquency of lower class males. Specifically, the theory explores group adaptations to strain and the development of the delinquent subculture. Although the theory comports with Merton's conceptualization of strain as the motivation for delinquent behavior, it was developed under the premise that strain theory does not adequately account for delinquent adaptations (Cullen, 1988). As Cloward and Ohlin assert:

> "It should not be inferred that there is a perfect positive correlation between pressures toward deviance and rate of deviance. Other variables intervene to influence the outcome of those pressures" (1960:85).

In tracing the progression to delinquency, opportunity theory combines traditional strain concepts with elements of differential association (Sutherland, 1947) and ecological theory to provide a more complete picture of delinquent subcultures (refer to Figure 2 for an illustration of the Cloward and Ohlin model).

Opportunity theory builds upon Merton's basic premise that a discrepancy between culturally accepted success goals and access to legitimate opportunities constitute strain and create the motivation for forming delinquent subcultures. With respect to success goals, a typology of lower class youth is developed on two distinct aspirations; one relates to a change in economic position and another that focuses on a desired change class in membership (middle versus lower class). The desire for a change in economic position is characterized purely by the acquisition of wealth, while a change in membership group involves the adoption of middle class value system and affiliation with members of the middle class. The typology is based on goals, where Types I and II aspire toward middle class membership and may or may not simultaneously desire a shift in financial acquisition. Type III youth, most likely to be found in delinquent subcultures, are primarily concerned with financial success and are unconcerned with attaining middle class status, while Type IV youth are not concerned with either goal (Cloward and Ohlin, 1960). The focus of opportunity theory is Type III youth who seek economic advancement but lack the legitimate opportunity to achieve that goal. The pressure for forming delinquent subcultures is greatest among the lower class, given restricted access to the legitimate opportunity structure and higher levels of strain. Therefore, the discrepancy between aspirations and legitimate opportunity systematically increases as one's position in the social structure decreases (as represented in Figure 2).

Formation of the delinquent subculture is seen as a specialized method of adaptation to goal frustration. Rather than assuming a direct relationship between strain and delinquency, however, opportunity theory captures the complex processes that stem from strain and result in delinquent adaptations (Hoffman and Ireland, 1995). The evolution of the delinquent subculture begins with a response to the discrepancy between goals and opportunity, and the attribution of blame for failure to achieve economic success. Some individuals may perceive the source of failure as internal or due to their own personal inadequacies. Others may externalize failure, attributing it to the social system which restricts access to legitimate means for certain groups. Cloward and Ohlin admit that "relatively little is known about the conditions that lead to external rather than internal attributions of causality" (1960:112), but suggest that blame is more likely to be externalized if barriers to economic success are highly visible. For example, among African Americans in the United States, feelings of discrimination or unjust deprivation are the expected response to visible barriers to success .[3]

Those individuals who experience strain and perceive that failure stems from the social structure may challenge the legitimacy of conventional methods of goal attainment. Once legitimacy is removed from behavioral norms, the individual is free from commitment to culturally prescribed means and may then choose alternate methods for goal attainment. The removal of legitimacy from conventional means may lead to a new code of unconventional conduct. A delinquent subculture is formed with its own norms that legitimize and reinforce delinquent behavior. Newly adopted delinquent values and activity are reinforced as one gains support from others who are similarly situated and who perceive the social structure as unjust.

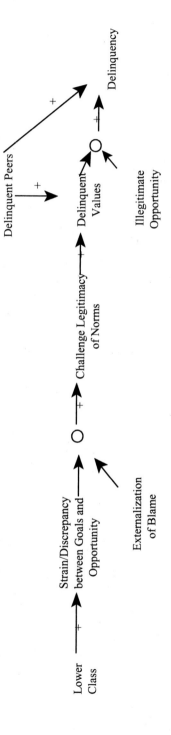

Figure 2. Traditional Strain Model Predicting Delinquency

Three types of delinquent subcultures are described by Cloward and Ohlin; criminal, conflict and retreatist. The *criminal* subculture is characterized by the commitment to economic success through illegal means (i.e. theft, fraud, etc.). The *conflict* subculture, on the other hand, is concerned with gaining status through force and violence. The *retreatist* subculture, similar to Merton's adaptation, places an emphasis on drug and/or alcohol consumption. Generally, adaptations stem from environmental factors; elements of the Chicago School are incorporated into opportunity theory to describe neighborhood level influences on delinquent behavior, and the process by which delinquent behavior is learned.

While the adaptation choice in anomie theory is based on non-specific social interaction, Cloward and Ohlin identify a specific variable that directly impacts upon the type of delinquent subculture that is formed; access to illegitimate means. In addition to socially structured availability of legitimate means, there is also variation in access to the *illegitimate* opportunity structure. It is this theoretical component, the availability of illegitimate means, that moderates the impact of delinquent values on delinquent behavior and influences the type of adaptation one is likely to make. The motivation for deviance is not sufficient in and of itself to result in deviant behavior. Instead, Cloward and Ohlin assert that the individual must have access to the proper learning environment and should be allowed to practice what has been learned. This learning structure stems from Sutherland's differential association and is relevant in determining adaptation outcomes generally, and the generation of the criminal subculture in particular.

The criminal subculture is likely to emerge in a neighborhood in which there are close bonds between offenders of different ages. This allows for the transmission of criminal values and skills from older offenders to younger delinquents. Integration among those who transmit conventional and criminal values is also important in determining criminal outcomes. Ties to conventional roles in society are deemed necessary for establishing criminal careers (Cloward and Ohlin, 1960:173). Specifically, associations among criminal and legitimate elements within the community are vital for the development and persistence of criminal roles. For example, semi-legitimate positions such as the fence or others who deal in stolen goods serve to sustain criminal occupations. Contact with legitimate elements, including law enforcement officials and politicians, can broaden the delinquent's knowledge of illegitimate activities, and further stabilize the criminal career.

The conflict subculture, on the other hand, evolves within an unorganized community which is unable to provide access to legitimate or illegitimate means for success. Discontent among youth is particularly strong in the community, as access to both legal and criminal opportunities are limited. Delinquent opportunities are rare, since the proper learning environment that is required for the transmission of criminal behavior from one generation to the next is more difficult to find in the unorganized community. In addition, informal social controls might also be weakened due to the lack of neighborhood integration in age and conventional and criminal values. As Cloward and Ohlin argue, "where opportunities are absent, patterns of social control are likely to be absent too" (1960:175). Deprivation of both legitimate and illegitimate opportunity contributes to disorganization, weakened controls, frustration and discontent, and ultimately results in the formation of the conflict subculture that seeks its status through violence and force.

The retreatist subculture centers around the consumption of drugs and alcohol. "Retreatist gang members have given up on both goals and means, whether conventional or illegal" (Akers, 1994:149). This adaptation is thought to result from a failure in the use of both legitimate and illegitimate means. Neither criminality nor violence prove successful for this group, which results in a pattern of drug and alcohol abuse.

OTHER EXTENSIONS OF STRAIN THEORY

In addition to the effort made by Cloward and Ohlin, strain theory has also been expanded upon by Cohen (1955), Agnew (1992), and Hoffman and Ireland (1995). Each has developed somewhat varying definitions of success goals and sources of strain which stray from Merton's original concepts. For example, Cohen (1955) utilizes Merton's framework of anomie and merges social structural forces of deviance with Sutherland's differential association to explain the formation of delinquent subcultures. Aspirations and norms of attainment in Cohen's view, are based on middle class values. "Rather than the inability to gain material success, in Cohen's view, it is the inability to gain status and acceptance in conventional society that produces the strain" (Akers, 1994:147). Failure to achieve middle class status, lower class youth experience frustration and may reject middle class values.

More recently, Agnew (1992) offered his elaboration on traditional strain, which resulted in the development of general strain theory (GST). This effort is designed to address both theoretical and empirical criticisms of traditional strain theory. New sources of strain are developed by Agnew in addition to the traditional concept of strain as resulting from the failure to achieve goals. Agnew's sources of strain are designed to include both actual and anticipated failure to achieve goals. Through expansion of the possible sources of strain, middle class delinquency may be explained by GST. Drawing from the stress and justice/equity literature, Agnew attempts to include all possible sources of adversity. Although his initial departure from economic success goals is not far removed from the original strain concept, the introduction of concepts other than goal attainment (for example, expectations of justice/equity) notably differ from Merton's and Cloward and Ohlin's conceptualizations of the sources of strain. Hoffman and Ireland (1995) also expand the sources of strain and consider complex relationships among strain and other theoretical concepts, including the externalization of blame and the influence of peers on delinquent outcomes. Since those models diverge from original strain theory premises, this paper will focus on the theory as it has been offered by Merton and developed by Cloward and Ohlin (Figure 2). This model provides a detailed description of the development of antisocial behavior during the adolescent years.

EMPIRICAL TESTS OF STRAIN THEORY
Empirical tests of traditional strain theory have provided mixed results, with the level of support varying by the measure of strain used (Burton & Cullen, 1992; Burton et al., 1994; Farnworth & Leiber, 1989; Hoffman & Ireland, 1995). A variety of delinquency measures and samples have also been utilized in studies of strain which are also likely to have affected findings. Delinquency measures range from minor delinquent behavior to more serious, violent crime; in some instances, strain has proven to be a stronger predictor of serious delinquency than non-serious or general delinquency (Bernard, 1984; Farnworth & Leiber, 1989). Bernard pointed out that studies with representative youth samples typically include minor delinquency items to achieve variation in the absence of serious delinquency. As a result, examinations of mainstream adolescents are not

deemed appropriate for testing strain theory, since it was designed to explain the behavior of seriously delinquent youth (1984:368). Indeed, support for strain theory is more likely to be found in studies which focus on serious delinquency (Bernard, 1984). In addition, studies comprised solely of middle class youth are criticized as inconsistent with traditional strain theory, since lower class delinquency is the traditional focus.

Empirical tests of traditional strain theory are criticized most recently for over-simplifying theoretical models. Opportunity theory is commonly reduced into a bivariate relationship between strain and delinquent behavior; as a result, a full test of Cloward and Ohlin's work is lacking (Hoffman & Ireland, 1995). Typically studies assume a direct relationship between strain and delinquency, and do not recognize that opportunity theory includes other important theoretical elements, such as the externalization of blame, the withdrawal of legitimacy from conventional norms, the influence of delinquent peers, and the availability of illegitimate opportunities. As Hoffman and Ireland comment:

> "Cloward and Ohlin did not state that strain leads directly to delinquent acts; rather a complex set of interactive and dynamic processes that begins with strain leads certain youths to pursue delinquent solutions to commonly perceived problems." (1995:248)

Without examining conditioning factors, previous research "constitutes an inadequate test of strain theory because the most proximate influence on illegal behavior is excluded from the model" (Menard, 1995:140).[4] In an effort to correct this oversight, recent examinations of strain theory include conditioning factors which represent the concepts Cloward and Ohlin contribute to Merton's theory of anomie (Agnew et al., 1996; Burton et al., 1994; Menard, 1995).

Operationalization of strain concepts is perhaps the most central issue in empirical examinations of the theory, and relates to a more general concern over the theory itself. Key concepts of strain theory have been described as vague and, as such, are open to various interpretations (Nettler, 1974). Varying conceptualizations of success goals and blocked opportunity have led to the creation of several different measures of goal frustration or strain. In various tests of the theory, no single measure of strain is employed; instead, studies include measures of goal disjunction, blocked opportunity, and relative deprivation (Burton et al., 1994).

In an effort to measure strain, researchers typically examine the discrepancy between goals and the means of achieving goals. In early tests of the theory, educational and occupational aspirations and expectations were utilized as a proxy for success goals and means (Elliott, 1962; Hirschi, 1969; Liska, 1971; Quicker, 1974; Short, 1964; Stinchcombe, 1964). Those goal discrepancy measures have produced conflicting results, and have provided minimal support for strain theory.

Since traditional strain theory describes success goals in terms of financial attainment, educational and occupational approaches to measuring strain are criticized for not truly representing traditional strain goals. The acquisition of wealth is described as the widest-reaching success goal in American society which serves as the primary source of strain, and ultimately, influences delinquent behavior. Given the criticism over occupational and educational goals, recent studies include measures of economic aspirations to capture strain as Merton originally intended (Agnew, 1994; Agnew et al., 1996; Burton et al., 1994; Farnworth & Leiber, 1989; Jensen, 1995).

Other attempts to create a more direct operationalization of strain involve measurement of perceptions of blocked legitimate opportunities. This measure essentially taps the perception that a person has available opportunities for achieving the economic success goal through legitimate means. Individuals are typically asked about perceived chances of educational and occupational advancement, such as graduation from high school and college, and securing a good paying job. In an evaluation of empirical tests of strain theory, Burton and Cullen argue that this approach "provides a more adequate operationalization of the essence of strain theory than 'aspirations-expectations'" (1992:14). Compared to the discrepancy between aspirations and expectations, perceived blocked opportunity has yielded more favorable results.

Along a similar line, relative deprivation is used to test strain theory propositions, and assesses one's opportunities for goal attainment as they compare with similarly-situated others. Although this measure serves as an adequate predictor of middle class, non-serious delinquency, it is also inconsistent with original strain theory propositions and will not be reviewed in the current section.[5] Studies which include common measures of strain will be reviewed in the remainder of the chapter.

OCCUPATIONAL GOAL DISCREPANCY

Occupational goal discrepancy (OGD) is a measure of strain which is designed to assess the disjunction between occupational goals and occupational expectations. Occupational aspiration measures capture the type of job one desires, and occupational expectations assess perceived access to that job. OGD represents the disjunction between occupational goals and means to measure goal frustration.

In early tests of strain, occupational goal discrepancy provided minimal support for the theory. Most studies employing OGD found the measure to be unrelated to delinquency, and were therefore nonsupportive of strain. In one instance, however, limited support for strain was provided by an absolute occupation disjunction measure (Short, 1964). Examination of the absolute disjunction between occupational aspirations and occupational expectations revealed that youth who are most involved with police have the highest mean discrepancy between aspirations and expectations. Relative occupation disjunction was also examined in this study by comparing boys' occupational aspirations and expectations with the occupational achievements of their fathers. Unlike the absolute disjunction measure, relative disjunction was not predictive of delinquent behavior.[6]

In an attempt to clarify basic strain issues, Quicker employed both occupational and educational goal discrepancy measures (1974). Educational goal discrepancy (EGD) is designed to assess the disjunction between desired educational attainment and actual expectations for school achievement. Quicker included educational goals in addition to occupational goals to address the concern that short-term aspirations are ignored by opportunity theory. Although Cloward and Ohlin define educational aspirations as a means to future occupational goals, Quicker argues that education represents a more proximal concern in an adolescent's life than one's future occupation:

"To be frustrated by inability to achieve occupational goals can produce strain which lead to delinquency, as Cloward and Ohlin argue, but to be frustrated from achieving more immediate goals such as educational goals, can also produce strain which can lead to delinquency as well" (1974:78).

In support of his argument, a weak correlation between occupational goal discrepancy and delinquency was found. Overall, short term educational goal discrepancies were more strongly related to delinquency. As a result, Quicker concludes that the concept of goal frustration in traditional strain theory is too narrow, and that immediate goals are important to consider. Conclusions drawn from these data, however, must be considered in light of certain shortcomings of the study to represent a true test of strain theory. For example, the design of the study included "considerable variation in the ethnicity and social class of (male high school) students" (p.78). Because of the variation in subjects' social class, this test of strain may be flawed. Since the theory is designed to explain lower class delinquency, inclusion of classes other than the one specified by strain, without proper control variables, might impact the strength of relationships and result in an inaccurate estimation of the utility of the theory.

EDUCATIONAL GOAL DISCREPANCY
In a number of studies on strain theory educational goal discrepancy has been evaluated. In an early test of theoretical constructs, Hirschi (1969) operationalized strain as such, with an assessment of educational aspirations (goals) and expectations (one's perception of what they are likely to attain in education). The relative gap between the two was utilized as an indication of strain, since the theory argues that a discrepancy provides the motivation for deviant behavior. The gap between educational aspirations and expectations, however, was found to be unrelated to delinquency. Other studies utilizing the same measure of strain provided minimal support for the theory (Liska, 1971; Quicker, 1974; Short, 1964; Stinchcombe, 1964), leading to a conclusion that strain theory is largely unsupported (Bernard, 1984; Burton & Cullen, 1992; Farnworth & Leiber, 1989).

Hirschi's study has produced other criticisms of strain; one which relates to the redundancy of the theory, and the other which focuses on relationship between social class and crime. The redundancy of strain stems from the finding that educational aspirations alone account for the relationship between delinquency and strain (Hirschi, 1969; Liska, 1971). Regardless of one's expectations, higher educational goals were found to result in higher levels of delinquent behavior. That finding was cited as evidence that control theory provides a better, more parsimonious, explanation for crime than strain, since the control concept (commitment to education) was more strongly related to delinquency than strain (disjunction between educational goals and expectations). Strain theory was regarded as redundant, since access to legitimate means is not necessary for understanding deviance. Given the class-based nature of strain theory, Hirschi also examined the relationship between social class and delinquency. Unable to find a significant relationship between the two variables, the most basic aspect of the theory was questioned. From all of the evidence obtained, Hirschi concludes that primary propositions of strain are not related to delinquency.

In a recent re-analysis of Richmond Youth Survey data, Greenberg's (1999) findings on educational strain contradict those found by Hirschi (1969). In evaluating the strength of control theory, Hirschi's original tables were utilized to examine control theory relationships. Greenberg included educational aspirations and re-examined the redundancy hypothesis that aspirations alone reduce delinquency, and not the discrepancy between aspirations and expectations. Through the creation of a strain index (educational aspirations - educational expectations), Greenberg found support for strain which Hirschi was unable to find. He demonstrated that strain is positively related to delinquent behavior; those who experience greater strain produce higher levels of delinquency. Upon closer examination, Greenberg found that the relationship between strain and delinquency is consistent across various levels of economic aspirations. Thus, holding aspirations constant, an impact of the strain discrepancy measure was found.[7] Within strain categories, higher aspirations produced lower levels of delinquency, which control theory predicts (1999). Beyond that, however, support for strain was also found; the discrepancy between aspirations and expectations influences delinquent outcomes.

The methodology employed by Hirschi's and other early tests of strain theory might also explain the lack of support for strain. First, it is important to point out that strain was measured as the discrepancy between *educational* goals and means, and not in terms of economic success as Merton and Cloward and Ohlin conceptualized it (Agnew, 1994; Bernard, 1984; Farnworth & Leiber, 1989). Because education was originally considered as a means toward an end and not an end in itself, problems arise when evaluating the theory with studies that employ educational goals. In addition, the self-reported delinquency scales used in Hirshi's examination of strain included minor delinquency items such as theft of something worth less than $2.00. Since strain theory was not originally designed to explain low-level, non-utilitarian crime, it is not surprising to find little or no support in predicting this measure of delinquency.

After finding little support for strain in a review of four empirical studies Liska (1971) also suggested that control theory may provide a better explanation of delinquency. In the studies that were reviewed, however, similar misinterpretations of the theory were made (Bernard, 1984). Everything considered, it stands to reason that the data support control theory in some instances; the methodology employed was not designed to test strain theory. Although early tests of strain find little support for the theory, it would be premature to dismiss the theory's value based on studies that poorly fit the theory they were designed to test.

ECONOMIC GOAL DISCREPANCY
In an examination of competing measures of strain, Farnworth and Leiber (1989) evaluate the various strain measures employed in empirical tests of the theory and argue that the most appropriate measure is one that captures the gap between economic aspirations and educational expectations. Those concepts most closely resemble Merton's depiction of culture goals and legitimate means of achieving success. Central to anomie theory is the economic success goal that is adopted by members of society, and the means of achieving that universal goal through education. Theoretically, the utilization of both educational aspirations and expectations does not accurately capture the strain described by original theorists. As Farnworth and Leiber suggest, "if strain is recast entirely in the educational realm, the educational means in Merton's original theory become both goals and means, and the central theoretical importance of economic goals is lost" (1989:265). The theoretical inconsistency that occurs with the utility of educational goals and means might account for some conflicting findings in early empirical tests of strain; Farnworth and Leiber suggest that empirical findings are likely to be affected by varying operationalizations of strain. In their investigation, they "explore the possibility that research interpretations differing conceptually from Merton's original statement contribute to the recent empirical failure of strain theory" (p.263).

To demonstrate the influence that differing operationalizations of strain have on outcome measures, Farnworth and Leiber replicated the educational goal disjunction measure that failed to provide support for strain in the past as well as a more traditional strain measure comprised of economic goals and educational means. In addition, various outcome measures were examined with prevalence and frequency measures of delinquency categorized by seriousness and utilitarianism. This study is unique in that varying operationalizations of both strain and delinquency are included in one comprehensive study.

Farnworth and Leiber found varying levels of support for the theory, depending upon the measure of strain employed. When strain was measured as the discrepancy between economic goals and educational expectations, it was significantly related to delinquency and proved to be a better predictor of delinquency than the educational goal frustration measure, in terms of both prevalence and frequency. Therefore, studies relying on educational goals and means alone have underestimated the true relationship between goal frustration and delinquency. When the variable was measured as it was originally intended, empirical support for the theory was provided. This finding led Farnworth and Leiber to conclude that "the apparent failure of strain theory in recent empirical study might well be a function of inappropriate operationalization" (1989:272).

In examining the redundancy of strain, support was found for the hypothesis only when strain was measured in terms of educational goals. Consistent with Hirschi (1969), school aspirations alone predicted delinquency, thus supporting control theory. When strain was measured as Merton's theory intended, however, the redundancy hypothesis was unfounded. Commitment to financial goals alone was not significantly associated with delinquency. Taken together these findings suggest "that operationalization strategies affect the nature of findings concerning the predictive value of strain for delinquency" (p.271). Therefore, it may be premature to dismiss strain theory based on studies that have inappropriately measured strain concepts.

Although Farnworth and Leiber shed light on inconsistent findings and provide hope for strain theory's future, their study has met with criticism. In an evaluation of their analysis, Jensen (1995) pointed out that the effect of educational expectations was not properly teased out from the impact of strain. Farnworth and Leiber demonstrated a relationship between strain and delinquency while controlling for the impact of economic aspirations alone, but did not introduce expectations into the analysis. Jensen argues that:

"support for strain theory requires evidence that the strain between goals and means has an impact independent of either goals or means. Thus, the data would have to show that youths with high economic aspirations and low educational expectations have a delinquency rate higher than that expected based on the effects of expectations or aspirations alone." (1995:141)

Jensen re-analyzed data used by Farnworth and Leiber and controlled for main effects of aspirations and expectations to determine whether an interaction measure of strain independently contributes to the explanation of delinquency. In a log-linear analysis, Jensen found no significant support for the interaction term once aspirations and expectations were introduced into the model. Regardless of expectations, however, economic aspirations were related to delinquency.

Jensen also criticized the study by Farnworth and Leiber for failing to examine the influence of social class on strain, or the distribution of strain in the sample. To adequately support strain theory, Jensen argues that empirical tests must reveal a negative relationship between social class and strain, and a positive relationship between strain and delinquent outcomes. In his re-analysis, a relationship between social class and strain was not found and strain did not predict delinquent outcomes when main effects of aspirations and expectations are controlled. These findings led to the conclusion that strain theory was not supported (Jensen, 1995).

In response to Jensen's criticisms, Greenberg argues that it is "mathematically and conceptually impossible to control for both aspirations and expectations while assessing the impact of strain" (1999:73). When utilizing a traditional disjunction measure, aspirations and expectations cannot be held constant or the difference between them cannot vary. The use of a strain interaction measure is also inappropriate because strain theorists do not posit an interaction, but rather define strain as a disjunction between aspirations and expectations (Greenberg, 1999).[8] In his re-analysis of Hirshi's data, Greenberg found support for the traditional strain disjunction measure.

In other recent studies that examine strain measures based on economic success goals, however, findings are mixed. In an examination of strain across various adolescent age groups, Menard found support for strain among the middle and late-adolescent groups (1995). Although the measure of success is described as economic, it included occupational goals. Goals and means were not kept entirely within the occupational realm, however. Educational expectations were also combined to reflect economic goal disjunction. Various modes of adaptation were included in the analysis and were defined as "acceptance of institutional norms governing means of achieving goals" (p.140), which is reminiscent of Cloward and Ohlin's concept of legitimacy withdrawal. Menard found strong support for the relationship between anomie and mode of adaptation. In addition, he found that adaptation mode is the strongest and most consistent predictor of minor, index, and drug using behavior across all age groups (but provides the greatest explanatory power in later adolescence), supporting opportunity theory.

Agnew (1994) and Agnew, Cullen, Burton, Evans, and Dunaway (1996) further expand research on the desire for economic success and delinquency. Agnew (1994) argues that previous tests of strain fail to capture one's immediate desire for money; instead, adolescents are typically asked about future economic success goals. In addition, expectations for educational attainment may not prove to be an accurate measure of one's perception of opportunity for goal fulfilment. To capture strain, he assessed the immediate desire for money (dollars desired per week) and actual goal achievement (dollars received per week). Strain was measured as the discrepancy between amount desired and amount received. In the analysis, Agnew did not find a relationship between strain and delinquency.[9] The main effect of goals was included, and contributed independently to higher delinquency scores (higher goals produce higher levels of delinquency). Overall, Agnew (1994) found weak support for strain theory among a general population sample. Perhaps the inclusion of high-risk youth would provide greater support for the theory, as others have suggested (Bernard, 1984). In addition, the conceptualization of strain as the disjunction between immediate goals and acquisition of money does not capture traditional strain theory precepts. The definition of strain differs from long term goals that the traditional model describes; therefore, conclusions cannot be drawn about traditional strain theory from this particular study.

Agnew et al. (1996) also assess one's dissatisfaction with financial status to create an individual strain measure. Dissatisfaction or frustration is an important component of classic strain theory which is frequently omitted from empirical examinations.[10] Rather than reducing the model into a single disjunction measure Agnew et al. argue that strain "is a function of multiple factors including the importance attached to monetary success and other goals, position in the stratification system, expectations for future success, and comparisons with the monetary situation of others" (1996:683). Six factors were included in the analysis, and their contribution to individual dissatisfaction was assessed.[11] The cumulative impact of all six factors was expected to produce strain, or dissatisfaction with financial achievement:

"strain, then, should be greatest when individuals 'put all their eggs in one basket' - placing a high relative and absolute emphasis on large sums of money and a low emphasis on all other goals - and when these individuals also lack money and the legitimate means for obtaining money, when they do not expect to obtain money in the future, and when their comparison others are better off financially than themselves." (1996:685)

Although an interaction effect of all predictors was expected to produce strain, the authors recognized that the most basic interaction originally proposed by strain theorists occurs between high economic aspirations and low achievement. Therefore, a traditional disjunction measure was examined in the analysis, and its relationship with dissatisfaction was estimated separately from other factors expected to predict strain. The traditional aspirations and expectations measures were assessed in dollar amounts, and the disjunction between them did not predict strain. In addition, no main effects of monetary aspirations or monetary expectations were found with these particular measures. Instead, strain was predicted by poor education, low family income, relative deprivation, and more general measures of economic aspirations and expectations (which were *not* based on specific dollar amounts). While not defining them as such, the goal of making a lot of money and the diminished expectation of making a lot of money clearly qualify as traditional strain measures, and were supported by this analysis. Main effects of these measures were uncovered, however the interaction between them was not found to predict strain when it was included with other interaction terms.[12]

In conjunction with predictors of dissatisfaction, the impact of strain on delinquent outcomes was evaluated. Agnew et al. (1996) included measures thought to condition the impact of strain on delinquent behavior such as blaming the social structure for failure, a weakened commitment to institutionalized norms, and delinquent peers.[13] Estimating a more complete strain model revealed that dissatisfaction (strain) interacts with criminal beliefs and criminal associations, and leads to greater delinquent behavior. The interaction term is a significant predictor of outcomes, even when controlling for aspirations, expectations, social control, and class.

Although this study did not find support for the traditional strain disjunction measure, it supports the notion that dissatisfaction/frustration with monetary status results in delinquency. This finding is significant, given that dissatisfaction with monetary status is a theoretical element that is often omitted from other tests of strain theory. The influence of dissatisfaction is compounded when combined with weakened commitment to institutionalized means and delinquent peers. In addition, a direct relationship between social class and frustration was revealed, producing an indirect relationship between class and delinquency. Upon close examination, social class is found to be the strongest predictor of economic expectations, which is consistent with opportunity theory.

Generally, support for the theory is provided by the influence of social class on the model, where "dissatisfaction or strain is found to be more common among those with less education and lower incomes" (Agnew et al., 1996:699). The study also highlights the impact of conditioning factors such as delinquent beliefs and criminal associations. However, the traditional economic disjunction measure, as defined by dollar amounts, was not supported by Agnew et al. (1996). Rather than abandon the classic strain theory measure, variables utilized in the study might be re-evaluated and properly tested. Measures indicative of the general economic success goal and expectations for achieving the goal were found to be significant predictors of strain in the study. Those measures were not recognized as elements of the traditional strain disjunction, however, and disjunction was operationalized with items related to desired and expected dollar amounts. The interaction between economic aspirations and expectations may have proved to be a proper operationalization of traditional strain, however, it was not examined separately in the analysis. Instead, its influence was potentially masked as it was examined in conjunction with several other interaction terms.

This investigation addresses several concerns raised by empirical tests of strain theory. Previous studies have identified the need for testing a more complete theoretical model, incorporating factors which condition the impact of strain on delinquency such as peers and the availability of illegitimate opportunities (Agnew, 1996; Hoffman & Ireland, 1995; Menard, 1995). Others have called for the examination of strain theory relationships over time with the use of panel data and the inclusion of high risk youth (Agnew, 1994; Farnworth & Leiber, 1989; Hoffman & Ireland, 1995; Jensen, 1995; Menard, 1995). Researchers also specify the need for testing the theory by gender, age and ethnicity (Burton & Dunaway, 1994; Jensen, 1995; Menard, 1995).

This study maintains adherence to the work of Merton and Cloward and Ohlin through the inclusion of an economic goal disjunction measure. In addition, the utilization of longitudinal data from the Denver and Rochester studies allows for the examination of strain theory over time with a sample of high risk youth. The current investigation also incorporates concepts of externalization of blame, legitimacy of norms, delinquent values, peer influence, and illegitimate opportunity to test a more complete theoretical model. Finally, the study breaks down analysis by gender and ethnicity, to assess the applicability of strain to various populations. This study also targets deficiencies in the literature related specifically to strain and ethnicity/race to be described in Chapter 3.

CHAPTER 3
Ethnicity and Traditional Strain Theory

The primary goal of this study is to assess the applicability of the traditional strain model, as presented in Chapter 2, to various ethnic groups. Although strain theory has been accepted as a general explanation of antisocial behavior, the potential influence of ethnicity on the model should be explored. Studies of Latino delinquency have emphasized the importance of teasing out effects of ethnicity on traditional theories of crime. In an effort to predict delinquency and drug use among Puerto Rican youth, Rodriguez and Weisburd (1991) and Rodriguez and Recio (1992) describe the importance of assessing the predictive value of theoretical models across ethnic groups. Ethnographic literature has illustrated sociocultural influences on delinquency; therefore, it is unclear whether Latino deviance can be explained with general models (Rodriguez & Weisburd, 1991). Traditional theories may apply similarly across ethnic groups, since Latinos share similarities with their White counterparts, including family and school problems, peer influences, and frustration due to aspirations and expectations. At the same time,

"Puerto Ricans are nonetheless raised in a culture different from that of the American population, occupy minority status, have much lower socioeconomic status than Whites or even Blacks, and often live in neighborhoods characterized by high levels of social disorganization" (Rodriguez & Weisburd, 1991:5).

33

Given the variation in sociocultural characteristics between Latinos and Whites, relationships within general models might be affected. This argument supports the aims of this study, where the focus is on testing the generality of strain theory and assessing the potential influence of Latino sociocultural factors on that general model of behavior.

Sociocultural differences among ethnic groups might influence strain relationships, and as a result, may have confounded previous empirical tests of the theory. For example, Quicker's (1974) study of strain theory included a collective examination of individuals from various ethnic backgrounds. Since little support was found for the theory, one might expect that the examination of multiple ethnic groups obscured results, particularly since other examinations of strain have illustrated differences between Whites and ethnic minorities (Jessor, Graves, Hanson, & Jessor, 1968; Perez y Gonzalez, 1993; Rodriguez & Recio, 1992; Rodriguez & Weisburd, 1991; Simons & Gray, 1989; Short, 1964; Short & Strodtbeck, 1965). Empirical examinations by race/ethnicity have illustrated differences between minority and White populations on various strain theory dimensions, including the perception of blocked opportunity, levels of strain experienced, externalization of blame, and adaptations to strain. Findings from those studies suggest the importance of teasing out the effects of race/ethnicity and serve as a cautionary statement in interpreting comments previously made about the theory.

In addition to the empirical investigations, theoretical links between Latino delinquency and strain theory have been made. Literature on Latino crime has cited strain theory as one possible explanation of general delinquency, gang membership, and substance use (Blea, 1988; Covey, Menard, & Franzese, 1992; Moore, 1978; Moore 1991; Vigil, 1988; Walker, Spohn, & DeLone, 1996). Such studies provide the theoretical framework for an empirical analysis of strain theory among Latinos. This chapter examines the literature on Latinos and strain theory, and utilizes findings of previous studies to explore the ways in which elements of the Latino culture might impact upon the traditional strain theory model.

ETHNIC DIFFERENCES IN THE STRAIN MODEL
Given the difference in socioeconomic status (SES) between Latinos and Whites in American society, traditional strain theory accounts for a certain degree of ethnic variation in the model. Strain theorists posit a direct impact of socioeconomic status on elements of the traditional model,

including the perception of blocked opportunity and strain, which ultimately leads to a greater involvement of lower class youth in delinquent behavior. Since Latinos experience greater structural disadvantage compared to their White counterparts, mean differences between groups are expected across the strain model due to variation in SES. For example, within the Denver and Rochester studies, 60 and 56 percent of Latinos are recipients of public assistance, compared to 40 and 22 percent of Whites, respectively.[1] Since Latinos experience greater socioeconomic disadvantage, there should be evidence of disadvantage throughout the model. As a result of social stratification, the Latino population is likely to produce a higher mean value of strain, since SES is so closely tied to the theory.

A crucial issue to be explored in this analysis is whether differences among ethnic groups exist above and beyond those due to class. In examining the history and culture of Latinos in the United States, group experiences might bear upon strain concepts. For example, the Latino experience has been characterized by physical and social isolation from the mainstream, which may impact the extent to which Latinos view their opportunities as limited (Peterson & Harrell, 1992; Vigil, 1988). Regardless of economic standing, Latinos are relegated minority group status; as members of an ethnic minority, they are likely to experience various forms of discrimination which may ultimately translate to higher levels of blocked opportunity and strain.

In addition to simple mean differences in strain concepts, therefore, variation might be observed in the *strength* of relationships across ethnic groups. If mean values of strain concepts differ among ethnic groups but the impact of variables is consistent, such a finding would suggest that strain theory applies similarly by ethnicity. On the other hand, concepts within the strain theory model might have a different impact among Latinos. Based on the literature identifying sociocultural differences, certain relationships within the model may be stronger for Latinos and others may be weaker compared to Whites. To illustrate hypothesized variation in relationships within the traditional strain model, a second causal diagram is generated in Figure 3. The model represents anticipated differences in strain relationships between Latinos and Whites. Separate causal paths for Latinos are presented in the model to illustrate anticipated differences in model pathways. Hypothesized slope variation is indicated with the letters LT or GT: when placed between the paths, LT indicates that the influence of the variable within the model is expected to be weaker for Latinos, and the slope is expected to be less than that of Whites. A stronger relationship for Latinos is indicated by GT, where the slope is expected to be greater than the slope for Whites.

Aside from slope variation, additional variables are expected to impact model pathways and influence the overall explanatory power of strain theory in predicting Latino delinquency. Sociocultural factors such as acculturation, language, family involvement, religiosity, and a history of marginality and discrimination are expected to influence traditional strain theory relationships, and are included in a modified strain model. Figure 3 illustrates the potential impact of such cultural factors on traditional strain theory.

HYPOTHESES

The influence of ethnicity on strain theory is explored in the following sections. Elements of the Latino experience are related to the traditional strain theory concepts offered by Merton and Cloward and Ohlin, including the acceptance of success goals, the perception of blocked opportunity, the externalization of blame, the removal of legitimacy from conventional norms, and the adoption of delinquent values. Hypotheses are specific to Latinos as they compare with Whites, the population which is typically included in empirical examinations of strain. Although a large African American population is included in the current study and a separate model is estimated for the group, the primary point of comparison in this chapter will be between Latino youth and their White counterparts. The modified strain theory model presented in Figure 3 is included to illustrate potential differences between Latino and mainstream youth and do not represent hypotheses about African Americans, primarily for the purpose of simplicity.

Potential differences among minority groups are not to be ignored, however. A general inquiry on the applicability of strain theory requires the inclusion of all three ethnic groups; as such, preliminary hypotheses on African American and Latino adolescents are reserved for the end of the chapter. Similarities between Latinos and African Americans are drawn along the lines of minority group status, and anticipated differences in strain are derived from cultural and historical variation among minority populations. Hypotheses represented in Figure 3 are provided in the next sections and are followed by minority group comparisons.

Figure 3. Modified Strain Theory Model Predicting Latino Delinquency

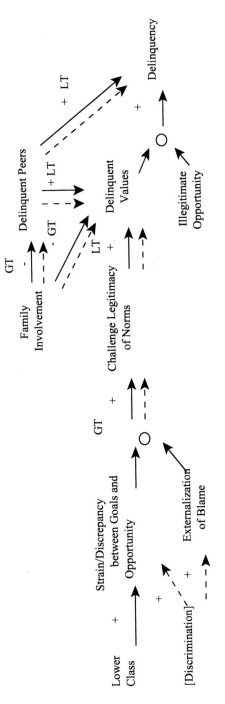

Paths:

White ⟶
Latino – – ▸

LT = slope expected to be lower among Latinos
GT = slope expected to be higher among Latinos

ETHNICITY AND SUCCESS GOALS

One of the most basic assertions made by traditional strain theory is the existence of a universal economic success goal. Empirical examinations of the theory typically consider the internalization of success goals to be constant. In the most recent revision of his theory, however, Merton (1968) argues that the economic success goal may not be as universal as he had previously argued. Instead, he suggests that it is a matter of inquiry to determine the extent to which individuals (or groups, for the purpose of this study) internalize success goals.

It is arguable that mainstream culture influences all classes in American society, emphasizing certain goals and values, including the aspiration for economic success. Mainstream values are likely to transcend class and racial lines through mass media, such that all members of society desire financial success regardless of ethnic background.[2] Support for the universality of goals is provided by various descriptions of Latinos and the American dream. Blea and others argue that societal goals of wealth and prestige have been internalized by Mexican Americans (Blea, 1988; Heller, 1971; Horowitz, 1983; Moore, 1978). Existence within a capitalist society and exposure to mainstream values via television, movies and newspapers has influenced Chicanos to aspire to economic success. Blea argues that Chicanos aspire to fulfill the American dream, which is characterized by home ownership and economic security (1988:64). Chicanos, along with members of all other ethnic groups, are encouraged to internalize financial success goals.

The extent to which mainstream values are internalized by Latinos, however, has been questioned. For example, Clark and Wenniger (1963) suggest that the ethnic composition of communities is related to goal orientation, although this influence was not empirically investigated. In another study, differences in mobility aspirations were directly linked with ethnicity (Heller, 1971). In ethnographic research, Heller observed that Chicano youth appear to value material success to the same or even greater extent than White American youth. In statistical analyses, however, she found that Mexican American youth value financial success to a *lesser* degree than their White counterparts. Due to the lack of clarity in survey wording, Heller concludes that Chicanos and Whites have similar aspirations.[3] Given the confusion over the measure, this issue remains unresolved.

In other examinations of the Latino population, cultural influences on mainstream goals have been explored. Various studies of Mexican Americans and Puerto Ricans in the United States describe the influence of mainstream American culture and traditional Latino culture on the generation of success goals (Blea, 1988; Horowitz, 1983; Moore, 1978; Perez y Gonzalez; 1992; Sowell, 1981). While Latino youth are somewhat isolated from the mainstream (physically and socially), they are constantly exposed to life outside the barrio which reinforces economic success goals. At the same time, Latino youth are also influenced by traditional Latino values which are more communal in nature, and may counteract desires for individualism and materialism. As Blea describes:

"Success in America usually means obtaining large amounts of many resources, especially money. In Chicano culture success means stability, growing old, and living in peace. Money and resources are also valued; but in contrast with most Americans, Chicanos do not live their lives continuously seeking progress and with profit in mind" (1988:17).

The dual commitment to traditional culture goals and American values may influence the degree to which the economic success goal is shared among ethnic groups.

The duality of the Chicano condition and its impact on attitudes and behavior is described by Horowitz (1983). Lives of 32nd Street residents in Chicago are characterized by two distinct but intertwined codes; the expressive code of honor and the instrumental code of the American dream. Personal and family honor conveys the importance of character and personal relations within the local Latino community. Success is determined by that community, and "the self, not a job or financial resources, is the currency of status" (Horowitz, 1983:22). Simultaneously, Chicanos are concerned with achieving the American dream through legitimate means that have been established by the mainstream. Education is thus described as a method of securing financial success. The uniqueness of the Latino condition lies in the balance between the codes. This process is described by Horowitz as continual; one that occurs through interactions between individuals and social institutions. As a result, values and norms are continually redefined (Horowitz, 1983).

It appears, therefore, that Latinos in the United States are influenced by two sets of values; individual-based American success goals and more communal values of traditional Latino culture. Given their status as a recent immigrant group, concentration in largely homogeneous areas, and close proximity to country of origin, it is reasonable to assume that traditional values are viable in the Latino community, and are likely to conflict with mainstream American values that are pervasive throughout the larger American society.[4] One might argue that Latinos, as a group, value economic success to a lesser extent than White Americans because of those competing interests.

ACCULTURATION AND SUCCESS GOALS
As a means of operationalizing competing values within the Latino culture, Perez y Gonzalez has examined the role of acculturation on Puerto Rican delinquency (1993). This cultural factor has been linked to Latino success goal adoption and may account for individual variation in internalizing the American dream.[5] In an examination of the integrated social control model (ISC), Perez y Gonzalez hypothesizes that acculturation and strain are positively related. She argues that more acculturated adolescents place a greater emphasis on economic success than their less acculturated counterparts. As migrant groups begin to assimilate and internalize American values, they also adopt mainstream success goals. At the same time, however, opportunities to achieve such goals are limited, since minority group status blocks legitimate opportunities for success. As a result, she argues that the more acculturated individual will experience a greater degree of strain.

Perez y Gonzalez also examines the influence of biculturalism on strain, arguing that the bicultural individual is likely to retain traditional Puerto Rican goals and place less emphasis on economic success. To clarify her argument, she provides the following scenario:

> "With regards to strain, if the adolescent (Rafaél) is bicultural, it is assumed that he has adopted some of the conventional goals and values of the mainstream American culture and retained some from the traditional Puerto Rican culture, which is more family oriented and does not stress the acquisition of an advanced education or a career-ladder job as a means of success" (1992:32).

As a result, biculturalism is expected to have a negative relationship to strain, such that lower aspirations would reduce the potential for goal disjunction and strain.

Perez y Gonzalez examined these relationships within the context of the ISC model, using data from the Puerto Rican Adolescent Survey (PRAS). Unable to assess the influence of acculturation and biculturalism on success goals which are not part of the ISC, she examined their direct influence on strain. In the analysis, Perez y Gonzalez was unable to find a direct impact of acculturation or biculturalism on strain in the ISC model. In terms of the traditional strain theory model, this particular issue has not been empirically examined. Acculturation and/or biculturalism might have a direct impact on goal orientation, and an indirect influence on strain among Latinos.

Since the universality of culture goals remains an important underlying assumption of strain theory, its relationship to ethnicity will first be addressed. In examining goal internalization, analyses will determine whether economic success is widely accepted by members of all ethnic backgrounds, or whether ethnic groups differ in the extent to which they adopt the American dream. Arguments have been made to support both positions, and the current analysis addresses the issue with a preliminary look at success goal internalization. Goals will be examined by ethnicity while controlling for class status, to determine whether findings are attributable to ethnicity or social class differences. The current investigation also aims to provide a preliminary examination of acculturation and goal orientation among Latinos. The acculturation influence can be examined in only one of the two sites (Rochester), however, the analysis will provide a preliminary look at the relationship between acculturation and goals.

ETHNICITY AND BLOCKED OPPORTUNITY

In addition to the internalization of success goals, ethnicity might influence one's perception of blocked opportunity. Cloward and Ohlin have argued that legitimate opportunities vary by class; this investigation extends that argument by suggesting an interaction between class and ethnicity.[6] Characteristics of the Latino condition may limit one's objective opportunities for success, and discrimination by various social institutions is likely to influence subjective perceptions of opportunity.

Sources of blocked opportunity among Latinos include socioeconomic factors, barrioization, language, and institutionalized discrimination. In a general comment on Latino crime, Flowers (1988) has asserted that unemployment, income and education put Latinos at increased risk for criminality. Although he does not specifically link this notion to strain theory, this assertion is clearly characteristic of the strain theory concept of blocked opportunity. Higher unemployment rates, lower median income and lower levels of education arguably limit the Latino's ability to succeed financially. Examinations of Chicano youth gangs have yielded similar conclusions about the social structure and limited access to legitimate means for success (Covey et al., 1992; Moore, 1978; Moore, 1991; Vigil, 1988). In describing the conditions of barrio life in East Los Angeles, Moore focused on the powerlessness of Mexican Americans in the city and the southwest generally. Employment within the barrio contributes to the powerlessness of Latinos and their failure to achieve economic success; Mexican American employees are typically found in the lowest paying jobs, since "the type of job always described in the American dream of normalcy (with security, good pay, and a career ladder) is relatively scarce" (Moore, 1978:20).[7] Describing the barrio as a "world of limited opportunities," Moore argues that Chicano youth find opportunity for economic success in the illegal drug market.

As mentioned previously, socioeconomic variation between Latinos and Whites is expected to influence legitimate means within the strain model. Structural disadvantage among Latinos is likely to restrict legitimate opportunity, and ultimately lead to increased levels of strain. Although socioeconomic disadvantage is not unique to Latinos, a number of other conditions also serve to limit legitimate opportunity and set the group apart from the mainstream population. Researchers of Latino gangs often depict the marginality of youth who are unable to achieve status in mainstream society turn to gangs for such rewards. With the concept of multiple marginality, Vigil (1988) describes ways in which Mexican Americans have been marginalized in the United States, and how that history of discrimination might impact deviant behavior. Sources of marginality include macro (group), meso (family), and micro (life) historical factors which cumulatively influence behavior. Vigil attempts to illustrate "through time how ecological and economic conditions create sociocultural stresses and ambiguities, which, in turn, lead to subcultural and psychological mechanisms of adjustment" (1988:11).

Macro level sources of Chicano marginality include barrioization, which is characterized by physical and social separation between Chicanos and the mainstream society. Aside from structural disadvantage, physical and social isolation is expected to impact upon one's perception of legitimate opportunities. Historically, life within the barrio has served as a reminder that the group has been isolated from the mainstream. Vigil argues that the marginal entrance of Mexican Americans into the United States is continually reinforced by barrio life.

Peterson and Harrell (1992) also describe several dimensions of isolation which act as barriers to the opportunity structure for inner city residents. Physical isolation refers to the separation of urban residents from suburban areas where jobs and resources are found. Social isolation is also common to those living in the barrio. Although specific indicators of social isolation remain open for discussion, the essence of this type of alienation is limited contact with individuals or institutions which represent mainstream society (Wilson, 1984). Residence within the barrio limits job and educational opportunities directly and indirectly by separating Latinos from the mainstream, where networks to legitimate opportunity are created and sustained.

In a theoretical link between strain theory and Latino delinquency, Blea argues that Mexican Americans are ascribed low status in American society, primarily on the basis of color, culture, and history (Blea, 1988). Further, she suggests that the dominant society has historically set minority groups up for failure; minorities are encouraged to aspire to the majority's goals and at the same time are kept from achieving success. She argues that the social system does not allow Chicanos near the standard that has been set by Anglos, and as a result, the Chicano is viewed as deviant. "Thus, it is normal for Chicanos to be abnormal within the context of White dominant American society, because much of it is dictated by Anglos" (Blea, 1988:95).

Discriminatory attitudes and practices may serve to separate Latinos from the mainstream, and may prevent members of the ethnic group from achieving economic success to some extent. This variable has, in fact, been offered as a potential source of criminality. Often neglected in criminological theory, discrimination has special significance for Latinos:

"An important factor often overlooked in causation or motivational approaches to Hispanic involvement in criminality is the mistreatment they and their ancestors have endured over the years, from an abusive, exploitative, prejudiced America, beginning with its early attitudes of Anglo-Saxon racial supremacy and superiority over Spanish colonists and any other ethnic or racial minorities, which manifested itself through colonialism, expansionism, and imperialism" (Flowers, 1988:99).

Although discrimination is marginally considered within the strain theory model as it relates to the externalization of blame (Cloward & Ohlin, 1960), discriminatory practices also serve to limit opportunities for advancement. Discrimination acts as a barrier to legitimate opportunity, and the visibility of that barrier leads to the externalization of blame; thus, indirectly leading to criminal activity within a strain theory perspective. In a study of a Chicago neighborhood, Horowitz found that outsiders' views of the Chicano community create distance between the mainstream society and the ethnic group and serve to limit Chicano success:

"Success...has been hindered by outsiders' appraisals and evaluations of the residents as poverty-stricken, untrustworthy, lazy, and dangerous, for their treatment is based on these attitudes, contributing to the gap between the limited success of residents and their desire to achieve and be respected" (1983:50).

Within that community, Horowitz observed inferior service provision to residents, which was attributed to negative attitudes toward Latinos. She describes the media portrayal of residents as violent, and the local banks and food stores as charging unnecessarily high prices for goods and services. In addition, the local school board failed to improve its deteriorating schools within the neighborhood (Horowitz, 1983). Therefore, it appears that discriminatory attitudes to some extent can influence the availability of services and resources, and ultimately the availability of legitimate opportunity, within the Latino community.

Others have also observed institutionalized discrimination toward Latinos within the educational system and have cited such treatment as limiting access to legitimate means for success (Blea, 1988; Mirandé, 1985; Moore & Pachon, 1985; Padilla, 1993; Vigil, 1988). Those who have examined the Latino experience in education often point out the failure on the part of American schools to properly serve members of the ethnic group. While some argue the insensitivity to language and culture in the classroom, others describe the education system as outright prejudiced and discriminatory.

Institutionalized prejudice against Latinos has been cited in the literature since the 1920's. Although prejudice has not always been overt, school practices that have led to unequal treatment of Chicanos; academic tracking, counseling strategies, and employment of teachers unable to properly handle cultural issues. Tracking, in particular, has been criticized for placing a disproportionately high number of Mexican American youth in remedial classes. In addition, certain counseling practices often result in Chicano students being guided toward a trade rather than college (Vigil, 1988), which serves to label Chicano students and separate them from their White counterparts.

Mirandé has characterized the educational system as discriminatory, arguing that education has been used as a tool to oppress Latinos. In his examination of the Mexican American experience, he describes the school as perpetuating the economic, educational, political, and cultural oppression of Chicanos (1985:91), thus maintaining the existing social order. The ideology of education is democratic and unbiased; it is advertised as the mechanism by which social advancement is achieved and the American dream is fulfilled. One's advancement is thought to be "based on achievement and the acquisition of appropriate credentials rather than on social or familial background" (p.95). At the same time, however, the educational system has engaged in discriminatory practices which serve to limit Latino success. Therefore, Mirandé concludes that "the ideal of equal opportunity is a myth, a cruel hoax perpetuated on the poor and on Chicanos and other minorities" (p.96). Other researchers agree that the social system leads Latinos to believe that education is the way to achieve success while engaging in practices that prevent members of the ethnic group from advancing (Blea, 1988).[8]

While such ideas about the motivations of the educational system are extreme, few would argue that the education experience of Latinos and their White counterparts are similar. Segregation, tracking, grade retention and failure to incorporate Latino culture into the classroom have put Latino students at a disadvantage for attaining success. Substandard education has been cited in various Latino communities. For example, the failure of the Chicago public school system to provide adequate services to Puerto Rican students directly limits opportunity for future success:

> "Relying on the system of public education to establish the academic foundation with which to pursue the educational credentials necessary for "good jobs" in the service economy is a handicap for Puerto Ricans and other low-income residents of Chicago" (Padilla, 1993:140).

In the face of limited manufacturing jobs in Chicago, available positions are more difficult for Puerto Ricans to acquire, since the education and training they have received within the Chicago public schools is lacking. Therefore, one can reasonably conclude that inferior education in the barrio coupled with potential discriminatory practices can prevent Latinos from achieving educational advancement and as a result, can serve to limit chances for occupational and economic success.

Although changes have taken place in the education system, Vigil asserts that Chicano youth still experience forms of discrimination and isolation from the mainstream. Many problems stem from language barriers and are heightened by prejudice. The language barrier has been described as "a difficulty that prevents group members from full participation in American society" (Bullington, 1977:33). As a result, language may impede academic progress, and have indirect implications for employment opportunities. Schools have been known to discourage the use of Spanish in the classroom, which may lead to inadequate knowledge of both languages, and may set Latino children back from their White and African American counterparts, in terms of academic achievement. The language barrier also has direct consequences for employment opportunities. Gaining employment in mainstream society may be especially difficult for those who lack proficiency in English.

Taken together, characteristics of the Latino experience are likely to impact perceptions of blocked opportunity. Cloward and Ohlin describe educational expectations of the lower class as adaptive; having been "scaled down to accord with the realistic limitations on access to educational opportunities" (1960:103). In much the same way, the social conditions of Latinos might influence expectations for success.

Socioeconomic disadvantage, residential segregation, discrimination, inferior education, and the language barrier are likely to limit legitimate opportunities and influence the extent to which Latinos anticipate success. The relationship between race and blocked opportunity in strain theory has been supported by empirical research. In a study of Chicago youth gangs, Short (1964) examined whether Black and White youth of varying classes and gang membership statuses were similarly situated, or ranked, in terms of their occupational goals and opportunities. A disjunction measure was utilized, representing the discrepancy between occupational aspirations and expectations for six groups (Black and White gang members, Black and White lower-class, and Black and White middle class). In conducting racial comparisons, Short found that the groups were ordered similarly on goal discrepancy and delinquency measures, with Black gang members having the highest level of goal discrepancy or strain and the greatest involvement with police. This group was followed by the White gang members, Black lower-class, White lower-class, and middle class groups. This study illustrates the impact of race on opportunity independent of SES, and leads Short to conclude that, "Negroes will have fewer opportunities than will Whites, as will lower class boys compared to boys who are middle class" (1964: 107). In terms of motivation for delinquent behavior, this finding also indicates that the greatest strain is experienced by lower class African Americans.

Addressing the issue with a sample that includes Latinos, Jessor et al. (1968) examined Merton's theory of anomie and Cloward and Ohlin's theory of differential opportunity within a tri-ethnic community. In addition to personality influences on deviant behavior, the opportunity structure was examined as a motivation for deviant behavior. Ethnicity and gender, in addition to class, are thought to limit one's access to legitimate opportunities. "Thus, being a member of the female sex, or the Negro race, or an ethnic minority, has implications for control, or possible control over access to culture goals" (p.58). In terms of access to legitimate opportunities, the authors expected Whites to have the greatest access relative to Latinos and Native Americans. The Latino group was expected to be the most limited in terms of legitimate opportunity, while Native Americans were expected to have access to a larger number of positions of power than Latinos, due to tribal bureaucracy and more economic resources.

In their assessment of an eight item measure of access to the legitimate opportunity structure, Jessor et al. found ethnic differences among adults in the study.[9] As expected, Whites held the highest position of access, Latinos the lowest, and Native Americans held the intermediate position. Although the measure was altered for age-appropriateness, similar findings were obtained among adolescents. These results led authors to conclude that the relative position of minority groups limits access to legitimate opportunities, and exerts greater pressure to utilize illegitimate means for success. Such findings also lead to the inclusion of discrimination into the modified strain theory model in Figure 3. Discrimination is expected to impact the discrepancy between goals and opportunity. As the discrimination experience serves to limit legitimate opportunities for success, it is expected to have a positive, direct relationship with strain.

Although discrimination is introduced into the modified strain model, that influence cannot be assessed with Denver Youth Survey or Rochester Youth Development Study data. Since objective and subjective measures of historical and contemporary discrimination are beyond the scope of the current analysis, it is expected that the influence of discrimination on the model would be observed through strain:

> **Hypothesis #1:** As a group, Latinos are expected to produce greater mean values of strain, thus reflecting the cumulative effect of sociocultural experiences and discriminatory factors on access to legitimate opportunity.

Hypothesized differences in mean values of strain are suggested above and beyond any differences due to varying levels of social class. Anticipated ethnic variation is based on a cultural argument of discrimination and social isolation which serve to limit opportunities for economic advancement. The current analysis controls for social class when comparing means across groups.

ETHNICITY AND THE EXTERNALIZATION OF BLAME

Discriminatory practices are also linked to the externalization of blame. Flowers argues that a history of discrimination in the United States has led to Latino "distrust, defiance, resistance, and alienation against the larger group" (1988:99). Hypotheses of discrimination and externalization in the current investigation are based on Cloward and Ohlin's discussion of race and system blame. In *Delinquency and Opportunity*, the visibility of blocked opportunity is identified as the mechanism by which African Americans are likely to externalize rather than internalize blame for failure to achieve economic success (1960). Cloward and Ohlin assert that visible barriers to legitimate opportunity, including discrimination, may result in feelings of unjust deprivation and a tendency to blame the system for failure. The modified strain model (Figure 3) incorporates the concept of discrimination and models its estimated impact on the externalization of blame.

In an empirical examination of strain theory, Simons and Gray (1989) explored the relationship between race and the externalization of blame. An interaction between race and socioeconomic status (SES) within the strain model was hypothesized; lower-class Blacks are likely to be the most prone to strain, followed by lower-class Whites, then upper class Blacks and Whites. While class is the primary determinate of opportunities for legitimate means of goal achievement, Simons and Gray recognize that race might impact strain as it bears on the externalization of blame. System blame for failure to achieve economic success is an important step in the progression to delinquency. Not all who experience strain commit delinquent acts; for delinquent outcomes to result, the legitimacy of conventional means must first be challenged. Those who perceive the social system as inequitable are likely to blame that system for their failure to achieve economic success, and subsequently challenge the system's rules.

Certain groups within society may be more likely to perceive the system as unjust, and are therefore more likely to challenge the system's conventional means and resort to delinquent methods of goal attainment:

"Individuals in lower-status positions, especially lower-class minorities, are more apt than persons of higher status to encounter situations in which opportunities are blocked upon what are perceived to be unjust and arbitrary institutional arrangements" (Simons and Gray, 1989:92).

The relationship between occupational opportunity and delinquency should be strongest among lower-class Blacks, since this group is most susceptible to strain (due to limited legitimate opportunities) and system blaming (due to discrimination and low-class status).

In their examination of adolescent males, this argument received some support.[10] Minor differences in perceived opportunity scores were observed across the four groups, with lower means found among the lower class groups compared to middle-class.[11] A moderate correlation between opportunity and delinquency was found only for lower-class Blacks. To determine whether the relationship was spurious or due to family influences, a regression equation was estimated holding family structure and parental rejection constant. The pattern among the groups remained consistent, revealing a significant relationship between opportunity and delinquency only among lower-class Blacks. Therefore, lower-class Blacks are likely to experience discrimination in addition to class barriers to success, and are therefore more likely to externalize blame (Simons & Gray, 1989). Once the legitimacy of conventional means is challenged, this group might adopt alternative methods of goal attainment, including delinquent activity.

The interaction between race and SES in the Simons and Gray study is significant to the current inquiry because it leaves the impression that SES alone is not enough to determine delinquent outcomes. The impact of cultural factors on the externalization of blame is a compelling notion; one which may influence the application of strain to groups of minority status, including Latinos. While the inclusion of this concept is to be commended, an important issue should be addressed. It appears as though Blacks have been identified as system blaming rather than self-blaming based on assumption alone; no attempt is made to support this argument with empirical evidence or previous research. The notion that groups of minority status are more likely to externalize blame for failure is a testable hypothesis, one that might have been more appropriately operationalized by Simons and Gray. Based on their findings, however, one can reasonably hypothesize that Latinos who share the minority status of African Americans are also likely to externalize blame for their failure. A positive relationship between discrimination and the externalization of blame is anticipated among Latino youth.

While Cloward and Ohlin describe this relationship in opportunity theory, it has yet to be incorporated into the traditional strain theory model. This study recognizes the potential influence of discrimination on externalization when applying strain theory to ethnic minorities in general, and to Latinos in particular. Therefore, a path between discrimination and externalization of blame is included in the modified model, however, it cannot be empirically tested, since neither the Denver nor the Rochester study contains measures which capture discrimination. Instead, the following hypothesis is to be tested:

Hypothesis #2: Latinos, as a group, are more likely than Whites to externalize blame for failure to achieve economic success, since societal-level barriers to legitimate opportunities (i.e. discriminatory practices) are more visible for them.

Cloward and Ohlin have pointed out that reform groups serve to illuminate the failures of the social system in providing all ethnic groups with adequate resources to attain the American dream. The Chicano movement of the 1960's may have evoked such sentiment on the part of Mexican Americans and other Latino populations, causing members to externalize blame for their failure to achieve economic success. In general, social scientists describe the development of negative attitudes toward social institutions, and have attributed such feelings to unequal treatment.

Discriminatory practices in education are identified as a source of distrust and defiance among Latinos (Vigil, 1988). Resentment toward school is described as a direct consequence of tracking and other methods of institutionalized discrimination which serve to segregate Chicanos from Whites. Vigil reports that Chicano students frequently develop negative attitudes toward education as a result of problematic school experiences. Negative attitudes toward education might also be harbored by parents, whose own experiences may have led to similar conclusions. Early immigrants who experience prejudice in education may influence attitudes of their children and may even encourage children to leave school in favor of employment (Vigil, 1988:57). System blaming among Latinos in this regard is likely to continue throughout generations, with feelings of futility toward institutionalized methods of goal attainment.

Evidence of the externalization of blame has also been found on a larger scale, directed at the social structure in general. Blea describes the influence of racism on Latinos as creating antagonism and ambivalence toward life outside the barrio and anything that is middle class (1988). Such sentiment is often the result of discrimination and racism, and clearly indicates a rejection of middle class values. In addition, attitudes toward junkies in the barrio express acceptance. They are not looked down upon by Chicanos, because "there seems to be a sense of understanding that they are not responsible for their condition" (1988:104). Placing responsibility for their condition outside of the individual is further evidence of externalization among Latinos.

ETHNICITY AND CHALLENGE TO LEGITIMACY OF NORMS
Cloward and Ohlin have closely tied race to externalization and the removal of legitimacy from conventional behavior. Specifically, they suggest that African Americans may be more likely than non-minorities to withdraw legitimacy from conventional modes of behavior in the following way:

> "A Negro may find it difficult to maintain his faith in the ideology of equality under social conditions which conspicuously bar members of his 'race' from access to legitimate opportunities for achieving success...an increase in the visibility of external barriers to the advancement of Negroes heightens their sense of discrimination and justifies the withdrawal of attributions of legitimacy from conventional rules of conduct" (1960:121).

In a similar way, it is expected that the interaction between strain and the externalization of blame influences the removal of legitimacy in the traditional strain model among Latinos:

> **Hypothesis #3:** As discrimination influences the externalization of blame among Latinos, it impacts the relationship between externalization and the removal of legitimacy from conventional means. Therefore, a stronger relationship between the strain/externalization interaction term and challenge to legitimacy is expected for Latinos compared to Whites.

ETHNICITY AND ADOPTION OF DELINQUENT VALUES

Within the traditional strain model, the withdrawal of legitimacy from conventional means of goal attainment can lead to the adoption of a delinquent belief system. From a traditional strain perspective, this relationship is consistent across youth of varying ethnic backgrounds. Cloward and Ohlin argue that the withdrawal of legitimacy provides the freedom to commit to an alternative value system which includes, but is not limited to delinquent values. While the adoption of delinquent values is one response to the withdrawal of legitimacy from conventional norms, the relationship may not be uniform across ethnic groups. There is reason to believe that cultural factors impact this portion of the traditional strain theory model and influence the potential for delinquent value internalization among Latinos.

As described earlier in the chapter, the Latino experience is characterized by duality in terms of traditional and mainstream American value systems (Horowitz, 1983). Traditional Latino values include personal and family honor, which convey the importance of character and personal relations within the community. The traditional sense of Latino community and group well-being competes with the American value of individual acquisition (Horowitz, 1983). Latinos are described as familistic, and tend to value family relationships over individual accomplishments (Moore & Pachon, 1985; Sommers, Fagan & Baskin, 1994). The ideology of familism transcends socioeconomic and generational status within the Latino population and represents a distinctive cultural element (Valenzuela & Dornbusch, 1996). The extended family network is also characteristic of the Latino culture, and includes close relations with godparents, or baptismal sponsors (Horowitz, 1983; Moore & Pachon, 1985). *Compadrazgo* is cited as an element of Latino kinship which represents the bond between parents and godparents:

"...the godparent was expected to take care of the physical and spiritual needs of the child in the event that the parents could not perform these essential duties. And reciprocal ties were formed between the parents and godparents. Both parties were expected to assist each other in time of social or economic need" (Williams, 1990:26).

The Latino family is also cited as a source for retaining and transmitting traditional culture. In an examination of inner city Chicano families, Valdez describes the use of familial strategies for retaining culture which, "enables the Chicano family to cope with persistent poverty conditions and pressure exerted by the dominant society to assimilate and conform to the 'American way of life'" (p.63). Cultural retention is described as a mechanism by which Chicano families cope with discriminatory experiences and social inequality.[12] Elements of traditional culture, such as familism, may also serve to constrain antisocial behavior (Rodriguez & Zayas, 1990).

Within the traditional strain theory model, cultural characteristics such as familism might reduce the likelihood of adopting a delinquent value system in response to strain and withdrawing legitimacy from conventional methods of goal attainment. Rather than adopt a delinquent belief system when legitimate norms are challenged, the Latino adolescent may be influenced by a traditional and familiar set of cultural beliefs. Given the duality of the Latino culture, traditional values may make Latinos *less* likely to adopt a delinquent value system when legitimacy is removed from conventional norms. As Gil, Vega, & Biafora assert, "historically, minority people and immigrants have used their cultural repertoire as mechanisms of adaptation to their immediate environment in the U.S." (1998:376). In responding to strain, traditional culture, as transmitted through the family, may provide an alternative to the adoption of a delinquent value system.

The influence of Latino culture on the strain model might be observed in several ways. First, the impact of cultural values might be illustrated through slope differences in the path between challenge and delinquent values among Latinos and Whites (see Figure 3) in the traditional strain model:

Hypothesis #4a: The relationship between challenge to legitimacy and delinquent values is expected to be weaker for Latinos in the strain theory model, due to the influence of traditional cultural values.

Second, the influence of culture might be operationalized by incorporating a new construct into the theoretical model. For example, in Figure 3, a variable is added to represent one aspect of the traditional

Latino culture. Family involvement is included in the current analysis, since it is commonly cited as a dimension of the larger Latino culture. It is reasonable to expect that the family exerts a similar influence across ethnic groups; involvement with family is likely to reduce delinquent values regardless of ethnic background (Rowe et al., 1994):

Hypothesis #4b: Traditional cultural values, as transmitted by involvement with family, are likely to decrease the likelihood of adopting a delinquent value system. A negative relationship between family involvement and delinquent values is anticipated for all ethnic groups.

Although family involvement is not necessarily unique to the Latino population, differences in family dynamics have been found between Latinos and Whites. In an examination of several dimensions of familism, Valenzuela & Dornbusch found that White and Mexican American youth produce high scores on familistic attitudes and evidence strong kinship networks. In contrast to their White counterparts, however, Mexican Americans were found to have stronger familistic attitudes, more frequent contact with extended family, and tended to live within close proximity to family members (1996:58).[13]

Ethnic variation in family relations might reflect immigration influences. While large-scale European immigration subsided in the 1920's, Latino immigration has remained constant (Chavez, 1991). Since Latinos are considered a recent immigrant group, the conflict between traditional and mainstream values is likely to be reflected among the ethnic group as a whole, when contrasted with Whites. In addition, the close proximity of Latino countries of origin might also influence the extent to which traditional values are maintained. "Proximity permits Hispanics to maintain their distinct culture and language to a far greater degree than other immigrants could do in the past" (Chavez, 1991:129). Based on variation in immigration and dual value systems, a difference in the strength of family influences between Latino and White adolescents is expected.

Previous research also provides evidence of differential family impacts on delinquent outcomes (Rodriguez & Weisburd, 1991; Smith, 1990; Smith & Krohn, 1995; Sommers et al., 1994; Vazsonyi & Flannery,

1997; Weber, Miracle, & Skehan,1995) and substance use (Gil et al., 1998; Murguia, Chen, & Kaplan, 1998; Rodriguez & Recio, 1992) by ethnicity. In terms of constraining delinquent behavior, Smith and Krohn (1995) observed that family variables as a group have a greater impact on Latino adolescents than on their White or African American counterparts. In estimating family influences on delinquency, Smith and Krohn found a greater amount of variance in Latino delinquency explained by family variables. In addition, the relationship between family involvement and delinquency was strongest among Latinos, compared to African Americans or Whites. Family structure was also directly related to Latino delinquency; a relationship not found among African Americans or Whites. Given their findings across ethnic groups, Smith and Krohn conclude, "family life is more central to the lives of Hispanic adolescents, and therefore, is a more important determinant of adolescent behavior among Hispanics than it is for other racial/ethnic groups" (1995:81).

Other examinations of Latino youth reveal unique family influences on delinquency and drug use. For example, a review of risk factors for drug use initiation demonstrated that family structure and environment are more highly associated with Latino drug use compared to African Americans and Whites. As a result, the authors conclude that "the relationship between family environment factors and... substance use are not inexorably correlated, but rather are altered by the social and cultural characteristics of different racial and ethnic groups" (Gil et al., 1998:388). In another comparison of ethnic groups, Vazsonyi and Flannery (1997) found comparable predictors of delinquency across Latinos and Whites, however, differences in parental monitoring were observed. Poor monitoring was more highly associated with delinquent behavior among White youth. The authors note that this finding is consistent with other studies of Latino families. They point out that other studies of Latino delinquency find no link between parental control and delinquency; instead, other family processes (such as involvement with family and family structure) are commonly identified as salient among the Latino population in reducing delinquent behavior.

Additional evidence of differential effects of family dimensions has been found. Among a multiethnic sample, Weber et al. (1995) examined several elements of the family bond and assessed their impact on delinquency. Like the observations made by Vazsonyi and Flannery, parental monitoring was found to be unrelated to Latino delinquency, although it was significantly related to delinquency among African Americans and Whites. In addition, a significant relationship between family pride and delinquency was found among Whites and Latinos only, with a stronger impact on Latino delinquency. A unique effect of female (caretaker) communication on Latino delinquency was also revealed.

In comparing a Puerto Rican sample to National Youth Survey respondents, Rodriguez & Weisburd (1991) also found differences in the impact of two separate family variables. Of the two family measures included in the study - family involvement and family normlessness - only family involvement was significantly related to delinquency among the Puerto Rican sample.[14] Neither of the family variables were significant among the NYS sample, which leads Rodriguez & Weisburd to conclude that the "family is likely to exert more independent influences among Puerto Rican youths than among mainstream American youths" (1991:476). Differences in family dimensions among the Puerto Rican sample might illustrate underlying qualities of Latino families. Family involvement in the study was expected to capture a psychological bond, while family normlessness was intended to measure "the extent to which the family has acted as a vehicle for transmitting conventional norms" (p.477). The authors conclude that involvement or bonding is more meaningful in the Latino family than the transmission of conventional norms. Therefore, the Latino family does not appear to serve as a reinforcement for mainstream values; that argument has been cited by others as well (Smith & Krohn, 1995).

Due to differential exposure to American values, White parents are more likely to reinforce the economic success goal, since European immigrant groups helped shape that goal and have experienced success within mainstream institutions. Given the relative inability of Latinos to achieve the same degree of success, involvement with family might lead to alternative sources of success among members of the ethnic group and decrease the chances of developing a delinquent adaptation to strain to achieve economic success. In explaining unique findings among Latinos, Smith and Krohn suggest differential exposure to stressors by ethnicity:

"perhaps for White and African American children, more mainstream American pressures for independence and autonomy for adolescents have resulted in reduced family influence over children in many instances" (1995:84).

Involvement in traditional culture is likely to serve as a protective factor against delinquent behavior by reducing the likelihood of internalizing delinquent values. Based on previous research, a stronger family influence is expected among Latinos, since the family is less likely to reinforce the mainstream values that are less familiar to them. Additionally, the Latino family is more likely to emphasize traditional values, such as family obligation and closeness:

Hypothesis #4c: The influence of family on delinquent value adoption is expected to be stronger for Latinos than Whites.

Traditional Latino culture also emphasizes communality which competes with the mainstream American ideal of individual accomplishment. As a result, Latino families are less likely to encourage the kind of independence that is often required for fulfilling American success goals.

This investigation also explores the impact of acculturation on one's involvement in traditional Latino culture. Sommers et al. (1993, 1994) describe the process of acculturation and its influence on the relationship between family and delinquency among Puerto Rican youth. Acculturation among Latinos "refers to the process whereby the behaviors and attitudes of an immigrant group change as a result of contact, exposure, and a move toward accepting the new dominant culture," and is primarily expressed through fluency in and preference for the English language (Sommers et al., 1994:210). Sommers et al. assert that as Puerto Rican youth are exposed to mainstream values, traditional culture goals and values may be neutralized (1994). In the integrated theoretical model, familism (traditional concepts of family bonding and obligation) is expected to reduce delinquency. At the same time, acculturation is expected to weaken the impact of family within the model. As mainstream values are internalized, Puerto Rican youth are less likely to be bound to traditional norms and expectations. In their analysis, Sommers et al. found that acculturation weakens family ties and indirectly increases delinquency:

"The increased risk of delinquency among more highly acculturated boys appears to be due to the loss or blurring of boundaries and roles in the structure of Puerto Rican families in which traditional cultural values are not upheld, family bonds are weakened, and contact with deviant peers increases" (1994:221).

In addition, a direct, positive relationship between acculturation and delinquency was found. Although a positive influence was not anticipated, Sommers et al. attribute increased delinquency among the more acculturated to greater exposure to delinquent influences, including delinquent peers.[15]

Other studies of Latino families do not support a neutralizing effect of acculturation on family relationships. Valenzuela and Dornbusch (1996) examined family attitudes (emphasis on family versus individual needs), structure (geographic proximity of kin) and behavior (contact with family) across three generations of Mexican Americans, and found familism to be generally stable. Acculturation does not appear to weaken one's sense of family obligation; no statistically significant differences in family attitudes were found across the groups. In addition, family contact appears to be greatest among third generation Chicanos.[16] Acculturation seems to increase rather than decrease the amount of contact with family; a finding which contradicts the notion that acculturation weakens family bonds over time. Valenzuela and Dornbusch argue that "no dimension of familism is declining as Mexicans are exposed to greater acculturation or to greater success in American society" (1996:61).

Conflicting findings across Latino groups may indicate variation in familism by country of origin. In a sample of Puerto Rican youth, Sommers et al. (1994) demonstrate that acculturation weakens family ties, although a similar relationship has not been found for Mexican Americans (Valenzuela and Dornbusch, 1996). Given the differences in the impact of acculturation on traditional values, the potential acculturation influence on the strain model is unclear. The current analysis will examine the relationship between acculturation and traditional values and determine whether exposure to mainstream culture decreases family involvement. Unfortunately, the acculturation influence cannot be assessed across Latinos in both sites, as the measure is only available in the Rochester study. The language-based measure of acculturation will allow for an examination of cultural influences among Puerto Ricans only. Based on the work of Sommers et al. (1994), the following is anticipated:

Hypothesis #5: As Latinos become more acculturated into the mainstream, traditional cultural values may be weakened. Therefore, a direct relationship between acculturation and family involvement is examined, and is expected to be negative.

If acculturation is found to neutralize family relations, the subsequent influence of the family in reducing delinquent values may be compromised. Ultimately, acculturation may indirectly impact delinquent behavior. As acculturation neutralizes involvement in the traditional Latino culture, delinquent values are more likely to emerge, and in turn, delinquency may increase. A direct influence of acculturation on delinquency is not included in the current analysis, however, given the inconsistency of previous findings (see Sommers et al., 1993).

ETHNICITY AND DELINQUENT PEERS
Delinquent peers is a significant element in strain theory, since Cloward and Ohlin assert that delinquent values and delinquent behavior are reinforced by the association with similarly situated peers (1960). Based on previous research, there is likely to be variation in peer influences across ethnic groups. Studies of Latino samples have demonstrated decreased peer influences among Latinos compared to Whites. In a comparison of samples from the Puerto Rican Adolescent Survey (PRAS) and the National Youth Survey (NYS), common predictors of delinquent behavior were found among Puerto Ricans and Whites, although peer influences were weaker among Puerto Rican youth (Rodriguez and Weisburd, 1991). Researchers suggest peer involvement may be less important in predicting delinquent outcomes among Puerto Ricans, since the influence of the family is particularly strong. Additional comparisons of the samples reveal a similar impact of peers on drug use (Rodriguez and Recio, 1992). In another study of Latino and White youth, Murguia et al. (1998) found that family warmth reduces the likelihood of associating with delinquent peers (which indirectly reduces delinquency) among Mexican Americans only.

In an attempt to replicate such findings, this study models a direct family influence on delinquent peer association. As family involvement is anticipated to influence delinquent values across all groups, the same is expected with regard to a family influence on delinquent peer associations (see Hypothesis #4b):

Hypothesis #6a: Involvement in family activity is expected to decrease the likelihood of developing delinquent peer associations. A negative relationship between family involvement and delinquent peers is anticipated for all ethnic groups.

At the same time, the importance of the family in the Latino culture and previous findings with regard to family influences on delinquency suggests a differential impact of the family by ethnicity:

Hypothesis #6b: The influence of family involvement on delinquent peer associations is expected to be stronger for Latinos than Whites.

Given the relative importance of the Latino family, it is expected that peers are less likely to influence the adoption of delinquent values and involvement in delinquent behavior in the strain theory model:

Hypothesis #6c: The influence of delinquent peers on *delinquent values* is expected to be weaker for Latinos than Whites, due to the relative impact of the family.

Hypothesis #6d: The influence of delinquent peers on *delinquent behavior* is also expected to be weaker for Latinos than Whites.

ETHNICITY AND THE ILLEGITIMATE OPPORTUNITY STRUCTURE
The relationship between ethnicity and illegitimate opportunity is one of the primary ways in which Cloward and Ohlin incorporate race into strain theory. In a discussion of migrant group assimilation and delinquent adaptations in lower-class communities, Cloward and Ohlin describe three stages of group assimilation which are characterized by access to the legitimate and illegitimate opportunity structure, and as a result, related to various delinquent adaptations (1960:194).

The process of assimilation begins with new immigrants settling in urban areas, facing restricted access to legitimate and illegitimate opportunity structures. Crime within such neighborhoods is characterized by violence; the seemingly sole source of status attainment. Over time, migrant groups develop ties to the community and the neighborhood becomes characterized by organized crime and political groups. As this assimilation process occurs, the slum becomes more integrated, providing greater access to illegitimate means for success. Since legitimate means remain limited for the lower class immigrant, pressure to resort to illegal means increases, and criminal adaptations ensue. Once success is achieved (either through legitimate or illegitimate methods), the immigrant transitions into the suburbs and the slum begins to deteriorate. Once again, it becomes disorganized and violent crime increases.

Although Cloward and Ohlin describe the detailed progression toward assimilation and delinquent adaptations, they recognize structural changes that have occurred in the lower-class neighborhood that might influence the African American experience. They admit that the sequence they depict might be more accurate in describing the experience of European immigrants than that of African Americans. They suggest that changes in the lower class community "have resulted in the disorganization of the slums, restricted opportunity, and lessened social control" (1960:202). The attempt by African Americans to gain power within the community that has been met with resistance, thus limiting potential legitimate opportunities for success. In addition, the decline of the urban political machine has shifted local power to the state and national levels. As a result, "the urban lower class has lost an important integrating structure and a significant channel for social ascent" (p.207). Other structural changes in the lower-class community include the growth of the welfare state and the development of public housing projects. Cloward and Ohlin argue that both serve to break down social integration and cohesion within the community. The emergent social disorganization in urban low-class neighborhoods is therefore characterized by limited access to opportunity, both legitimate and illegitimate. Social control also suffers in the disorganized community; overall, conditions in lower class urban areas are expected to produce conflict-oriented behavior and retreatism among lower-class youth.

As Cloward and Ohlin recognize, their representation group assimilation may not be applicable across all ethnic groups. Since the Latino population is characterized by a constant immigration flow, neighborhood characteristics described by Cloward and Ohlin may not accurately depict the Latino condition. For example, assimilation is expected to be accompanied by opportunities for illegitimate activity. The process of assimilation appears to assume a degree of homogeneity within the group; as the group establishes ties within the neighborhood, opportunities for illegal behavior increase. Given immigration trends, the influx of individuals into a neighborhood may not be constant. Instead, Latino neighborhoods may comprise individuals who establish ties and discover illegitimate opportunities at different times. The idea of group assimilation within the Latino community may not be as obvious as that process has been in the past for other immigrant groups.

To test hypotheses, Short and Strodtbeck (1965) examined racial and community differences in adaptations to strain to determine whether Black gangs are more likely to adopt conflict-oriented adaptations to strain than White gangs. "That is, both legitimate and illegitimate economic opportunities seem objectively more limited for Negroes than for Whites - hence, the expectation of greater conflict orientation among Negro than among White gangs" (Short & Strodtbeck, 1965:93-95). Variation in delinquent adaptations was observed by race; African American gangs are reported to be the most conflict-oriented in the study, while White gangs rate most highly on retreatism. Short and Strodtbeck argue that differences are due, in part, to differences in the community. Socialization within the White neighborhoods appears to be more formalized, characterized by conventional institutions such as the church and local political associations. On the other hand, "community life for adults as well as children and adolescents, was largely informal and quasi-public in the Negro areas" (Short & Strodtbeck:107).

Regarding illegitimate opportunity among Latinos, Sullivan (1989) examined neighborhood influences on Puerto Rican youth crime in La Barriada, an ethnically diverse New York neighborhood. His observations of youth crime do not appear to reflect the illegitimate opportunity structure that Cloward and Ohlin define (refer to Chapter 2 for a description of the illegitimate opportunity structure). For the most part, youth recruit their peers for involvement in crime in La Barriada. Unlike Cloward and Ohlin's assertion of age integration among criminals (adult criminals recruit and train younger delinquents), Sullivan found that youth organize and train themselves to carry out various criminal activities, primarily theft. Adults in the neighborhood are indifferent to youth and do not appear to take an active role in their delinquent involvement. Although little criminal activity involves both adults and youth, Sullivan describes an environment of permissiveness within the community.

Adults appear to be indifferent to youth crime; often they are reluctant to call police when they suspect that a crime has been committed, and support youth delinquency indirectly by purchasing stolen goods.[17]

The dynamics of auto theft and drug sales appear to be quite different from other crime in the neighborhood. The structure of opportunity for auto theft, in particular, is more congruent with Cloward and Ohlin's assertions. In La Barriada, auto theft is characterized by adult recruitment, specialized training, and opportunity for advancement. Within the organized business, there is sustained interaction between adults and youth: older criminals recruit, train, and work with delinquents. In addition to the integration of offenders of various ages, Sullivan also describes an overlap between legitimate and illegitimate auto work in the neighborhood, which exemplifies a second element of Cloward and Ohlin's legitimate opportunity structure. Auto workers might be legally employed in a garage where legal and illegal business is done.

In an examination of illegitimate opportunity among multi-ethnic youth, Jessor et al. (1968) estimated ethnic differences in exposure to deviant role models and opportunity for deviance. Within a tri-ethnic community, they found that Whites have the least access to illegitimate means, and Native Americans the greatest, with Latinos ranking in between. Findings are consistent between their sample of adults in the community and high school students. Latinos have less access to illegitimate means than Native Americans because "of their relatively greater participation in church activities and social groups, and secondarily, because of lesser likelihood of exposure to deviant behavior during their socialization experience" (Jessor et al., 1968:265).

Applying the argument to the current analysis, Latinos who engage in activities related to their traditional culture are expected to have limited access to the illegitimate opportunity structure. Although the relationship is not directly examined in the current analysis, family involvement is expected to influence the adoption of delinquent values, and indirectly, delinquent behavior. Additionally, a direct relationship between traditional culture and illegitimate opportunity is not examined since other factors, such as neighborhood structure, are likely to impact the accessibility of illegitimate opportunity. As Cloward and Ohlin assert, neighborhood level influences are perhaps the most important source of illegitimate means of goal attainment. It is reasonable to argue that an individual might be deeply involved in family and religious activity and still have illegitimate opportunities present in their neighborhood.

Given the empirical findings and characteristics of the Latino experience in the United States, criminal opportunity appears to vary by Latino neighborhood. Because of class differences and barrioization (residential segregation from the mainstream), Latino youth are likely to reside in neighborhoods characterized by criminal opportunity. The influence of ethnicity on illegitimate opportunity is unclear, however, given population heterogeneity and immigration patterns. Therefore, no specific hypotheses will be made about this particular strain concept in the current analysis.

MINORITY GROUP DIFFERENCES

Although the primary focus of this chapter is the applicability of strain to Latinos as they compare with White youth, comparisons can also be drawn between Latinos and African Americans. This section offers preliminary hypotheses about similarities and anticipated differences within the minority group population on various strain theory concepts, including the internalization of goals, the perception of blocked opportunity, the externalization of blame, the challenge to legitimacy of conventional means of goal attainment, and the role of culture in inhibiting delinquent outcomes.

In describing the Latino experience, one can draw a parallel to the history and current condition of African Americans. Latinos and African Americans share elements of minority group status, including a history of discrimination and prejudice, limited opportunity for financial and educational advancement, exclusion from the mainstream political and social arena, and primary concentration in American inner cities (Aguirre & Turner, 1995; Mann, 1995). By definition, minority groups are excluded from full participation in mainstream society.[18] The minority experience is characterized by discrimination, where members of the dominant majority deny members of less powerful groups full access to the valued resources of education, employment, income, prestige, and power (Aguirre & Turner, 1995:4). Institutionalized discrimination is also cited as a primary contributor to minority crime (Mann, 1995); the impact of discrimination on criminal behavior is illustrated in the modified strain model, and is likely to apply to both minority groups.

From a strain theory perspective, Latinos and African Americans are limited in terms of access to legitimate opportunities; a similarity due to shared minority group status. Although the specific history of each differs, historical and contemporary exclusion is common, resulting in fewer legitimate opportunities to achieve economic success. In separate examinations, limited opportunities among African Americans (Short, 1964) and Latinos (Jessor et al. 1968) have been demonstrated. In the current analysis, the influence of discrimination on the traditional strain theory model is expected to apply to both minority groups:

Hypothesis #7: Due to shared minority status, African Americans and Latinos are expected to demonstrate stronger perceptions of blocked opportunity, and as a result, higher levels of strain compared to their non-minority counterparts.[19]

Although the role of discrimination is likely to strengthen perceptions of blocked opportunity and lead to greater strain among Latinos and African Americans, there are additional considerations to be made. Differences between minority groups exist in terms of identifiability, language, immigration patterns, and advances in the mainstream. Those differences are likely to shape discrimination experiences and might ultimately influence the fit of the traditional strain model across minority groups.

With regard to identification, physical characteristics are likely to make minority groups identifiable and therefore, vulnerable to discrimination. "Even when socioeconomic standing and/or culture are not obvious, skin color serves as a basis of discrimination" (Aguirre & Turner, 1995:61). Since African Americans are more likely to be identified as members of an ethnic minority by their physical characteristics, they are more easily targeted for discrimination than Latinos, who tend to have greater variation in skin color and physical characteristics. At the same time, however, Latinos are subject to identification and discrimination by language, which can limit educational and employment opportunities.

In addition to language, the consistent immigration of Latinos from various countries of origin contributes to the current Latino experience. Migration patterns of ethnic minority groups have been linked to overall group achievement. In accounting for differences in economic success between African Americans, Asians, and European immigrants Wilson describes:

> "The dynamic factor behind those differences and perhaps the most important single contributor to the varying rates of urban and racial ethnic progress in the twentieth century, is the flow of migrants" (1984:94).

Since the 1970's, the migration issue has become more salient to Latinos than to African Americans. Due to the differences in migration patterns and the continual growth of the Latino population, Wilson cites decreasing disadvantage among Blacks and increased joblessness, crime, discrimination and antagonism directed toward Latinos (1984:97). A certain degree of antagonism might also lie in the voluntary nature of current Latino immigration. Tides of immigration and deportation have been linked to the U.S. economy and the fear on the part of citizens over losing employment opportunities (Aguirre & Turner, 1995). Voluntary immigrants are seen as direct competitors for American jobs and might therefore be treated with hostility in a way that African Americans might not experience. Because of illegal immigration issues, Latinos might be treated with suspicion and hostility; limiting opportunities for advancement, and ultimately impacting the applicability of strain theory (as seen in Figure 3).[20]

Immigration patterns have also been tied to the traditional strain concept of economic aspirations. In a discussion of race and the American dream, Hochschild notes that the involuntary nature of African American immigration essentially forced members of the ethnic group to "come to terms with a dream that was not originally theirs" (1995:15). She notes that African Americans did not originally move to America in the pursuit of a dream as voluntary immigrants have. As a result, the internalization of economic success goals may be weaker among African Americans compared to Latinos, since their current immigration rate is much lower. Assuming all voluntary immigrant groups hold faith in the American dream, Latinos as a group may demonstrate higher success goals than African Americans.[21]

Hochschild also ties current African American economic success goals to historical failure to achieve success. She argues that the persistent failure of certain groups to achieve success serves to weaken the ideology of the dream: "when people recognize that chances for success are slim or getting slimmer, the whole tenor of the American dream changes dramatically for the worse" (1995:27). Since African American and Latino experiences have been characterized by disadvantage and blocked opportunity, the lack of success may have resulted in lowered aspirations compared to non-minority youth. As mentioned previously, the current analysis will examine success goal orientation by ethnicity, testing the strain theory assumption that goals are universal.

Social isolation from the mainstream culture (in terms of residential segregation, educational and occupational gaps between majority and minority groups, and the lack of minority group participation in the political arena) is expected to impact group expectations for achieving goals. Cloward and Ohlin describe that process with regard to class and education:

"What we are suggesting is that lower-class attitudes toward education are adaptive; that is, expectations are scaled down to accord with the realistic limitations on access to educational opportunities. Educational attainment and related forms of goal striving are thus eschewed not so much because they are inherently devalued as because access to them is relatively restricted" (Cloward and Ohlin, 1960:103).

In the same way, perceptions of limited legitimate opportunity among minority groups can result from the historical lack of success in mainstream society.

In spite of that similarity between minority groups, it appears as though African Americans have experienced a greater degree of mainstream success than Latinos. Recent demographic data depict the growth of the African American middle-class, a decreasing gap in educational and occupational attainment between Blacks and Whites, and a greater African American participation in politics (Aguirre & Turner, 1995; del Pinal & Singer, 1997; McMillen & Kaufman, 1997; Sowell, 1981). This is not to say that African Americans enjoy full participation in American society; in many areas they remain underrepresented. In comparison to the Latino population, however, their presence is felt in areas where Latinos are virtually invisible. For example, Latinos are noticeably absent in the political and professional arenas, and remain the least educated minority group (del Pinal & Singer, 1997).[22] The lack of Latino visibility is likely to be reflected in group perceptions of legitimate opportunity. Comparatively speaking, Latinos are likely to perceive fewer opportunities for advancement given the relative lack of success the ethnic group has enjoyed:

Hypothesis #8: While minority status is likely to depress perceptions of opportunity in both minority groups, Latinos are likely to demonstrate the strongest perceptions of blocked opportunity and highest levels of strain. Differences are likely to reflect decreased opportunities due to language, immigration patterns, and the history of success among Latinos in the U.S.

The influence of intra-minority group differences on the *strength* of relationships is less clear. Although higher levels of blocked opportunity and strain are anticipated among Latinos, the discrimination experience is likely to play out in a similar way for both minority groups:

Hypothesis #9a: Latinos and African Americans are more likely than whites to externalize blame for failure to achieve economic success, since societal-level barriers to legitimate opportunities (i.e. discriminatory practices) are visible among minority populations.

Among African Americans and Latinos, stronger relationships are anticipated between the strain/externalization of blame interaction and subsequent challenge to legitimacy. That relationship is likely to reflect the influence of discrimination on the model, and would therefore be stronger among minority groups compared to Whites:

Hypothesis #9b: Based Cloward and Ohlin's assertion that the visibility of barriers to legitimate opportunity leads to externalization and challenge to legitimacy of African Americans, a stronger impact of the strain/externalization interaction on the challenge to legitimacy is anticipated among both minority groups.

Ethnic differences represented in the front half of the modified model pertain primarily to minority group status. Minority status is characterized by historical and contemporary discrimination and is expected to influence relationships within the model similarly among Latinos and African Americans. Within the second half of the modified strain model cultural factors are introduced. Involvement in family is expected to reduce the adoption of delinquent values among all ethnic groups (Hypothesis #4a), and is expected to have a stronger influence among Latinos (Hypothesis #4b) compared to Whites. The literature on minority groups suggests that the influence of the family may be similar among Latinos and African Americans. According to Gil et al., minority groups are likely to evidence a stronger family influence on drug use initiation since their cultural background serves as an adaptation mechanism to discrimination experiences in the United States (1998). Similarly, Krohn and Thornberry argue:

"Perhaps because of their minority status and the discrimination that may limit the range of their social networks, Hispanics and African-Americans rely more on their families for social support than do whites" (1993:105).

Given the history and experience of minority groups in the United States, the family is likely to serve as an adaptation aid to both Latinos and African Americans. Additional research suggests that Blacks and Latinos are more likely than Whites to live in an extended family, where members help protect against drug use or delinquency (Amey & Albrecht, 1998).

The significance of the family in reducing Latino delinquency (compared to Whites and African Americans) has been supported by empirical research. Comparisons between African American and White families have also been made which reveal higher scores on family control and family intimacy among Blacks (Giordano et al., 1993). Higher levels of parental control and intimacy are attributed to the role of the Black family in American society, in which "Black youths may see their families as a particular important 'safe haven' or anchor" (1993:280). Findings among African Americans and Latinos suggest that the family plays a unique role in the socialization experience of minority youth:

Hypothesis #10a: Compared to the majority, African American and Latino families serve as a source of strength in response to discrimination, and may ultimately serve as a protective factor against delinquent adaptations to strain. In the current analysis, the influence of the family in reducing delinquent values is expected to be stronger among minority groups compared to Whites.

In the current analysis, Latino involvement in family activity is expected to demonstrate a stronger influence on the development of delinquent values compared to African Americans. Theoretically, the duality of the Latino culture (which incorporates both mainstream and traditional values) might set the ethnic group apart from other minority and non-minority youth (Horowitz, 1983). The immigration pattern of the Latino population is also likely to support the maintenance of traditional values of communality and familism. As a whole, the group is less likely to have been influenced by the mainstream ideals of independence, as Smith and Krohn (1985) have suggested. Their findings are described earlier in the chapter: the strongest influences of family involvement and family structure on delinquency are found among Latinos. Other studies support a stronger influence of family among Latinos when compared to African Americans (Brook, Whiteman, Balka, & Hamburg, 1992; Krohn & Thornberry, 1993).[23] Based on a differential impact of family by ethnicity, Smith & Krohn observe that "Hispanic family life appears to have a more pervasive effect on adolescent behavior than is suggested by the results on African American and White families" (1985:84). They attribute this finding to the differences in ethnic group exposure to mainstream pressures for independence and autonomy, which are congruent with the economic success goal described by strain theorists. Compared to other ethnic groups (minority and non-minority), Latino families may be less likely to reinforce a mainstream value system; instead, the family may cultivate traditional values:

Hypothesis #10b: Based on previous empirical findings, the influence of the family on delinquent values is expected to be strongest for Latinos. The Latino family may be less likely to reinforce mainstream ideals, and instead, provide other avenues of success for adolescents which are based on traditional values.

Within the modified strain model, cultural factors are also expected to impact peer effects on delinquency. Latinos are likely to experience a decreased peer effect on delinquent values and delinquent behavior compared to Whites, since the family is expected to be the most influential among the ethnic group. In a similar way, Latino peer relations might differ from African Americans. Since the impact of the family is expected to be strongest among Latinos, peer differences might also be observed across minority groups:

Hypothesis #11a: Between minority groups, Latinos are expected to evidence a weaker influence of peers on *delinquent values*, given the anticipated impact of the family.

Hypothesis #11b: Between minority groups, Latinos are also expected to evidence a weaker influence of peers on *delinquent behavior*.

Although a strong family influence is anticipated for both minority groups, similar peer influences are not hypothesized. Empirical findings on peers by race are mixed; some report decreased peer involvement among African Americans compared to Whites (Giordano et al., 1993). Other studies demonstrate similarities among Whites and African Americans, and cite Latino social networks as unique (Krohn & Thornberry, 1993). Support for lower peer influence among Latinos is provided by Curry and Spergel (1992), who studied predictors of gang involvement among Latinos and African Americans. In their analysis, Latino gang involvement was associated with *intra personal* variables, such as self-esteem and educational frustration. On the other hand, African American gang involvement was associated with *interpersonal* or social variables, including exposure to other gang members. Those differences suggest that African Americans are more likely to be influenced by relationships with others, including peers. Although the study by Curry and Spergel does not support the hypothesis that the family is most important among Latinos, it does demonstrate that peer influences may vary among minority groups.

Hypothesized differences among Latinos and Whites, and Latinos and African Americans presented in this chapter may not be the only differences revealed in the current analysis. Although theory has guided expectations of cultural influences on the strain model (listed on Table 3a), there may be unanticipated differences by ethnicity that are uncovered by statistical analyses. It is also important to keep in mind that the primary goal of the study is to examine the theory as it has been offered by Cloward and Ohlin. Although a modified model has been offered which incorporates additional variables, traditional strain theory will first be tested by ethnicity to determine its overall explanatory value in accounting for the delinquency of various ethnic groups. The theory has been accepted as a general explanation of crime, and as such, it is likely to apply similarly to Whites, Latinos, and African Americans.

CHAPTER 4
Data and Methods

This study utilizes data from the Denver Youth Survey (DYS) and the Rochester Youth Development Study (RYDS) to examine strain theory across various ethnic groups. These studies are appropriate for the current analysis because they are longitudinal in nature and have large minority populations, allowing for a test of strain theory among Latino, White, and African American males. The DYS and the RYDS are part of the Program of Research on the Causes and Correlates of Delinquency, which is designed to examine the developmental processes and experiences that lead to deviant behavior.[1] Each study utilizes a multidisciplinary approach and considers the influences of social and psychological factors on delinquent outcomes (Huizinga, Loeber, & Thornberry, 1993a).

Unlike most other delinquency studies, each site includes a substantial proportion of Latino youth; members of the ethnic group comprise approximately 45 and 17 percent of the total DYS and RYDS samples, respectively. Given the paucity of data on Latinos, the ethnic composition of the studies provides the unique opportunity to examine Latinos of two countries of origin; the DYS permits the examination of Mexican American youth, while the RYDS includes Latinos of Puerto Rican descent. Of Latinos in the DYS sample, 66% indicate that they are of Mexican descent and two percent describe their ethnicity as Puerto Rican (33% describe themselves as Hispanic or Spanish-American and do not indicate country of origin). In the RYDS sample, Puerto Ricans comprise 93% of all Latinos. These studies permit a comparative inquiry among ethnic groups generally, and at the same time allow for a comparison within the Latino population. In addition to the demographic composition of the samples, the studies contain parallel measures which are also necessary for comparative analyses. A detailed discussion of sampling designs and measures will follow in this chapter.

The DYS and the RYDS "were selected to work collaboratively and cooperatively in conducting longitudinal studies to examine the development of serious delinquency and drug use" (Huizinga et al., 1994:1-3). Both are based on a prospective longitudinal design, which involves periodic interviews with probability samples of different birth cohorts and their parents. The primary benefit of the longitudinal design is its ability to capture the sequence of events preceding delinquent involvement. As suggested by Huizinga et al.:

"the strength of the longitudinal investigation is that it permits researchers to sort out which factors precede changes in offending, to predict such changes, and to do so independent of other factors. With the aid of repeated measures, it is possible to identify the pathways to delinquency, each with unique causal factors that, like delinquency itself, may change over time" (1994:2).

Through the examination of cohorts at regular intervals, developmental pathways leading to delinquency can be identified. Compared to cross-sectional studies, longitudinal investigations are instrumental in distinguishing factors throughout the life course that are related to the development of delinquent behavior (Huizinga et al., 1993b). Longitudinal data are ideal for testing strain theory, since the progression to delinquency follows a sequence of events over time (Cloward & Ohlin, 1960).

Another benefit of the Program of Research on the Causes and Correlates of Delinquency is the coordination of the projects which allows for the replication and cross validation of findings. In their collaborative efforts, the DYS and the RYDS include a set of core measures in addition to site-specific items. The consistency of measures allows for comparisons across sites; this is particularly beneficial to the current investigation as it permits an examination and comparison of Latinos of Puerto Rican and Mexican origin. In addition, each site contains unique items which may strengthen the measurement of theoretical constructs, thus allowing for the comparison of multiple strain theory measures.[2]

Strain theory is examined utilizing DYS and RYDS data from 1990 to 1992 (indicated by Time 1, Time 2, and Time 3).

Table 4a. Total Male Sample Characteristics*

	Time 1 (1990)		Time 2 (1991)		Time 3 (1992)	
	DYS	RYDS	DYS	RYDS	DYS	RYDS
Student Interviews	(n=429)	(n=684)	(n=418)	(n=663)	(n=412)	(n=623)
% of initial sample	93%	97%	91%	94%	89%	89%
Parent Interviews			(n=402)	(n=613)		
Average Age	15.0	15.22	15.96	16.26	16.95	17.23
Ethnicity:						
White	6.7%	27.8%	7.0%	27.7%	7.0%	28.2%
Latino	46.2%	17.1%	47.6%	17.3%	48.4%	17.2%
African American	37.0%	55.1%	36.5%	54.9%	37.4%	54.6%
Other (DYS Only)	10.1%	- -	8.9%	- -	7.2%	- -
Social Class:						
Receive Public Assistance	49.5%	48.1%	48.6%	47.9%	42.8%	46.8%

*Note: Data are weighted to represent Denver high risk neighborhoods and Rochester public school seventh and eighth grade cohorts of 1988.

SAMPLING

DENVER YOUTH SURVEY

The DYS consists of annual interviews with a probability sample of five different birth cohorts and their parents. To gain a complete picture of juvenile delinquency, the DYS includes a substantial number of chronic offenders, which allows for a contrast to more trivial juvenile delinquents. The overrepresentation of individuals from Denver high risk areas is designed to "ensure enough serious, chronic offenders for analysis of their development, and, at the same time provide control data on normal developmental patterns" (Huizinga et al., 1994:3). High risk samples are appropriate for examining strain theory, as previous research suggests (see Chapter 2). Bernard (1984) has pointed out the lack of strain theory support among general population samples, whose criminal involvement may be restricted to less serious delinquency. Since strain theory was originally intended to explain serious delinquency among lower class, urban males, the high risk sample in the DYS is useful for testing strain theory. As a consequence, findings are applicable to youth found in similar demographic areas; results are not intended to generalize to mainstream samples in lower risk neighborhoods.

In the DYS, high risk areas were identified on the basis of social disorganization and high official crime rates. Initially, a social ecology analysis was conducted, which indicated areas with housing and population characteristics associated with delinquency (Huizinga et al., 1994). Specifically, 35 variables were selected from census data to represent seven conceptual areas related to social disorganization, including family structure, ethnicity, socio-economic status, housing, mobility, marital status, and age composition. Eleven distinct factors were identified and a cluster analysis was subsequently conducted to classify similar block groups of the city (Esbensen & Huizinga, 1991:699). Three clusters were identified as socially disorganized, although each had varied ecological characteristics. One cluster is described as 'traditional' in possessing characteristics commonly associated with social disorganization, such as a high poverty rate, unemployment, school dropout, and ethnic/racial heterogeneity. Other clusters vary on mobility, housing density, and racial composition. Using official arrest data, neighborhoods within the three disorganized clusters which ranked in the upper one third of the crime distribution were then selected for inclusion in the study (Esbensen & Huizinga, 1991).

Of all households available in the selected neighborhoods 20,236 were eligible for inclusion in the study. From a probability sample of households in the three disorganized areas, individuals were selected for participation in the study. Youth were oversampled from the 'traditional' disorganized area; as a result, the data are weighted to reflect a true random sample. A final sample of 1,530 adolescents was derived, which consists of equal numbers of males and females from five age cohorts who were 7, 9, 11, 13, and 15 years old when the study began. Although the inclusion of multiple birth cohorts allows for an examination of the full adolescent age span at any given year, the current analysis includes males of the 11, 13, and 15 year old cohorts since they provide a proper match with the age of the RYDS sample. For more detailed information on sampling techniques of the DYS see Huizinga et al. (1993a).

Strain theory is examined utilizing three waves of data from 1990 to 1992 which corresponds with waves 3 through 5 of the DYS (see Table 4a for a total sample description at each wave). Latino, White, and African American males who completed interviews at all three time periods and whose parents completed an interview at Time 2 are included in the current analysis (see Table 4b for final sample characteristics). A total of 345 males from the DYS are included, which represents 75 percent of the original 464 DYS males in the 11, 13, and 15 year old cohorts. The percentage of males included in the current investigation does not reflect the retention rates of the DYS. Over five waves of data collection, the study retained between 89 and 93 percent of males interviewed in Wave 1. The number of males in the current analysis is restricted because the selection criterion also includes parental interview completion at Time 2 (which results in a loss of 62 cases). Since this study is primarily concerned with Latino, White and African Americans, twenty males in the DYS who identify their ethnic background as Native American, Asian American or 'other' are excluded from the analysis.

The average age of males at Time 1 is 15.0 years, and at Time 3 it is 17.0 years. Examination of males during middle adolescence is supported by previous research that finds support for strain among middle and late adolescent groups (Menard, 1995). Within the DYS sample, there is a large number of African American and Mexican American youth which permits an analysis of multiple influences on delinquency, including ethnicity, social status, family characteristics and peer-related factors (Huizinga et al., 1993a). In the current analysis, African Americans and Latinos represent forty and fifty percent of the total DYS sample, respectively. Unfortunately, the number of White males in the DYS is small, and does not permit multivariate analyses. Group means and bivariate correlations are examined among White males and comparisons made to other groups where possible.

ROCHESTER YOUTH DEVELOPMENT STUDY
The RYDS sample consists of 1,000 students who were seventh and eighth graders in the Rochester, New York public schools during the Spring 1988 semester. To ensure that serious, chronic offenders and drug users are included in the study, the sample overrepresents high-risk youth in several ways. First, the city of Rochester, New York was chosen as a study site because of its ethnic and class diversity and its substantial crime

rate.[3] Second, males are oversampled (75 percent versus 25 percent) in the study because they are more likely to be chronic offenders and engage in serious delinquent behavior than are females. Third, students living in high crime areas are also oversampled, since they are expected to be at greater risk for offending (Farnworth, Thornberry, Lizotte, & Krohn, 1991).

Selection began with all seventh and eighth graders enrolled in the Rochester Public School System during the Spring of 1988 (n=4013), students were excluded from the study if they lived outside Monroe County prior to Wave 1; if the language spoken in the home was neither English nor Spanish; if a sibling was already in the pool, or if they were fifteen years or older at Wave 1. In addition, White females were initially excluded, since tract-by-sex stratification resulted in a very small subsample which was thought to be inadequate for subgroup study (Farnworth et al., 1991). This disparity was later corrected with the inclusion of White females in replacement cases at Wave 2.

Among those eligible for inclusion in the study (n=3,372), students were selected proportionate to resident arrest rates of the census tracts in which they resided during the first wave of data collection. These rates estimate the proportion of each tract's total population that was arrested in 1986. Students from tracts with the highest rates are proportionately overrepresented, since they are at highest risk for serious delinquency; students from the lower rate tracts are proportionately underrepresented. In fact, all students in the highest arrest rate tracts were selected for participation in the study, while those in all other tracts were selected according to tract arrest rate. Highest arrest rate tracts were determined by the distribution of arrest rates, where there appeared to be a natural break at three arrests per 100 residents; those above the cutoff were selected with certainty, while those below were selected according to the tract's arrest rate (Farnworth et al., 1991).

Households were selected by arrest rate within each tract, with half drawn from the seventh grade and half from the eighth grade student population. An initial sample of 1,334 potential participants was drawn with an expectation of deriving a final sample of 1,000, based on an anticipated nonparticipation rate of approximately 25%. Of those target cases, parents of 42 potential participants could not be reached, 45 parents did not respond prior to Wave 1, and 12 cases were not fielded before the deadline for drawing Wave 1 cases (Farnworth et al., 1991). In addition

248 parents refused to participate in the study, which generated a refusal rate of 20 percent. When compared across groups (by age, ethnicity, gender, and grade), refusal rates are relatively consistent. A total of 987 households constitute the total base panel for the study; 956 student interviews and 980 parent interviews were completed at Wave 1 (representing 97 and 99 of the base panel, respectively). Both parent and child were interviewed in 949 of the total cases.

Because the true probability of youth living in a particular census tract is known, cases can be weighted to represent the total seventh and eighth grade population (Farnworth et al., 1991). Students and their primary caretakers (typically mothers) were interviewed at six month intervals. The current analysis utilizes data from 1990 to1992 interviews which correspond with RYDS waves four through nine: waves four and five comprise Time 1, waves six and seven comprise Time 2, and waves eight and nine are combined to represent Time 3 (see Table 4a for sample characteristics at each time period). Males who completed interviews at all three time periods and whose parents were interviewed at Time 2 are included in the analysis (n=578), and represent 82 percent of all males interviewed at Wave 1. Across waves in the three time periods, the RYDS retains 89 to 97 percent of the original male sample. The number of cases reflects several waves of student interview data as well as parental participation at Time 2 (n=613).[4] The average age at Time 1 is 15.2 years and the age at Time 3 is 17.2 years (see Table 4b for final sample characteristics). More detailed information on sampling techniques of the RYDS can be found in Farnworth et al. (1991).

The city of Rochester was chosen in part for its ethnic diversity. Given that diversity and disproportionate stratification by census tract and sex, ethnic minorities are overrepresented in the RYDS sample; in the current study, sixteen percent of males are Latino, thirty percent are White, and fifty four percent are African American (see Table 4b). Sample diversity is particularly important for the current study which examines groups independently. Sample retention is important to note, since researchers have argued that respondent attrition may be particularly problematic among African Americans and Latinos. Analysis of retention rates in the RYDS has shown that overall retention among students and parents remains high across ten waves of data collection, although Puerto Ricans have somewhat lower retention rates than either Whites or African Americans.[5] In spite of ethnic differences, analyses reveal minimal selection bias. Correlations among risk factors and delinquency and drug use for those retained were not statistically different from correlations of the original panel (Krohn & Thornberry, 1999).

Table 4b. Total Sample Characteristics (weighted)

	Denver Youth Survey	Rochester Youth Development Study
	(n=345)	(n=578)
Average Age:		
Time 1	14.92	15.17
Time 2	15.87	16.20
Time 3	16.88	17.20
Ethnicity:		
White	9.4%	29.9%
Latino	50.4%	15.9%
African American	40.2 %	54.2%
Social Class:		
Receive Public Assistance	60.5%	45.5%

MEASUREMENT

This study utilizes three years of DYS and RYDS data to examine strain theory, as depicted in Figure 4. Strain measures are assessed at Times 1 and 2, and outcome measures are assessed at Time 3. Since RYDS interviews are conducted every six months, attitudinal measures are taken from the latter waves included in Time 1 and Time 2. For example, RYDS waves four and five correspond with Time 1. To allow for the most current attitudinal measures of the time period, data from wave 5 are used. If information from that wave of data collection is missing, measures from wave 4 are substituted. Similarly, measures from wave 7 are utilized for Time 2; missing information is substituted from wave 6. Since delinquency measures at Time 3 are strictly behavioral, a cumulative measure is created from RYDS waves eight and nine. It should be noted that substitution is necessary for only a handful of cases, and does not compromise temporal ordering.

Strain theory concepts are defined in Table 4c along with a brief description of the identical and site specific measures of the DYS and the RYDS. The contrast between identical and site specific measures is important for understanding the manner in which data are analyzed. First, the traditional model is estimated using only identical measures, to uncover differences in the applicability of traditional strain by ethnicity. Findings are compared within and across sites, to determine whether differences exist among ethnic groups generally, and among Latinos of varying countries of origin. Second, the traditional model is estimated using site specific measures. Findings are compared to those generated by identical measures, to determine whether more comprehensive variables improve model estimation. Third, the modified strain model is examined using identical measures across sites. The traditional strain theory model is compared to the modified model, and the utility of cultural factors to better understand Latino delinquency within a strain theory perspective is assessed (identical measures are utilized to make the comparison). If the modified strain model provides a substantial improvement over traditional strain, then a final estimation of the modified model will be conducted using site specific measures.

As Figure 4 illustrates, strain measures at Time 1 relate primarily to success goals and opportunities for achieving them. In addition, a measure of strain is calculated from Time 1 measures as the disjunction between the internalization of success goals and one's perceived opportunity for goal attainment. Strain measures assessed at Time 2 relate to one's removal of legitimacy from conventional norms of goal attainment and the adoption of delinquent values. Such measures include the externalization of blame, the challenge to the legitimacy of norms, and the adoption of delinquent values. Access to the illegitimate opportunity structure is also assessed during Time 2, in an effort to determine whether the combination of a delinquent value system and one's access to illegitimate means results in delinquent behavior. A variety of delinquent outcomes are assessed at Time 3.

Figure 4. Measuring the Traditional Strain Model with DYS and RYDS Data

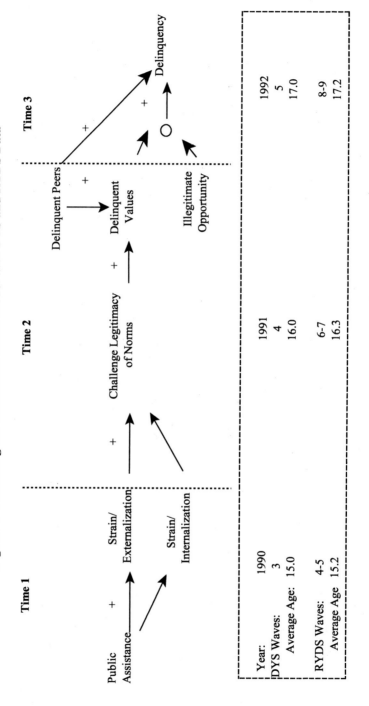

Table 4c. Traditional Strain Theory Concepts and Measures by Site

Strain Concept	Concept Definition	Identical Measures	DYS Only	RYDS Only
Social Class	Merton, Cloward and Ohlin were primarily concerned with examining lower class opportunities and adaptations.	Receipt of public assistance		Lower Class measure constructed from parent's income <u>and</u> public assistance receipt
Acceptance of Success Goals	Merton, Cloward and Ohlin were primarily concerned with acceptance of *economic success* goals.	High Income Aspirations measure		
Perception of Blocked opportunity	Merton, Cloward and Ohlin describe education attainment athe primary vehicle to upward mobility and economic advancement.	Academic Performance	Blocked Opportunity Index	
Strain	The discrepancy between culturally accepted success goals and access to legitimate opportunities for achieving them.	Disjunction term constructed from economic success goal orientation and academic performance		

Table 4c. Traditional Strain Theory Concepts and Measures by Site (cont.)

Strain Concept	Concept Definition	Identical Measures	DYS Only	RYDS Only
Externalization of Blame	Whether one attributes failure in achieving success goals through legitimate means to external sources (society) versus internal sources (self).	Parallel measures which captures reasons for failure to advance academically (RYDS) or make a lot of money (DYS).		
Challenge Legitimacy of Norms	Individual removes legitimacy once held in conventional means and essentially frees him/herself to commit to alternative belief system.	Conventional Beliefs	Comprehensive Conventional Beliefs Index	
Adoption of Delinquent Values	Once legitimacy is removed from conventional modes of behavior, the individual is free to commit to an alternative value system, including delinquent values.	Delinquent Values Scale	Comprehensive Delinquent Values Index	
Delinquent Peers	Association with delinquent peers serves to reinforce delinquent belief system, which ultimately leads to delinquent behavior.	Peer Delinquency and Drug Use		

Table 4c. Traditional Strain Theory Concepts and Measures by Site (cont.)

Strain Concept	Concept Definition	Identical Measures	DYS Only	RYDS Only
Illegitimate Opportunity	One's access to illegitimate opportunities. Also interested in lack of access to illegitimate means, since that is thought to influence violent behavior.	Access to Alcohol/ Drugs		
Family Involvement	Internalization of traditional Latino values, including participation in family activities.	Family Involvement		
Acculturation	Adoption of mainstream values and norms by ethnic groups.			Language of Parent Interview
Delinquency	Merton tended to focus on utilitarian crime, while Cloward & Ohlin describe pathways to utilitarian delinquency as well as violent crime.	General Delinquency Alcohol Use Drug Use Property Crime Violent Crime		

88 *Understanding Latino Delinquency*

STRAIN MEASURES AT TIME 1

Table 4d lists all measures employed in the current analysis along with variable ranges by site. Within the Denver and the Rochester studies there are various indicators of success goals. Each site includes several items that assess the importance of various goals, including economic and educational aspirations. In presenting anomie theory, Merton defines American culture goals in terms of monetary success. Similarly, Cloward and Ohlin focus their theoretical analysis on individuals who seek to improve their economic position. In opportunity theory, delinquent subcultures are thought to be primarily concerned with gaining wealth and achieving higher status within their own cultural milieu, rather than gaining membership in the middle class population (Cloward and Ohlin, 1960). Aspirations toward economic success, therefore, is utilized in the current analysis to test the traditional strain theory model. Use of the measure is supported by the work of Farnworth and Leiber (1989) who argue that economic aspirations most closely represent Merton's conceptualization of success goals. In their analysis, they found that strain, when defined in terms of financial goals, is a more accurate predictor of delinquent outcomes than measures based on educational goals.

Economic aspirations items in the current analysis are comparable across the two sites where each respondent is asked how important it is to make a great deal of money. Responses range from 'very important' (4) to 'not important at all' (1). To ensure comparability of measures across sites, the five category response set of the DYS is reduced to four to match that of the RYDS. Responses of 'somewhat important' and 'pretty important' are combined to reflect the 'important' category of the RYDS. All other categories are identical, and include 'not important at all,' 'not very/too important,' and 'very important.' It is worth noting that the wording of the RYDS measure appears to be more future oriented than that of the DYS and asks the importance of having a great deal of money *someday*, while the DYS does not specify any given time (see Appendix A for items as they appear in the DYS and the RYDS interview schedules).

Table 4d. List of Measures by Site

Variable Identical Variables	Description	Range	
		DYS (n=323)	**RYDS** (n=573)
PUBASST	Public Assistance Receipt	0-1	0-1
Time 1			
ASPIR	Aspirations for Economic Success	1-4	1-4
GRADES	Self-reported Grade Average	0-4	0-4
STRAIN	Traditional Disjunction Measure	0-4	0-4
Time 2			
EXTBLAME	Externalization of Blame	0-1	0-1
CHLEGIT	Challenge Legitimacy of Norms	1-4	1-4
DELVAL	Delinquent Values	1-4	1-4
DELPEERS	Peer Delinquency & Drug Use	1-4	1-4
DRUGACC	Access to Drugs	1-4	1-4
FAMINVOL	Family Involvement	1-5	1-4
Time 3			
GENI	General Delinquency Index	0-999	0-850
GENIL	Natural log	0-6.91	0-6.75
ALCI	Alcohol Use Index	0-500	0-480
ALCIL	Natural log	0-6.22	0-6.18
DRUI	Drug Use Index	0-388	0-480
DRUIL	Natural log	0-5.96	0-6.18
SERI	Serious Delinquency Index	0-169	0-60
SERIL	Natural log	0-5.14	0-4.11
PROI	Property Crime Index	0-294	0-100
PROIL	Natural log	0-5.69	0-4.62
PERI	Violent Crime Index	0-103	0-136
PERIL	Natural log	0-4.64	0-4.92

Table 4d. List of Measures by Site (cont.)

VARIABLE	DESCRIPTION	RANGE DYS (N=323)	RANGE RYDS (N=573)
TRANSFORMED VARIABLES			
STREXT	STRAIN/EXTERNALIZATION	0-4	0-4
STRINT	STRAIN/INTERNALIZATION	0-4	0-4
CDELVAL	CENTERED DELINQUENT VALUES	-.75-1.95	-.52-1.48
CDRUGACC	CENTERED ACCESS TO DRUGS	-1.35-1.65	-2.06-.94
CDELXILL	INTERACTION TERM (CDELVAL*CDRUGACC)	-1.56-3.22	-.99-1.39
CFAMINV	CENTERED FAMILY INVOLVEMENT	-2.46-1.54	-2.15-.85
DYS			
BLKDOPP	BLOCKED OPPORTUNITY INDEX	1-5	- -
BKOPEXT	BLOCKED OPPORTUNITY/ EXTERNALIZATION	0-4	- -
BKOPINT	BLOCKED OPPORTUNITY/ INTERNALIZATION	0-4	- -
CHLEGIT2	CHALLENGE LEGITIMACY - 11 ITEMS	1-4	- -
DELVAL2	DELINQUENT VALUES INDEX - 19 ITEMS	1-4	- -
CDELVAL2	CENTERED CUMULATIVE DELINQUENT VALUES	-.84-1.81	- -
CDL2XILL	INTERACTION TERM (CDELVAL1*CDRUGACC)	-1.40-2.99	- -
RYDS			
LOWERCL	LOWER CLASS MEASURE	- -	0-1
T2SPAN	PARENT COMPLETED SPANISH INTERVIEW	- -	0-1

Merton and Cloward and Ohlin describe educational attainment as the primary vehicle to the realization of the economic success goal. As such, the most reasonable gauge of one's perception of blocked opportunity would be a measure of one's educational expectations. This measure has been utilized in a number of empirical tests of strain theory, and is appropriate for the current analysis (see Hirschi, 1969; Liska, 1971; Quicker, 1974; Short, 1964). The DYS and the RYDS includes items which assess respondents' expectations for educational attainment. Multiple indicators from the RYDS are collapsed into a single item to match the DYS, indicating the level of education one is expected to achieve, which ranges from less than high school to completion of college.

In a previous examination of the RYDS educational expectations measure, Ireland (1996) discovered that the item had limited variance, since the majority of the sample expects to attain some college education. As a result, Ireland substituted academic performance for the potentially inflated educational expectations measure. Measures of educational expectations were examined for use in the current analysis and confirmed Ireland's findings; approximately 85 % of the RYDS sample and 74% of DYS students expect to graduate college. Therefore, this study adopts Ireland's measure of academic performance as an alternate indicator of blocked opportunity. The use of grade point average is supported by the work of Menard who asserts that, "GPA may be expected to affect perceptions of educational opportunities, which may in turn affect economic opportunities" (1995:142; see also Stinchcombe, 1964). In an empirical examination of strain theory, Menard (1995) finds a statistically significant relationship between GPA and perceptions of blocked opportunity, which further supports the use of this measure in the current analysis.

Self-reported grade average is consistent across the two sites. In the DYS, students are asked to describe the grades they are getting in school, allowing them to characterize academic performance as mostly A's, B's, C's, D's, or F's. The RYDS also asks students to evaluate their performance during the previous semester, and to characterize themselves as an A, B, C, D, or F student. Grades across sites are coded from 0 (F) to 4 (A), with higher values indicating increased access to legitimate opportunity.

While grades have been used as a measure of access to legitimate opportunity in other studies of strain theory, the variable may not be the ideal measure of blocked opportunity. On one hand, the measure can be criticized as somewhat removed from the economic success goal; that is, grades might not directly influence one's perceptions about chances to get ahead. This may be particularly true of Latinos, who have a history of limited educational attainment in the United States. Academic performance can generally indicate where one is standing in relation to the economic success goal. It may not represent the same in the Latino population, since Latinos have experienced limited educational success in the past and may not consider grades a predictor of success. Instead, lower grades may be considered to be a consequence of a discriminatory educational system. For the purpose of examining strain theory, however, the perception that grades are the consequence of the system is appropriate to consider. While Latinos may not view lower grades as a closed door to future opportunity/success, they may perceive the system as unfair or unjust. That experience of unjust deprivation might then lead to externalization of blame and the consequences for delinquent behavior that Cloward and Ohlin describe.

The DYS also includes an index of perceived blocked opportunity (Cronbach's Alpha=.80). Respondents are asked to report their level of agreement with a series of statements about legitimate opportunities to get ahead (see Appendix A for a complete listing of items). For example, students are presented with the following statement, "*you probably won't be able to do the kind of work that you want to do because you won't have enough education.*" Responses range from strongly disagree (1) to strongly agree (5). The mean of all items is assessed, and higher values indicate a stronger perception of blocked opportunity.[6] The index is based on nineteen separate items (see Appendix A), and provides a more comprehensive perspective of blocked opportunity than academic performance, which is comprised of only one indicator of opportunity. The index is examined in the analysis of site-specific items to determine whether it is a more accurate characterization of the strain concept. Ethnic groups are compared to determine whether differences exist on the more comprehensive measure of blocked opportunity.

The final measure assessed at Time 1 is strain, or the disjunction between success goals and access to legitimate means. Merton defined strain as the discrepancy between culturally accepted success goals and one's access to culturally legitimized opportunities. More precisely, frustration or strain is expected to result when an individual aspires to economic success, but has limited access to the means of achieving the goal. As such, the current analysis utilizes a traditional disjunction measure which is based on aspirations and academic performance. There are two options for computing a strain disjunction measure; one involves a simple subtraction of items, and the other involves the creation of a strain index. Both are designed to capture the difference between aspirations and expectations and are consistent with the traditional strain concept.

A simple disjunction measure (STRAIN) was first created using economic aspirations and academic performance items. Aspirations are coded low to high (ranging from 1 to 4), and self reported grades are coded high to low (F is coded zero and A is coded four). In keeping with previous economic disjunction measures, the blocked opportunity measure (GRADES) is subtracted from aspirations to produce a strain value (Farnworth & Leiber, 1989; Greenberg, 1999; Ireland, 1996). Raw strain scores range from -3 to 4, with higher values indicating greater strain (see Table 4e). Those who place the highest value on strain and have the lowest opportunity for achieving economic success receive the highest strain score (4). Negative values are recoded as zero: aspirations do not exceed legitimate opportunity, hence, individuals do not meet the criteria for strain. Other values of strain appear to overlap; a score of 3 captures individuals who either rate money as 'very important' and earn an average 'D' grade or those who rate money as 'important' and earn failing grades. Similarly, scores of 1 or 2 on STRAIN represent individuals who attach varying degrees of success goal internalization. Given the nature of the computation, individuals who report that money is 'not very important' or 'not important at all' can earn a score of 1 or 2 on STRAIN, depending upon their grades. This overlap in strain values causes some concern, since theoretically strain should be experienced only if one attaches importance to economic success. In the current example, strain is achieved even if one does not value economic success.

An alternate strain measure was constructed to reduce these problems (STRAIN2). Like the simple disjunction measure, this variable is based on both aspirations and academic achievement. To assess one's level of strain, individuals are first ordered by aspirations; those who rate money as 'not very important' or 'not important at all' are coded zero, since they do not meet the basic criterion for strain. Those who earn the highest average grade (A) are also coded as zero, since they have the greatest access to legitimate opportunity and cannot experience a discrepancy between academic performance and aspirations which would produce strain. Those who rate money as 'very important' or 'important' and report an average grade of 'B' or less are then ordered according to self-reported grades and assigned a strain value (see Table 4e). This measure produces nine strain values, which allows for greater variance in strain in comparison to the simple disjunction measure which has half the number of categories. STRAIN2 also avoids overlap across values, and codes those with lower aspirations as zero since they do not meet the criteria for strain.[7]

Table 4e. Traditional Strain Measures

Simple Strain Disjunction Values (STRAIN)*

		Self-reported Grades			
Aspirations	**F**	**D**	**C**	**B**	**A**
Very Important (4)	4	3	2	1	0
Important (3)	3	2	1	0	-1
Not Very Important	2	1	0	-1	-2
Not Important at All	1	0	-1	-2	-3

**Note: negative values are recoded as zero for final strain measure.

Strain Index (STRAIN2)	
Aspirations / Grades	**Value**
Money Not Important / A	0
Important / B	1
Very Important / B	2
Important / C	3
Very Important / C	4
Important / D	5
Very Important / D	6
Important / F	7
Very Important / F	8

Empirically, the disjunction measures are strikingly similar; a comparison of the two produces a Pearson correlation coefficient of .94 in the DYS and .96 in the RYDS. The two strain measures are also similar in their relationships with other strain variables and delinquency outcomes. Given the consistency in strain disjunction measures, this analysis utilizes the simple disjunction measure (STRAIN), which is most consistent with other studies of strain theory (Farnworth & Leiber, 1989; Greenberg, 1999; Ireland, 1996). In fact, those studies which utilize a simple economic disjunction measure most closely resemble Merton's conceptualization of the concept and find the strongest support for strain (see Chapter 2).

STRAIN MEASURES AT TIME 2

Indicators of the externalization of blame are less straightforward than other strain measures, as neither study contains a specific measure of this concept. For this reason, the current analysis reproduces a RYDS measure that has been previously used and creates a similar DYS measure. Ireland (1996) created a measure to assess the extent to which one attributes failure in achieving success goals through legitimate means to external sources (society) or internal sources (self). Using the externalization measure, Ireland captures the respondent's reasons for not advancing academically. In a similar way, the current analysis utilizes reasons for failing to advance academically as a dichotomous measure of externalization for the RYDS (see Appendix B for a list of items). Reasons for failure to graduate high school, failure to attend college, and failure to graduate college are examined and categorized as external or internal. External items are those related to financial difficulties, dislike of school, peer dropout, and non-supportive parents. Internal, or self-blaming reasons for not advancing academically, include personal life events such as marriage, pregnancy, joining the armed forces, and trouble with the law. Those individuals who provide any external reasons for failure to advance are identified by Ireland's measure as externalizing blame.

Since the DYS does not include an identical measure at Time 2, a reasonable proxy is adopted. The measure includes two items from the DYS interview schedule which tap into the perceived source of blocked opportunity, or reasons for not achieving the economic success goal. Students in the DYS are asked if they anticipate making a great deal of money someday; those who do not expect to achieve that goal are asked to provide a reason why. At the same time, those who anticipate making money are asked if achieving that goal will be difficult. If difficulty is expected, then respondents are asked to report perceived obstacles. Individuals cite various impediments to economic success, which are categorized in the following domains: personal limitations, family limitations, formal educational limitations, societal limitations, anticipated difficulty in finding a good job, and personal attitudes toward money, such as a lack of desire for money or an inability to save. Sources of difficulty are coded as internal or external. Those reasons which pertain to family, peers, or societal limitations are considered external (see Appendix B for specific responses). A dichotomous measure is constructed from the two DYS items, with those who report any external source of blocked opportunity coded as one and those who report personal limitations as zero.

In opportunity theory, Cloward and Ohlin posit an interaction between strain and the externalization of blame, such that those who experience strain *and* blame others for failure to achieve economic success then challenge the legitimacy of norms (1960). In the current analysis strain is assessed during Time 1 and externalization is captured during Time 2. The measures are taken from different waves since externalization is thought to occur as a reaction to strain. Strain does not cause externalization, but precedes it; over time, individuals are likely to attribute blame for their failure to achieve goals.

To capture the interaction between strain and externalization, new measures are constructed. The externalization dichotomy allows for the construction of two separate measures which represent strain scores for those who internalize and those who externalize blame. The first term (STREXT) identifies individuals who externalize blame and examines the impact of their strain experience within the model, coding internalization as zero. The second measure (STRINT) represents strain values among those who internalize, and codes externalization as zero. The measures are examined simultaneously in predicting the challenge of legitimacy; the first interaction term is expected to be statistically significant since it captures those individuals who experience strain *and* externalize blame. That group is most likely to challenge legitimacy of conventional norms, and should demonstrate a positive relationship between strain/externalization and challenge. The second interaction term is not expected to achieve significance in predicting challenge of legitimacy since it represents the internalization of blame, which theoretically, has no relationship with the legitimacy construct.

As mentioned in previous chapters, individuals who fail to achieve economic success via legitimate opportunity and blame society for that failure are expected to challenge conventional methods of goal attainment. As such, a measure is included which represents an attitudinal challenge to the legitimacy norms. Challenge to legitimacy is assessed at Time 2 using DYS and RYDS measures of conventional beliefs. The conventional belief scale consists of four items which assess the importance of conventional values, including a good reputation in the community, studying hard for good grades, working hard to get ahead, and saving money for the future (Cronbach's Alpha, DYS=.77, RYDS=.82). This measure is used as an indicator of the challenge to legitimacy, such that lower levels of importance attributed to each item are considered to be indicative of challenge to conventional methods of goal attainment. It should be noted that the measure is designed to capture challenge to conventional norms exclusively. Attitudes toward institutionalized methods of goal attainment are included, while indicators of the economic success goal are excluded. The success goal is thought to be maintained through the process; Cloward and Ohlin (1960) argue that conventional norms are challenged and alternative strategies are employed to fulfill that goal.

It seems unlikely that an individual would attribute high importance to an act that is not considered valid or legitimate to them. In a global sense, however, an individual may believe that such values are important, but have little relevance to their own behavior. The particular wording of items in the conventional values index varies slightly across sites and may influence respondents' reference point for answering the question. For example, the DYS asks, *"how important is it to...,"* while the RYDS asks, *"how important is it to you..."* The RYDS scale, compared to the DYS, may be more appropriate in capturing a sense of one's personal attitudes toward conventional methods of goal attainment.

Since the measure captures a challenge to legitimacy, items have been reverse coded to represent categories of 'very important'(1), 'important'(2), 'not very important'(3), and 'not important at all'(4); higher scores indicate weakened commitment to conventional values. Within the DYS, the five category response set is reduced to four, with categories 'somewhat important' and 'pretty important' combined to reflect the RYDS 'important' category. The DYS assesses the importance of seven additional items, including a college education, owning a home, having a good paying job, and planning ahead. In the site specific analysis, all are included in a more comprehensive index of challenge to legitimacy (Cronbach's Alpha=.88). See Appendix C for a complete listing of items across sites.

Traditional strain theory asserts that once legitimacy is removed from conventional modes of behavior, the individual may become committed to an alternative value system, including delinquent values. Both the DYS and the RYDS include a delinquent belief scale which is comprised of eleven items which determine how wrong the respondent believes various delinquent acts are. Item responses range from 'not wrong at all' (1) to 'very wrong' (4). The index (DELVAL) assesses the mean of all eleven items which range in seriousness from skipping school to assault (for a complete list of items, see Appendix D). To assess the strength of delinquent values, items have been coded so that higher values indicate stronger delinquent values (Cronbach's Alpha, DYS=.89, RYDS=.89). The full DYS delinquent values scale contains a total of 23 items, therefore, a site-specific measure will also be examined (Alpha=.93). This expanded measure includes a wide range of delinquent items, including use of tobacco, teen pregnancy, and assault of a spouse or partner (See Appendix D).

The current analysis also employs a measure of peer delinquency as an indicator of peer isolation from conventional society, which maintains consistency with previous examinations of strain theory. In the analysis of identical measures, association with delinquent peers is assessed. Respondents in both the DYS and the RYDS have been asked to report the proportion of friends who have engaged in a variety of delinquent behaviors, including substance use. This scale corresponds with the delinquent acts of the delinquent values index (DELVAL) and includes eleven items (See Appendix E for a complete listing of items).[8] While the RYDS includes four response categories of 'none' (1) to 'most' (4), DYS responses range from 'none of them' (1) to 'all of them' (5). The index ranges from one to four, with the DYS category 'all' collapsed with 'most' to ensure identical measures. In both sites, higher values indicate a greater proportion of friends that have engaged in delinquent behavior.

In developing the peer delinquency and drug use scale in the RYDS, some students responded 'don't know' to one or more items. Since strain theory focuses on the impact of peer behavior on one's delinquent value system, the current measure attempts to capture those who respond positively to peer delinquency. 'Don't know' responses do not qualify as a positive response in the current analysis; as such, they are recoded as 'none.' If an individual is unaware of delinquent peer activity, then they would not be expected to be impacted by it. This coding scheme also keeps the number of missing cases in the RYDS to a minimum.[9]

Access to Illegitimate Means

As described in Chapter 2, Cloward and Ohlin introduced the concept of the illegitimate opportunity structure to strain theory. Access to illegitimate opportunities is expected to influence delinquent adaptations in two ways: First, it is expected that individuals who fail to achieve economic success through legitimate means will engage in criminal behavior if they have access to illegitimate means. Second, the *absence* of both legitimate and illegitimate means is expected to result in an increased reliance on violent behavior as a method of status attainment (Cloward and Ohlin, 1960).

Criminal outcomes are determined in part by the presence of a proper learning environment, where delinquent behavior is learned and reinforced. Opportunity theorists point to the significance of age integration within neighborhoods as the primary means by which delinquent behavior is transmitted from one generation to the next. In addition, they describe the integration of deviant and conventional roles within the community, whereby delinquents are closely tied to those who convey more traditional values. Since neighborhood level measures such as age and role integration are not collected by the DYS or the RYDS, they are not included in the current analysis. Instead, the illegitimate opportunity measure is based on Cloward and Ohlin's more general argument concerning high crime neighborhoods, that "only those neighborhoods in which crime flourishes as a stable, indigenous institution are fertile criminal learning environments for the young" (1960:148). Criminal adaptations are expected to occur in neighborhoods characterized by high levels of crime.

The DYS and the RYDS contain consistent measures of neighborhood crime. Parent evaluations of neighborhood crime are available, along with student evaluations of neighborhood drug use and access to drugs.

Neighborhood level crime is assessed in both the DYS and the RYDS by asking the primary caretaker whether delinquent behavior is problematic in the neighborhood. Parents are asked about a variety of criminal acts, ranging from vandalism to neighborhood assault. Parents are also asked to assess the problem that gangs may present in the neighborhood. A total of eleven items are used, with parental ratings ranging from 'not a problem' (1) to 'a big problem'(3). A neighborhood crime index is constructed by taking the mean of all items (see Appendix F for a complete list).

In addition, neighborhood drug use is assessed in student interviews across both sites; DYS and the RYDS students are asked about levels of neighborhood drug use. The DYS includes a series of items which assess the prevalence of a variety of substances ranging from alcohol to crack in the neighborhood. The RYDS, on the other hand, asks about the extent to which neighborhood residents within the respondent's age group use alcohol, marijuana and hard drugs (three items), with responses ranging from 'none'(1) to 'a lot'(4). Perceived opportunity for substance use is also evaluated in student interviews; each respondent is asked about the ease of purchasing alcohol, marijuana, and hard drugs, with responses ranging from 'very difficult'(1) to 'very easy'(4).

Of the three available measures of illegitimate opportunity, parental evaluation of neighborhood crime provides information on a wider variety of neighborhood criminal activity. In spite of that, however, parent impressions of neighborhood crime (and the illegitimate opportunity they may provide) are likely to be formed independently of adolescents. In determining delinquent outcomes, Cloward and Ohlin describe the importance of *adolescent perceptions* of both legitimate and illegitimate opportunity (1960). Student measures of illegitimate opportunity are most important to consider, since their perception of such opportunities is likely to be a stronger predictor of behavior than perceptions of other individuals, such as parents. Parents and children may also have differing perceptions of neighborhood criminality; therefore, student measures are most appropriate for use in the current test of strain theory. Although student measures are primarily concerned with access to drugs and alcohol, such items may also be indicative of more general access to criminal opportunity in the neighborhood.

A principal components factor analysis was conducted with all six student measures of illegitimate opportunity to determine whether they are indicative of a general 'access to illegitimate opportunity' construct. The analysis revealed two separate factors in both the DYS and the RYDS, distinguishing neighborhood substance use from student access to drugs. Given those findings and differences in neighborhood drug use items across sites --DYS prevalence measures compared to RYDS indicators of the number of individuals who consume substances-- the current analysis utilizes student access to drugs as the final indicator of illegitimate opportunity. The mean of three items is utilized as a measure of illegitimate opportunity, and its interaction with delinquent values is assessed in the traditional strain theory model (Cronbach's Alpha, DYS=.84, RYDS=.93).

The interaction between delinquent values and illegitimate opportunity provides the motivation for a variety of delinquent behaviors, according to Cloward and Ohlin (1960). As such, the current analysis includes a second interaction term into the traditional strain theory model. The interaction between delinquent values and illegitimate opportunity can be modeled in several ways. One approach would mirror the strain/externalization interaction previously described and include two separate terms in the analysis. This, however, requires that one of the two components of the interaction is dichotomous, where the final terms represent groups of the dichotomy. Given the fact that both delinquent values and illegitimate opportunity are continuous, this solution seems less appropriate. While it is possible to dichotomize illegitimate opportunity into 'high' and 'low' categories and create two interaction terms, it requires that information is collapsed (and essentially lost).

Researchers who have examined interactions in multiple regression suggest the inclusion of a multiplicative product term when the two primary components are continuous (Aiken & West, 1991; Jaccard, Turrisi, & Wan et al., 1990). This approach is suggested for estimating interaction effects in regression and structural equation analyses, and is appropriate for use in LISREL in the current study (Jaccard et al., 1990). Prior to multiplying delinquent values (DELVAL) and illegitimate opportunity (DRUGACC), the continuous variables are first centered. This requires that the total sample mean is subtracted from an individual's delinquent values and access to drugs scores; resulting in the creation of two new variables (CDELVAL, CDRUGACC). Transforming the measures in this way produces two variables with a mean of zero, and preserves the units of the scale (West, Aiken, & Krull, 1996). This statistical approach has various advantages in analyzing interaction terms, including interpretation clarity and simplification, and the reduction of multicollinearity in a model (Aiken & West, 1991; Jaccard et al., 1990; West et al., 1996). Once delinquent values and illegitimate opportunity measures are centered they are multiplied to create the interaction term (CDELXILL). This interaction term is included in the model along with its centered components, to determine whether the interaction between the two is significant after controlling for main effects of goal internalization and blocked opportunity.[10]   For DYS site-specific analyses, the cumulative delinquent values measure (DELVAL2) has also been centered (CDELVAL2) and an additional product term has been computed (CDL2XILL).

DELINQUENCY MEASURES AT TIME 3

Cloward and Ohlin present their theory as it relates to the generation of delinquent subcultures, which are criminal, conflict, or retreatist-oriented. In the current study, their arguments are adapted to explain individual behavior. Self-reported delinquency items are available for both the DYS and the RYDS, and are primarily based on the National Youth Survey (Elliott, Huizinga, & Ageton, 1985). Delinquency indices represent core measures which are identical across the two sites. Self-reported delinquency is assessed at Time 3 and consists of thirty two items that tap a wide range of behaviors from truancy to aggravated assault. RYDS delinquency measures combine data from two separate waves to obtain a cumulative index of delinquent behavior for 1992 to match the DYS annual assessment. Students at both sites are asked at each interview if they had engaged in a particular behavior since the last interview, and if they had, they were asked to report the frequency of that behavior. A variety of indices have been constructed to assess the incidence of general delinquency, violent crime, and property crime. Substance use indices are also available, which assess consumption of alcohol, marijuana, and a variety of hard drugs. Given the skewness of frequency data, a natural logarithmic transformation is computed for all delinquency scales.[11]

Since strain theory proposes variation in delinquent outcomes given the presence of strain and one's access to the illegitimate opportunity structure, several delinquency scales are utilized to examine criminal and retreatist outcomes. *General delinquency* is comprised of all delinquency items which range in seriousness from runaway to assault. Although previous tests of strain have had limited success in predicting minor delinquent offenses (Hirschi, 1969, for example), this measure is employed in the current analysis to determine whether that finding is consistent across ethnic groups. Two separate substance use scales are also included to assess involvement with alcohol and drugs. A two item *alcohol use scale* and a ten item *drug use scale* are included in the analysis to assess the impact of strain on retreatist behaviors among all ethnic groups (see Appendix G for a listing of all self reported delinquency indices).

To determine whether findings are generalizeable to other outcome behaviors, models are estimated to predict property crime and violence. A *property crime* index is included to determine whether strain theory predicts utilitarian crime, including theft and forgery. As mentioned previously, the absence of illegitimate opportunities is expected to result in violent behavior, as Cloward and Ohlin have suggested (1960). To assess the influence of strain on violent behavior, a six item violent crime index is employed.

ADDITIONAL MEASURES
Social class is an integral part of the traditional strain theory model, since it is expected to directly influence one's legitimate opportunities for goal attainment. Merton and Cloward and Ohlin were primarily concerned with examining lower class opportunities and adaptations. As such, a dichotomous class measure is employed in the current analysis. Both the DYS and the RYDS collect data on the receipt of public assistance; as such, those who report receiving welfare, AFDC or food stamps are coded as one. Those who do not receive any form of government assistance are coded as zero.

The influence of social class on the strain model will be explored through an examination of the relationship between public assistance and strain interaction terms (described earlier in the chapter). Although strain measures incorporate the externalization of blame, which is not directly linked to social class in the model, class is expected to influence both equally. Class is thought to increase blocked opportunity and strain, regardless of the manner in which blame is attributed; therefore a positive relationship is anticipated between class and each strain measure. Bivariate relationships between class and components of strain (aspirations and expectations) will be also explored, to determine whether the relationship between lower class and strain is due to class influences on blocked opportunity as Cloward and Ohlin assert (1960). The bivariate relationship between lower class and blocked opportunity is expected to be positive and statistically significant.

In an effort to include a more complete measure of class, the RYDS site specific analysis utilizes a dichotomous lower class variable, which is characterized by the presence of one or more economic hardships, including parental receipt of public assistance, unemployment, and income below poverty level. All class measures are taken from parent interviews prior to Time 1 to construct the background measure which is thought to influence blocked opportunity directly, and strain indirectly.

Since specific cultural measures have not been included in either the DYS or the RYDS, the analysis includes a proxy measure related to the family, which is a central element of the Latino culture. Although the available measure is not ideal for a full examination of the influence of cultural factors on strain theory, it may be satisfactory in providing a preliminary examination of the alternative strain model. As described in Chapter 3, findings from the literature have illustrated variation in family influences among Latinos and Whites. In several instances, family measures proved to be significant for Latino youth, but did not have the same influence on Whites (Rodriguez & Recio, 1992; Rodriguez & Weisburd, 1991; Smith, 1990; Smith & Krohn, 1995). Therefore, it is vital to replicate such an analysis and assess the influence of family involvement across various ethnic groups.

Given such empirical findings, and a theoretical link between Latinos and family relations, measures in the current analysis were chosen based on an adolescent's involvement in family activity. To assess family involvement, the DYS and the RYDS include items which assess the amount of time spent with family. The DYS asks youth to report time spent playing, talking, or doing things with the family, with responses ranging from 'less than once a month'(1) to 'every day'(5).[12] Although the RYDS question is less specific, respondents are also asked the frequency of doing things with members of the family, which can range from 'never'(1) to 'often'(4). Since measures across sites differ in terms of the metric used to capture one's involvement, they are centered. Measures are handled according to the guidelines set for other measures, where the total sample mean is subtracted from an individual's response.

Since this study seeks to investigate the potential influence of cultural factors on traditional strain theory and makes hypotheses about Latinos and strain, it is important to include a measure of acculturation. As outlined in Chapter 3, acculturation is expected to influence elements of the strain theory model. In particular, acculturation is thought to impact involvement in traditional Latino culture and family, which has implications for the development of delinquent values and delinquent adaptations. Since neither the DYS nor the RYDS include specific measures of acculturation, a proxy must be utilized. The RYDS interview schedule includes several language-based proxy measures of acculturation. First, the language in which the parental interview is conducted is included as a proxy measure of acculturation. At Time 2, approximately 9 percent of all parent interviews and 59 percent of Latino interviews were conducted in Spanish. This measure of parent language is not the ideal measure of acculturation, however, it may be appropriate for gaining a preliminary look at the relationship between acculturation and delinquent outcomes.

In this investigation, the traditional strain theory model is tested on Latino, White, and African American adolescents of the DYS and the RYDS. In addition, a modified model is examined, which introduces cultural factors to the traditional model. All analyses are conducted with males, since the number within each ethnic group provides the statistical power that is needed at each stage of the analysis. The inclusion of males in the analysis is consistent with the focus of Merton and Cloward and Ohlin on male delinquency. Cloward and Ohlin (1960) have pointed out that strain theory may be more salient among males who typically face greater pressure to attain economic success (see also Stinchcombe, 1964).[13]

Site specific analysis allows for the inclusion of theoretically relevant measures which are not available in both the DYS and the RYDS. In most instances, unique measures will be examined separately, however, in some cases, the site specific measure will be combined with common indicators to create cumulative indices. Each test of site specific measures will be compared to the original estimation based on the identical measures. In analyzing Denver survey data, a blocked opportunity index is used in place of the common measure of academic achievement. In capturing one's access to illegitimate means, the DYS includes student evaluations of neighborhood crime and the presence of gangs in the neighborhood.

Such student-based measures are used in site specific analyses in place of specific drug use measures available in both sites.

Of the total of 345 males selected for inclusion in the current analysis, 22 cases have been dropped due to missing data. Since DYS measures represent annual assessments, it is not possible to substitute missing cases with data from the same time period as in the RYDS (which contains two interviews in one year). The number of missing cases per variable is relatively small (maximum number of cases missing in a single variable is six), and the deletion of missing cases poses no threat to data representation.[14]

Within the traditional strain theory model, the Rochester study allows for a more comprehensive measure of socioeconomic status. In addition, the RYDS includes a language-related measure to be used in the modified strain model as a proxy for acculturation. Of all the unique RYDS measures, acculturation is perhaps the most theoretically relevant to the current investigation. Inclusion of this measure in site specific analysis provides a preliminary examination of the influence of acculturation on the traditional strain model, allowing for a more complete test of the modified model presented in Chapter 3.

Data substitution is necessary for a handful of RYDS cases. Among Time 1 measures, missing data on economic aspirations and academic performance from wave 5 have been replaced with wave 4 data. Due to missing information at wave 7, data from wave 6 are utilized for Time 2 measures, including the externalization of blame, conventional beliefs, delinquent values, peer delinquency and drug use, and student access to drugs.[15] There are no missing data on cumulative delinquency indices from waves 8 and 9.

DESCRIPTIVE STATISTICS
Identical and site specific measures are listed in Table 4d along with value ranges for each variable by site. Descriptive statistics for all measures have been calculated for DYS and RYDS total samples. The following chapter presents summary statistics by ethnicity and describes mean differences between Latino, White, and African American males within each site. Mean differences are also explored across sites, in an effort to determine whether similar patterns emerge by location.

CHAPTER 5

Univariate and Bivariate Analyses

As an initial step in testing strain theory, univariate and bivariate analyses of strain measures were conducted. All identical and site specific measures were examined separately by ethnicity to determine if consistencies exist across groups. Generally, comparable descriptive statistics and bivariate relationships across ethnic groups might serve as a preliminary indicator that the theory is universally applicable. Statistically significant differences in group means or correlation coefficients, on the other hand, might foreshadow ethnic differences in the application of the strain theory model.

Descriptive statistics for all measures are listed in Table 5a by site.[1] Variable means and standard deviations have been calculated for each ethnic group within the DYS and RYDS samples.[2] The first section of this chapter reviews summary statistics by ethnicity and describes mean differences between Latino, White, and African American males within each site. A comparison of mean values across groups within each site allows for a preliminary examination of strain concepts and a test of specific hypotheses related to mean differences by ethnicity (as offered in Chapter 3).

Bivariate analyses are covered in the second half of the chapter. Pearson correlation coefficients provide a preliminary look at relationships within the strain model which will ultimately be examined via structural equation modeling. A comparison of coefficients across ethnic groups will identify relationships within the strain model which may potentially vary in the LISREL analysis.

TABLE 5A. DESCRIPTIVE STATISTICS BY ETHNICITY (WEIGHTED)

VARIABLE	DENVER YOUTH SURVEY						ROCHESTER YOUTH DEVELOPMENT STUDY					
	LATINO (N=161)		WHITE (N=30)		BLACK (N=132)		LATINO (N=92)		WHITE (N=172)		BLACK (N=310)	
	MEAN	S.D.	MEAN	S.D.	MEAN	S.D.	MEAN	S.D.	MEAN	S.D.	MEAN	S.D
PUBASST	.59[a]	.49	.40[c]	.50	.65	.48	.56[a]	.50	.22[c]	.42	.55	.50
TIME 1												
ASPIR	3.32	.56	3.17	.71	3.32	.58	3.49[a]	.57	3.34[c]	.69	3.57	.61
GRADES	2.38[a]	.93	2.86[c]	.81	2.28	.74	2.05[a]	.93	2.52[c]	.79	2.19	.74
STRAIN	1.05[a]	.89	.64[c]	.80	1.09	.85	1.49[a]	.68	.94[c]	.89	1.42	.88
TIME 2												
EXTBLAME	.27	.45	.23	.42	.24	.43	.35[b]	.48	.32[c]	.47	.17	.38
CHLEGIT	1.48[b]	.41	1.51	.46	1.38	.37	1.56[ab]	.49	1.74[c]	.48	1.45	.49
DELVAL	1.74[a]	.53	1.95[c]	.64	1.72	.53	1.53	.51	1.53	.41	1.47	.46
DELPEERS	1.86[a]	.77	1.64[c]	.50	1.85	.63	1.41	.55	1.44	.40	1.42	.55
DRUGACC	2.29[ab]	1.08	1.87[c]	.91	2.54	1.08	2.98[b]	.93	2.83[c]	.89	3.20	.99
FAMINVOL	3.55	1.21	3.39	1.13	3.33	1.29	3.19[a]	.63	2.91[c]	.75	3.19	.78

[a] Latinos significantly different from Whites, [b] Latinos significantly different from African Americans, [c] African Americans significantly different from Whites

TABLE 5A. DESCRIPTIVE STATISTICS BY ETHNICITY (CONT.)

| | DENVER YOUTH SURVEY | | | | | | ROCHESTER YOUTH DEVELOPMENT STUDY | | | | | |
| | LATINO (N=161) | | WHITE (N=30) | | BLACK (N=132) | | LATINO (N=92) | | WHITE (N=172) | | BLACK (N=310) | |
VARIABLE	MEAN	S.D.	MEAN	S.D.	MEAN	S.D.	MEAN	S.D.	MEAN	S.D.	MEAN	S.D.
TIME 3												
GENI	32.95[AB]	97.70	15.13	19.87	29.64	99.46	29.99	84.42	15.51[c]	58.85	32.18	94.41
GENIL-NATURAL LOG	1.68	1.71	1.94	1.44	2.07	1.52	1.26	1.77	.91	1.48	1.37	1.83
ALCI	25.50	56.95	20.79	28.38	31.82	89.29	26.76	63.68	15.44	40.36	18.62	46.63
ALCIL-NATURAL LOG	1.64	1.81	1.98	1.67	1.53	1.77	1.64	1.76	1.41	1.51	1.39	1.64
DRUI	12.10	48.90	20.61	71.83	11.22	52.00	13.42	50.81	20.46	61.35	12.90	41.95
DRUIL-NATURAL LOG	.67	1.44	1.07	1.67	.61	1.33	.70	1.41	.83	1.65	.83	1.52
PROI	4.61	25.80	.98[c]	2.54	2.24	5.10	1.81[A]	6.37	.53	1.87	1.32	7.32
PROIL-NATURAL LOG	.49	1.00	.30	.72	.60	.90	.38	.83	.20	.51	.26	.69
PERI	1.56	8.23	.43	1.17	1.10	2.99	.91[A]	2.02	.44[c]	1.25	2.18	10.73
PERIL-NATURAL LOG	.34	.75	.21	.47	.37	.69	.38	.63	.19	.49	.43	.82

[a] Latinos significantly different from Whites, [b] Latinos significantly different from African Americans, [c] African Americans significantly different from Whites

TABLE 5A. DESCRIPTIVE STATISTICS BY ETHNICITY (CONT.)

| | DENVER YOUTH SURVEY | | | | | | ROCHESTER YOUTH DEVELOPMENT STUDY | | | | | |
| | LATINO (N=161) | | WHITE (N=30) | | BLACK (N=133) | | LATINO (N=92) | | WHITE (N=172) | | BLACK (N=309) | |
SITE-SPECIFIC VARIABLE	MEAN	S.D.	MEAN	S.D.	MEAN	S.D.	MEAN	S.D.	MEAN	S.D.	MEAN	S.D.
DYS												
BLKDOPP	2.37[a,b]	.37	2.14	.39	2.26	.41						
BKOPEXT	.66	1.10	.48	.94	.58	1.06						
BKOPINT	1.71	1.10	1.65	.95	1.68	1.01						
CHLEGIT2	1.46[b]	.35	1.49[c]	.39	1.35	.33						
DELVAL2	1.83[a]	.49	2.01[c]	.59	1.81	.51						
CDELVAL2	-.01[a]	.49	.17[c]	.59	-.03	.51						
CDL2XILL	.22	.54	.05	.53	.17	.58						
RYDS												
LOWERCL							.66[a]	.48	.32[c]	.47	.64	.48
T2SPAN							.59	.49	–	–	–	–

[a] Latinos significantly different from Whites, [b] Latinos significantly different from African Americans, [c] African Americans significantly different from Whites

Before any comparisons are made, it must be recognized that the number of White males in the DYS is relatively small compared to the number of Latinos and African Americans in the sample. In spite of variation in group size, findings are fairly consistent with those found in the RYDS.

MEAN DIFFERENCES BY ETHNICITY

Mean differences between groups are discussed in the order in which concepts appear in the traditional strain theory model. Of primary concern to traditional strain theory is class status, which determines one's access to legitimate opportunities and serves as the motivation for delinquent behavior. Within the DYS, Latinos and African Americans differ significantly from Whites in the percentage within each group that receives public assistance (significance indicated at $p<.05$, one-tail test).[3] As anticipated, minority groups appear to experience economic disadvantage at a greater rate compared to their non-minority counterparts: 59% of Latinos and 65% of African Americans receive public assistance, compared to 40% of Whites in the sample. Although they both differ significantly from Whites, minority groups in the DYS do not differ significantly from one another. A similar pattern emerges in the RYDS, where 22% of Whites receive aid, while 56% and 55% of Latinos and African Americans also receive public assistance, respectively. In both sites, Whites are least likely to receive public assistance.

TIME 1 MEASURES

Strain measures assessed at Time 1 include economic aspirations and academic performance, which constitute the strain disjunction measure. In the DYS, all groups evidence similar aspirations for economic success. In the RYDS, however, Latinos and African Americans have significantly *higher* aspirations compared to their White counterparts. In terms of academic performance, Whites in both samples report higher grade averages. Overall, males in both the DYS and the RYDS report average grades of 'C' or higher, however, White males in both samples have significantly higher grades than either of the minority groups.

As a consequence of lower grades and higher aspirations (in RYDS), minority groups across both samples produce higher mean values of strain. In the DYS, White males have an average strain score of .64, while Latinos and African Americans have scores of 1.05 and 1.09, respectively. In RYDS, the mean of Whites is also the lowest across ethnic groups in the sample (.94 compared to 1.49 for Latinos and 1.42 for African Americans).

As described in Chapter 3, Latinos and African Americans, on the whole, are expected to demonstrate higher levels of strain as the result of structural disadvantage and blocked opportunities for economic success related to the minority group experience in the United States. Within minority groups, Latinos are expected to have limited legitimate opportunities for success and higher mean values of strain compared to African Americans. Specifically, the following was posited:

> **Hypothesis #1:** As a group, Latinos are expected to produce greater mean values of strain (compared to Whites), thus reflecting the cumulative effect of socio-cultural experiences and discriminatory factors on access to legitimate opportunity.
>
> **Hypothesis #7:** Due to shared minority status, African Americans and Latinos are expected to demonstrate stronger perceptions of blocked opportunity, and as a result, higher levels of strain compared to their non-minority counterparts.
>
> **Hypothesis #8:** While minority status is likely to depress perceptions of opportunity in both minority groups, Latinos are likely to demonstrate the strongest perceptions of blocked opportunity and highest levels of strain. Differences are likely to reflect decreased opportunities due to language, immigration patterns, and the historical lack of success among Latinos in the U.S. compared to African Americans.

Based on initial mean difference tests, as presented in Table 5a, support is provided for Hypothesis #1 and Hypothesis #7. In both the DYS and the RYDS, Latinos and African Americans demonstrate significantly higher strain values compared to Whites. With regard to Hypothesis #8, it appears that while minority groups differ from Whites, Latinos do not significantly differ from African Americans in the degree of strain experienced. Although Latinos have the highest strain score in the RYDS and African Americans have the highest score in the DYS, the difference between the two minority groups in each site does not achieve statistical significance. Both ethnic groups appear to have comparable levels of strain, as evidenced by findings across sites.

Differences between minority and non-minority groups reflected in Table 5a do not control for social class. The higher levels of strain observed among Latinos and African Americans may simply be a function of class. To determine whether variation in strain reflects class differences as opposed to ethnic differences, additional analyses were employed. Given the dichotomous nature of the class measure (public assistance), a t-test of means was run across ethnic groups separately for those who receive government aid and for those who do not (see Table 5b). In Chapter 3, factors other than class were described as potentially decreasing opportunity for economic success among Latinos and African Americans. Elements of the minority experience, including discrimination, are expected to contribute to diminished legitimate opportunity. As such, differences between ethnic groups should emerge across ethnic groups within each class category, and would reflect a main effect of ethnicity on strain.

After estimating mean differences across ethnic groups by class, an interactive effect of class and ethnicity on strain was found. Among those who receive public assistance, no significant differences in the level of strain were observed by ethnicity. Economic disadvantage appears to influence all ethnic groups similarly. As Merton and Cloward and Ohlin have posited, individuals within a lower class strata are vulnerable to strain, regardless of ethnic background. Among those who do not receive government aid, however, ethnic differences in the strain experience are found. Minority groups who do not rely on government support have significantly higher strain values compared to their non-minority counterparts. Taken together, findings across sites suggest an interaction between social class and ethnicity on strain. While preliminary findings support traditional strain theory's propositions on the influence of class on strain, they also suggests that elements of minority status, aside from those related to structural disadvantage, are also related to strain.[4]

To examine this issue more closely, it is necessary to examine group differences on the components of strain, namely aspirations and academic performance. In Hypothesis #7 it is asserted that minorities in general are more likely to experience strain due to blocked opportunity; an analysis of academic performance across ethnic groups will determine whether that is the case. In addition, differences in aspirations might also exist, which can contribute to mean differences in strain between minority groups and Whites.

Table 5b. Comparing Time 1 Variables by Ethnicity and Class

RECEIVE PUBLIC ASSISTANCE

	DENVER YOUTH SURVEY			ROCHESTER YOUTH DEVELOPMENT STUDY		
	LATINO (N=96)	WHITE (N=12)	BLACK (N=85)	LATINO (N=51)	WHITE (N=38)	BLACK (N=171)
ASPIRATIONS	3.28	3.41	3.40	3.45	3.44	3.56
GRADES	2.34	2.59	2.25	1.95[A]	2.24	2.13
STRAIN	1.05	1.00	1.22	1.53	1.27	1.46

DO NOT RECEIVE PUBLIC ASSISTANCE

	DENVER YOUTH SURVEY			ROCHESTER YOUTH DEVELOPMENT STUDY		
	LATINO (N=65)	WHITE (N=18)	BLACK (N=47)	LATINO (N=41)	WHITE (N=133)	BLACK (N=139)
ASPIRATIONS	3.38[AB]	3.01	3.17	3.55[A]	3.31[C]	3.59
GRADES	2.45[A]	3.04[C]	2.34	2.17[A]	2.60[C]	2.26
STRAIN	1.06[A]	.40[C]	.88	1.44[A]	.84[C]	1.37

[a] Latinos significantly different from Whites, [b] Latinos significantly different from African Americans, [c] African Americans significantly different from Whites

Initial mean difference tests indicate that minorities indeed have decreased legitimate opportunities for success, as indicated by academic performance. In both the DYS and the RYDS White males have significantly higher self reported grades compared to minority groups. Once social class is introduced, differences between ethnic groups exist only among those who do *not* receive public assistance. This finding is consistent with mean differences in strain levels across groups; among those who are disadvantaged economically (receive public aid), opportunities for educational advancement are blocked, regardless of ethnic background (Table 5b). Among those who do not rely on government assistance, however, differences exist by minority status. Note that African Americans and Latinos both have significantly lower grades compared to their White counterparts, however, minority groups do not differ from one another. These findings suggest that in addition to class, minority status serves as an additional source of strain. Although strain theorists were originally concerned with blocked opportunity by class, there may exist an interaction between minority status and class which serves to restrict educational opportunities among Latinos and African Americans who are not economically disadvantaged.[5] Social class does not appear to be the sole mechanism by which legitimate opportunities are blocked; the findings thus far suggest that class and race are intertwined. Restricted access to legitimate means produces higher levels of strain among the minority population who do not receive public assistance.

Although no previous hypotheses were offered regarding ethnicity and aspirations, differences may exist, which can contribute to variation in strain levels among ethnic groups. Within the DYS sample, no ethnic differences are observed in the desire for economic success. In the RYDS, however, Latinos and African Americans have significantly higher aspirations than Whites. Once social class is taken into consideration, differences in both sites emerge. Among those receiving public assistance in both sites, there are no significant differences between groups in their desire for money. Among those who do not receive aid, Latinos have significantly higher aspirations than both Whites and Blacks in the DYS, and in the RYDS, aspirations of Latinos and Blacks differ from Whites.

There exist differing hypotheses on the internalization of the 'American Dream' by Latinos (see Chapter 3). Some have argued that Latinos are just as likely as other groups to have high aspirations for economic success, as all groups are influenced by popular culture and media sources of goal transmission (Blea, 1988; Heller, 1971). Others argue that Latinos may be less likely to adopt economic goal orientations which can conflict with traditional Latino values (Horowitz, 1983). Findings from the RYDS suggest that minority groups, in general, differ in their goal orientation; across all ethnic groups, minorities demonstrate higher aspirations than non-minorities. Once aspirations are examined by class, consistent findings on Latino goal internalization emerge across sites. Latinos from the upper classes have higher aspirations than Whites (DYS also finds Latino aspirations higher than Blacks). Among those who receive public assistance, aspirations do not vary.

In the RYDS, a language measure is utilized to assess the potential impact of acculturation on aspirations. As described in Chapter 3, some have argued that as Latinos become acculturated, they are more likely to adopt a value system that is consistent with the mainstream American culture. Comparisons between children of Spanish and English speaking parents in the RYDS indicate that aspirations do not vary significantly by level of acculturation (3.53 compared to 3.43, respectively). Differences by acculturation were also examined by class, to determine whether higher aspirations by Latinos who do not receive aid are a consequence of the acculturation process. Findings by class indicate that those Latinos of Spanish speaking parents who receive public assistance have *higher* aspirations than those of English speaking parents, whereas no differences were observed across Latinos who do not receive public assistance. Those Latinos who are considered to be more acculturated have lower aspirations; therefore, greater immersion into mainstream culture (i.e. acculturation) does not seem to explain higher aspirations among the ethnic group.

TIME 2 MEASURES
Strain measures assessed at Time 2 include the externalization of blame, challenge to legitimacy of conventional norms, delinquent values, peer delinquency and drug use, student access to drugs (illegitimate opportunity), and family involvement. In keeping with Cloward and Ohlin's (1960) assertion that externalization is related to the visibility of barriers to economic success, Latinos and African Americans are expected to externalize blame more than White males.

> **Hypothesis #2:** Latinos, as a group, are more likely than Whites to externalize blame for failure to achieve economic success, since societal-level barriers to legitimate opportunities (i.e. discriminatory practices) are more visible for them.
>
> **Hypothesis #9a:** Latinos and African Americans are more likely than Whites to externalize blame for failure to achieve economic success, since societal-level barriers to legitimate opportunities (i.e. discriminatory practices) are visible among minority populations.

Barriers to minority group success are likely to be more visible given minority group status and discrimination; therefore, Latinos and African Americans are more likely to externalize blame. Initial mean difference tests across groups suggest that Latinos are most likely to externalize blame. In both sites Latinos have the highest percentage of males that externalize blame (27% in DYS, 35% in RYDS), however, differences across ethnic groups in the DYS are not statistically significant. In the RYDS, the externalization of blame among Latinos differs only compared to African Americans. Black males in the RYDS are the least likely to externalize blame for failure to achieve economic success (17%); both Latinos and Whites have significantly higher mean externalization. Neither Hypothesis #2 nor Hypothesis #9 receive support in the current examination. Contrary to expectations, minority groups in general are *not* likely to externalize blame to a greater extent than Whites. While Latino externalization differs significantly from African Americans, there is no corresponding distinction with Whites. In fact, Latinos and Whites in the RYDS appear to externalize blame to a similar extent, and are more likely to externalize blame than Blacks.

　To determine whether the higher percentage of externalization among Latinos is due to their experience of economic disadvantage, groups were compared across class categories. Across class groups, ethnic differences in the externalization of blame remain consistent. Latinos and Whites in the RYDS are more likely to externalize blame for failure to advance academically than are African Americans, regardless of class. In the DYS, no differences in externalization across ethnic groups were observed in either class category.

　The variation in findings across sites may reflect a difference in externalization measures. Although an identical measure was desired, it was necessary to utilize two separate but related measures, as neither site includes a specific measure of externalization. The DYS asks students to identify reasons for difficulty in making money, and the RYDS asks participants to attribute blame for failure to advance academically. As mentioned previously, the concept of externalization is a vital component to the strain model; given the difference in data collected within each site, it is necessary that the current analysis employs slightly different measures of externalization. Based on mean difference tests, Latinos and Whites in the RYDS are more likely to identify external sources which impede opportunities for educational advancement. In the DYS, all ethnic groups are similar in externalizing blame for failure to make money. Latinos and African Americans in both sites are no more likely than Whites to identify external sources of blocked opportunity. This finding is inconsistent with Cloward and Ohlin's assertion about African Americans and blocked opportunity. Minority groups in the sample have decreased opportunities for success, however, they do not externalize blame to a greater extent than Whites. Although mean differences do not vary as anticipated, differences between minority groups and Whites may emerge once the relationship between the strain/externalization interaction and the challenge to legitimacy is examined.

As described in Chapter 4, higher values on the weakened conventional beliefs measure indicate a challenge to legitimacy of conventional norms. Those who experience strain and externalize blame for failure to achieve economic success are most likely to withdraw legitimacy from conventional methods of goal attainment. In both the DYS and the RYDS, Whites have the highest mean values of challenge, Latinos have the second highest challenge average, and African Americans appear to be the least likely to withdraw legitimacy from conventional norms. In the RYDS, all three groups differ significantly from each other, however, in the DYS, only differences between the minority groups are significant. In the describing the progression to delinquency, Cloward and Ohlin (1960) posit that the legitimacy removed from conventional norms may be replaced by a delinquent value system. In adopting delinquent values, Whites in the DYS score higher than either Latinos or African Americans. In the RYDS all of the groups appear to be quite similar in delinquent value adoption.

In the traditional strain theory model, peer delinquency is expected to reinforce both delinquent values and delinquent outcomes. In a preliminary examination of peer delinquency and drug use, minority groups in the DYS differ from Whites in the number of delinquent peers reported; both Latinos and African Americans have higher mean values (1.86 and 1.85, respectively) compared to their White counterparts (1.64). In the RYDS, all ethnic groups report similar involvement with delinquent peers and no statistically significant differences emerge. In both sites, African Americans report the greatest access to drugs across all groups (2.54 in DYS, 3.20 in RYDS). Latinos in both sites are second highest (2.29 in DYS, 2.83 in RYDS). In the DYS, differences between all ethnic groups are statistically significant, whereas in the RYDS, Whites and

Latinos differ from African Americans, but not each other in the ease of acquiring drugs. A final measure assessed at Time 2 is involvement with family, which will be used to test for cultural influences on the strain model. Family involvement is included in the modified strain model as an indicator of the traditional Latino culture. Scholars have documented the importance of the family in the lives of Latinos, and have demonstrated the influence of the family on delinquency (Rodriguez & Weisburd, 1991; Smith, 1990; Smith & Krohn, 1995). The family measure is introduced into the theory as a potential alternative to the route to delinquency that might be traveled by those who experience strain. A comparison of family involvement in the DYS demonstrates that all ethnic groups are relatively similar in the amount of time spent in family activity. In the RYDS, however, Whites differ from both Latinos and African Americans on family involvement; on the average, Whites spend less time with family.

TIME 3 MEASURES
A variety of delinquent outcomes are assessed at Time 3, including general delinquency, alcohol use, drug use, serious delinquency, property crime, and violent crime (see Appendix for a complete list of item in each index). No previous hypotheses have been offered regarding the impact of ethnicity on delinquent outcomes, however, some differences emerge across groups in both sites. In the DYS, ethnic groups differ on half of all delinquency indices, including general delinquency, serious delinquency, and property crime. A t-test of mean values indicates that Latinos have the highest involvement in general delinquency (average number of delinquent acts is 33) compared to Whites (15) and African Americans (30). A comparison of average serious delinquency scores demonstrate higher values across minority groups which are significantly different from Whites. The mean score of property crime incidence is the highest among Latinos, but the only statistically significant comparison is between Latinos and their African American counterparts.

Within the RYDS, delinquency indices illustrate group differences on general delinquency, serious delinquency and property crime as in the DYS. However, violent crime in the RYDS also differs across groups. Latinos differ only from Whites on the means of both property and violent crime, and have higher incidence on both measures. African Americans also differ from Whites on violent crime, as well as general and serious delinquency indices. Latinos and African Americans do not differ on any delinquency indices in the RYDS, and only differ on general delinquency scores in the DYS.

SITE-SPECIFIC MEASURES

Among the DYS site-specific measures are two variables which represent more comprehensive indicators of challenge to legitimacy and delinquent values than those included in the analysis of identical measures. In addition to items used to create identical indices, the DYS includes a total of eleven items which reflect challenge to conventional beliefs (captured by CHLEGIT2). A site-specific comprehensive measure of delinquent values is also included in the current analysis which combines a total of eighteen items, compared to the eleven item index used for comparison with the RYDS. On the comprehensive challenge measure, both Latinos and Whites differ significantly from African Americans (1.46 and 1.49 compared to 1.35, respectively). The comprehensive challenge measure indicates a difference between Whites and African Americans, which was not captured by the identical measure. Within the more comprehensive delinquent values measure (DELVAL1), a pattern similar to the identical measure emerges; Whites have the highest mean value followed by Latinos and African Americans. Differences between minority groups and Whites are statistically significant.

The DYS data also include two unique strain measures; one of blocked opportunity and a student evaluation of neighborhood crime. On the blocked opportunity index, Latinos perceive the greatest obstacles to legitimate opportunity and differ significantly from Whites and Blacks in the DYS. The index provides support for Hypothesis #1 and Hypothesis #8, which posit that Latinos are most likely to have the strongest perceptions of blocked opportunity. In comparison to the identical measure of academic performance, the index does not reveal a statistically significant difference between Blacks and Whites (although both minority groups score higher on the blocked opportunity index). Instead, Latinos experience the greatest obstacles to legitimate opportunities, compared to minority and non-minority groups. Differences between minority groups and Whites on the identical measure might reflect more objective or structurally-based obstacles to legitimate opportunity. Minority groups are less likely to succeed in school than Whites, and the academic performance measure appears to reflect this. When a subjective measure is assessed, however, differences between Blacks and Whites are not found. Instead, Latinos emerge as the group which faces the greatest obstacles to legitimate opportunity, which supports the hypotheses. The neighborhood crime measure, intended to serve as an alternative measure of illegitimate opportunity, indicates that African Americans face the greatest exposure to illegitimate opportunity (report the most serious problem with neighborhood crime), while Whites have the lowest group mean. Only differences between Latinos and African Americans are statistically significant.

Within the RYDS lies a comprehensive measure of social class status which is utilized in the analysis of site-specific measures (for a complete description of the measure, see Chapter 4). A comparison of mean differences across ethnic groups reveals that minority groups differ significantly from Whites in the percentage which qualifies as lower class (Latinos, 66%; Blacks, 64%; Whites, 32%). Minority groups in the RYDS do not differ on the comprehensive SES measure.

BIVARIATE RELATIONSHIPS BY ETHNICITY
Pearson correlation coefficients provide a preliminary look at relationships within the strain theory model. Although full correlation matrices are provided for Time 1 and Time 2 variables and for Time 2 and Time 3 variables (see Appendix H), only those modeled by traditional strain theory will be discussed in the following section (see Table 5d for a reduced listing of coefficients). In addition, the influence of family involvement, as introduced by the modified strain model, will also be examined by ethnicity.

Traditional strain theorists presume that strain relationships across groups are equivalent, as the theory is expected to apply equally to individuals, regardless of ethnic background. Bivariate analyses allow for a test of that assertion across all strain relationships. A comparison of correlation coefficients across ethnic groups in both the DYS and the RYDS also permits an initial test of hypotheses offered in Chapter 3. Based on previous research and the literature on Latinos, certain relationships in the traditional strain model are expected to vary across groups. In the following sections, relationships are presented in the order in which they appear in the strain model.

CLASS AND STRAIN

Traditional strain theory posits a direct relationship between class status and strain.[6] The influence of class provides the foundation for strain theory; one's position in the social structure determines access to legitimate opportunities, and therefore, influences strain. In the current analysis, class is assessed with information on public assistance (0=no aid, 1=receives public aid), therefore, the relationship is expected to be positive; an increase in PUBASST will lead to an increase in STRAIN. Strain theorists would assert this relationship to be uniform; as one becomes more economically disadvantaged, legitimate opportunities diminish, regardless of ethnic background. Findings of bivariate analyses indicate that on the whole, class is *not* a consistent determining factor of strain across groups. Class is associated with strain among White males in the DYS and the RYDS, however, findings among minority groups are mixed. Class is not related to strain among Latinos in either site; among African Americans, the relationship is significant only in the DYS.

Overall, the most basic strain hypothesis holds true only for Whites. The receipt of public assistance in the White population significantly increases strain disjunction scores. Among Latinos in both the DYS and the RYDS and African Americans in Denver, public assistance is unrelated to one's level of strain. One possible explanation for this finding is that class is unrelated to strain across minority groups because minorities do not experience strain. However, descriptive statistics indicate that Latinos and African Americans do experience strain, and at a higher level than their White counterparts. An alternative explanation is that factors other than class contribute to strain among minority groups. Previous analyses in this chapter illustrate varying levels of strain across class groups (Table 5b), which is consistent with a null finding of the relationship between class and strain for Latinos. Taken together, these preliminary findings indicate that factors other than economic disadvantage may be related to strain among minorities.

To get a closer look at the class influence on strain, the bivariate relationship between class and the perception of legitimate opportunity (self reported grades) is examined. Recall that in the traditional strain model, class is expected to influence strain by limiting opportunities for success.

TABLE 5C. COMPARING CORRELATION COEFFICIENTS BY SITE

TRADITIONAL STRAIN THEORY RELATIONSHIPS	DENVER YOUTH SURVEY			ROCHESTER YOUTH DEVELOPMENT STUDY		
	LATINO (N=161)	WHITE (N=30)	BLACK (N=132)	LATINO (N=92)	WHITE (N=172)	BLACK (N=310)
IDENTICAL MEASURES						
PUBLIC ASSISTANCE —>STRAIN	.01	.37*	.19*	.04	.20*	.05
PUBLIC ASSISTANCE —> GRADES	-.06	-.28	-.06	-.12	-.19*	-.08
CHALLENGE LEGITIMACY —> DELINQUENT VALUES	.29*	.41*	.29*	.40*	.46*	.30*
DELINQUENT PEERS —> DELINQUENT VALUES	.41*	.68*	.52*	.49*	.51*	.36*
FAMILY INVOLVEMENT —> DELINQUENT VALUES	-.25*	-.08	-.22*	-.13	-.08	-.13*
DELINQUENT PEERS —> GENERAL DELINQUENCY	.31*	.58*	.53*	.46*	.46*	.37*
DELINQUENT PEERS —> ALCOHOL USE	.14*	.47*	.55*	.36*	.37*	.30*
DELINQUENT PEERS —> DRUG USE	.27*	.52*	.46*	.29*	.53*	.32*
DELINQUENT PEERS —> SERIOUS DELINQUENCY	.32*	.58*	.45*	.11	.30*	.31*
DELINQUENT PEERS —> PROPERTY CRIME	.32*	.63*	.28*	.27*	.51*	.17*
DELINQUENT PEERS —> VIOLENT CRIME	.30	.54*	.50*	.31*	.36*	.35*

*p less than or equal to .05 (one-tail test)

TABLE 5C. COMPARING CORRELATION COEFFICIENTS BY SITE (CONT.)

TRADITIONAL STRAIN THEORY RELATIONSHIPS	DENVER YOUTH SURVEY			ROCHESTER YOUTH DEVELOPMENT STUDY		
	LATINO (N=161)	WHITE (N=30)	BLACK (N=132)	LATINO (N=92)	WHITE (N=172)	BLACK (N=310)
SITE-SPECIFIC MEASURES - DYS						
PUBLIC ASSISTANCE —> BLOCKED OPPORTUNITY	.26*	.33*	.21*	--	--	--
CHALLENGE LEGITIMACY 2 —> DELIN. VALUES	.25*	.50*	.26*	--	--	--
CHALLENGE LEGITIMACY —> DELIN. VALUES 2	.27*	.42*	.37*	--	--	--
CHALLENGE LEGITIMACY 2 —> DELIN. VALUES 2	.25*	.50*	.32*	--	--	--
DELINQUENT PEERS —> DELIN. VALUES 2	.43*	.73*	.54*	--	--	--
FAMILY INVOLVEMENT —> DELIN. VALUES 2	-.27*	-.10	-.20*	--	--	--
SITE-SPECIFIC MEASURES - RYDS						
LOWER CLASS —> STRAIN	--	--	--	.14	.08	.05
LOWER CLASS —> GRADES	--	--	--	-.17	-.07	-.09
ACCULTURATION —> FAMILY INVOLVEMENT	--	--	--	.11	--	--

*p less than or equal to .05 (one-tail test)

Across sites the receipt of public assistance is negatively related with grades among all males. While the relationship between class and grades is statistically significant among White males, it is not significant among minority groups.[7] Rather than representing a consequence of lower class membership, limited legitimate opportunity and strain may be related to other elements of minority status, such as discrimination. Based on these initial findings it appears that the hypothesized primary source of strain, economic disadvantage, is not consistent across groups. This may indicate that strain theory is not a universal explanation of behavior, as it has been previously accepted. Sources of strain may extend beyond economic causes and may be indicative of larger structural relationships in society (i.e. race relations, minority status).

CHALLENGE LEGITIMACY OF NORMS AND DELINQUENT VALUES
Cloward and Ohlin (1960) depict a positive relationship between the challenge to legitimacy and delinquent values; as individuals remove legitimacy from conventional methods of goal attainment, they are more likely to adopt an alternative value system, including delinquent values.[8] Pearson correlation coefficients of the relationship between the current measure of challenge (weakened conventional beliefs) and delinquent values are positive and statistically significant across all ethnic groups in both the DYS and the RYDS. Generally, this indicates support for the effect of challenge on a delinquent value system. Across all ethnic groups, however, Whites males evidence the strongest correlation coefficients between challenge and delinquent values.

In a previous discussion of ethnicity and strain (see Chapter 3), anticipated differences in the adoption of delinquent values across ethnic groups were outlined. A primary element of the Latino culture, family involvement, was introduced into the model and its potential impact on traditional strain theory was described. Based on previous studies of family relations and delinquency, the relative influence of the family among Latinos was expected to weaken the impact of challenge on the adoption of delinquent values:

Hypothesis #4a: The relationship between challenge to legitimacy and delinquent values is expected to be weaker among Latinos in the strain theory model, due to the influence of traditional cultural values.

While the general strain assertion applies to all ethnic groups, support is also found for Hypothesis #4a. Results of bivariate analyses suggest that the strength of the relationship between challenge to legitimacy and delinquent values is *not* consistent across ethnic groups. Other factors which theoretically contribute to the development of a delinquent value system are examined in the current analysis, and include the impact of delinquent peers.

DELINQUENT PEERS AND DELINQUENT VALUES

In the traditional strain theory model, peer delinquency and drug use is expected to strengthen delinquent values. However, the strength of that relationship is expected to vary by ethnicity:

> **Hypothesis #6c:** The influence of delinquent peers on *delinquent values* is expected to be weaker for Latinos than Whites, due to the relative impact of the family.
>
> **Hypothesis #11a:** Between minority groups, Latinos are expected to evidence a weaker influence of peers on *delinquent values*, given the anticipated impact of the family.

Although family involvement is expected to influence relationships across all ethnic groups, prior research suggests that the influence of the family will be strongest among Latinos (Rodriguez & Weisburd,1991; Smith & Krohn,1995). Given the relative importance of family, the impact of peers is expected to be weaker among Latinos compared to both Whites and African Americans.

Generally, the relationship holds for all groups in both sites; all Pearson correlation coefficients between delinquent peers and values achieve statistical significance. As in other relationships, this finding is strongest among White males in both sites. Hypothesis #6a is supported by both the DYS and the RYDS, as Latinos have a smaller correlation coefficient than Whites (.41 compared to .68 in the DYS, and .49 compared to .51 in the RYDS). Minority group differences are not consistent across sites: in the DYS, the relationship between peer delinquency and delinquent values is smaller for Latinos compared to Blacks (.41 versus .52), which supports Hypothesis #13a. In the RYDS, however, the association is stronger among Latinos (.49 versus .36).

FAMILY INVOLVEMENT AND DELINQUENT VALUES
Latinos are also expected to evidence a stronger family influence on the adoption of delinquent values. In Chapter 3, family involvement is introduced into the traditional strain model as an alternate route for strained youth, and is expected to discourage the adoption of a delinquent value system and involvement with delinquent peers:

Hypothesis #4b: Traditional cultural values, as transmitted by involvement with family, are likely to decrease the likelihood of adopting a delinquent value system. A negative relationship between family involvement and delinquent values is anticipated for all ethnic groups.

Hypothesis #6a: Involvement in family activity is expected to decrease the likelihood of developing delinquent peer associations. A negative relationship between family involvement and delinquent peers is anticipated for all ethnic groups.

Although the influence of family is anticipated for all youth, the impact of family involvement is expected to be strongest among Latinos in the following way(s):

Hypothesis #4c: The influence of family and religion on delinquent value adoption is expected to be stronger for Latinos than Whites.

Hypothesis #6b: The influence of family involvement on delinquent peer associations is expected to be stronger for Latinos than Whites.

Hypothesis #10a: Compared to the majority, African American and Latino families might serve as a source of strength in response to discrimination, and may ultimately serve as a protective factor against delinquent adaptations to strain. In the current analysis, the influence of the family in reducing delinquent values is expected to be stronger among minority groups compared to Whites.

Hypothesis #10b: Based on previous empirical findings, the influence of the family on delinquent values is expected to be strongest for Latinos. The Latino family may be less likely to reinforce mainstream ideals, and instead, provide other avenues of success for adolescents which are based on traditional values.

In the current analysis, support for Hypothesis #4b is not found, since the relationship between family involvement and delinquent values is not consistent across ethnic groups. In the DYS and the RYDS, a substantial impact of family is uncovered only among Latino and African Americans.[9] Differences between minority and non-minority youth support Hypothesis #11 and Hypothesis #4c; a significant buffering effect of the family is found only among minority groups in the DYS. Latinos and African Americans in the RYDS also demonstrate a significant impact of the family in reducing delinquent values, unlike Whites. Differences between minority groups are less consistent across sites. A comparison of minority groups in the DYS supports Hypothesis #12, where the influence of family is strongest among Latinos. In the RYDS, however, the impact of family is strongest among Blacks; the magnitude of the family effect is the same (-.13), however, the Latino coefficient is only marginally significant.

DELINQUENT PEERS AND DELINQUENT BEHAVIOR
In addition to serving as a reinforcement of delinquent values, peer delinquency and drug use is also expected to contribute to delinquent behavior. Cloward and Ohin's opportunity theory would assume this relationship to be equal across ethnic groups. As indicated previously, however, scholars have argued that the peer influence on Latino delinquency may be comparatively weaker due to the significance of the family in the lives of Latino youth. Chapter 3 describes anticipated differences in the relationship between peer delinquency and delinquent outcomes by ethnicity. Specifically, a strong family influence is anticipated within the Latino population, as evidenced by previous research and supported by findings described earlier in this Chapter. At the same time, peer effects are expected to be weaker among minorities than mainstream youth in the following manner:

Hypothesis #6d: The influence of delinquent peers on *delinquent behavior* is also expected to be weaker among Latinos than Whites (due to the relative impact of the family).

Hypothesis #11b: Between minority groups, Latinos are expected to evidence a weaker influence of peers on *delinquent behavior*, given the anticipated impact of the family.

As described, the influence of peers on delinquent value adoption is found to be strongest among White males. Similar findings are anticipated in the relationships between delinquent peers and various delinquency indices. Compared to both African Americans and Whites, the influence of peers among Latinos is expected to be weakest.

Generally, those hypotheses are supported by DYS data. On five of the six delinquency indices Latinos produce the smallest correlation coefficients of all ethnic groups (coefficients vary on general delinquency, alcohol use, drug use, serious delinquency and violent crime indices). In the RYDS, the Latino peer influence appears to be weaker compared to Whites, which supports Hypothesis #6b. On the majority of delinquency indices, the peer impact is weaker among Latinos compared to Whites, but is stronger than relationships among African Americans. Hypothesis #13b is only partially supported by the RYDS data, as the correlation coefficients vary in strength between African Americans and Latinos.[10] Relationships between peer delinquency and delinquent outcomes may not hold once other components of the model are examined in multivariate analyses. In predicting delinquent outcomes, the influence of peers is examined along with the interaction effect of delinquent values and illegitimate opportunity.[11]

SITE SPECIFIC MEASURES

Bivariate results presented to this point include identical measures across sites. In additional to identical measures, site specific variables have been examined using bivariate analyses. In the following section, strain relationships are examined with site specific measures and are compared to results derived from analysis of identical measures.

DENVER YOUTH SURVEY

The Denver Youth Survey introduces a blocked opportunity index as an alternative measure of strain. The relationship between public assistance and blocked opportunity was first examined to determine whether ethnic differences emerge as they do when using the strain disjunction measure. Unlike the findings from the identical strain measure, consistencies in correlation coefficients were observed across all ethnic groups in the DYS. The relationship between class and the blocked opportunity index is positive and statistically significant across Latino, White, and African American males; as one receives public aid, perceptions of blocked opportunity increase. The relationship between class and blocked opportunity holds true for all ethnic groups, whereas the association between class and the strain disjunction measure was true only for Whites and African Americans. Differences between strain measures might account for this finding. While the strain disjunction variable is based on a simple measure of blocked opportunity (academic performance), the DYS blocked opportunity index includes multiple questions about one's perceived chances for getting ahead. Legitimate opportunity in the index is not restricted solely to the educational realm, as it is in the disjunction measure. In addition, the blocked opportunity index taps into subjective perceptions of access to legitimate opportunity, where the strain disjunction measure cannot. Educational attainment is interpreted as an indicator of the likelihood that one will achieve economic success, however, it does not provide a subjective assessment as does the blocked opportunity index.[12] It should also be noted that Latino academic performance in the DYS may not be attributed to class status, but instead, may relate more broadly to the historical educational challenges faced by all Latinos in the United States. Inclusion of factors other than education in evaluating one's perceived opportunities might allow for the link between social class and opportunity to emerge.

In addition to the unique strain measure included in the DYS, the study also includes comprehensive measures of challenge to conventional values and delinquent values. Bivariate analyses of strain relationships were re-examined using those comprehensive measures, and findings were compared to those obtained with identical measures. With regard to the comprehensive challenge variable, an impact similar to that of the identical challenge measure was observed, however, differences between ethnic groups become more distinct. All ethnic groups demonstrate a positive, statistically significant association with the identical delinquent values measure. In keeping with previous findings, Whites evidence the strongest relationship among all ethnic groups. Inclusion of the comprehensive measure highlights the difference in magnitude of the association across ethnic groups, however (White=.50, Latino=.25, Black=.26). When identical challenge measure is coupled with the comprehensive delinquent values measure, findings are consistent to those generated with the identical DELVAL measure. All ethnic groups demonstrate positive and significant correlation coefficients, with Whites producing the highest coefficient. When the DYS comprehensive measures are assessed simultaneously, findings are nearly identical to those generated with the comprehensive challenge measure; ethnic differences are evident, with the strongest association emerging among White males.

Other relationships involving delinquent values were also examined, including peer and family effects. Findings of the peer delinquency influence on DELVAL1 are similar to those generated with the identical DELVAL measure, however coefficients are higher across all ethnic groups using the comprehensive measure. Again, White males demonstrate the strongest association between peer delinquency and drugs and delinquent values, although all are significant. The impact of family involvement on the comprehensive delinquent values measure is consistent with findings from the identical variable; a significant, negative effect is found only among Latinos and Blacks in the DYS.

ROCHESTER YOUTH DEVELOPMENT STUDY

The Rochester Youth Development Study includes a unique measure which is vital for estimating an acculturation influence on the traditional strain theory model. Parent completion of a Spanish interview is utilized as a proxy for acculturation, and is available only in the RYDS. As described in Chapter 3, acculturation is expected to influence the extent to which Latinos are enmeshed in traditional cultural activities, including involvement with the family:

> **Hypothesis #5**: As Latinos become more acculturated into the mainstream, traditional cultural values may be weakened. Therefore, a direct relationship between acculturation and family involvement is examined, and is expected to be negative.

Researchers have argued that as Latinos become acculturated, they may spend less time involved with family. Using bivariate analyses, a positive relationship between acculturation and family involvement emerges; as Latinos become more acculturated, the *more* involved they are in family activities. Since the zero order correlation is not statistically significant, there appears to be no support for Hypothesis #5; acculturation does not appear to influence family involvement.

The final site specific measure found in the RYDS is a comprehensive assessment of class status. LOWERCL combines public assistance, principal wage earner employment status, and household income to arrive at an alternative measure of class. Using bivariate analyses, the comprehensive measure was examined to determine its impact upon strain and legitimate opportunity. Inclusion of the site specific measure produces findings which differ from those found using public assistance. Specifically, no impact of class is found among any ethnic group when LOWERCL is included. Recall that public assistance is significantly related to strain and grades among Whites. Those findings do not hold when a comprehensive measure is utilized; lower class status is unrelated to strain and academic performance.[13]

The preliminary findings described in this chapter demonstrate support for several hypotheses regarding ethnic differences in strain theory relationships. Latinos and African Americans are more likely to receive public aid and experience higher levels of blocked opportunity and strain. Minority groups are more vulnerable to strain than Whites, however, the primary source of strain among minorities is not consistent with traditional strain theory. Merton (1938) and Cloward and Ohlin (1960) have argued that class is the primary mechanism by which access to legitimate opportunity is restricted. This appears to be the case only among White males. The fundamental strain theory relationship between class and level of strain does not hold true for Latinos and African Americans as it does for non-minority youth. Limited legitimate opportunity and higher levels of strain are not simply a function of economic disadvantage. Instead, an interactive effect of class and ethnicity is suggested, and other sources of strain among minority groups should be considered.

With regard to group adaptations to strain, all ethnic groups appear somewhat similar. Minority groups do not externalize blame to a greater extent than Whites. This finding contradicts hypotheses of the current analysis and those originally posited by Cloward and Ohlin, who suggested that African Americans are more likely to externalize blame. On other strain theory measures, findings are relatively consistent across groups; challenge to legitimacy and delinquent peers lead to delinquent values among Latinos, Whites, and Blacks. In addition, peer delinquency is related to the majority of delinquent outcomes.

Peer influences are stronger for Whites, but significant for all groups. Although minorities report a greater incidence of peer delinquency, they are not as strongly influenced by peers as their non-minority counterparts. This finding lends support to hypotheses related to the family influence on delinquent values. Peer effects among minority groups may be weaker due to the importance of the family; across Latinos and African Americans in both sites, family influence is stronger than Whites, as hypothesized. White males report less time spent in family activities, and no bivariate relationship between family and delinquent values is found among the population in either site. Initial findings suggest that cultural factors, as introduced by the modified strain model, are important for understanding delinquent adaptations to strain among Latinos.

While preliminary findings provide a glimpse into the consistency of individual relationships proposed by strain theory, it is necessary to estimate the strain model as a whole. Structural equation modeling provides an appropriate mechanism by which to examine strain relationships simultaneously. Using LISREL, models are simultaneously estimated by ethnicity, allowing for a comparison of path coefficients and the overall model fit across Latino, White, and African American males.

CHAPTER 6

Testing Traditional Strain Theory

This chapter describes structural equation analyses of the traditional and modified strain theory models of the total male sample within each site. The examination of males in the aggregate serves to replicate other studies which do not examine ethnic groups separately. It evaluates traditional strain theory as a general explanatory model, and assesses its utility in predicting delinquency across all groups. The traditional strain theory model does not assert variation by ethnicity, and as such, requires a preliminary examination across all males in the DYS and the RYDS.

All structural equation models are estimated using the Maximum Likelihood (ML) method of estimation found in the SIMPLIS program of LISREL 8.30. Initial evaluation of the traditional strain theory model will determine the utility of the theory in explaining delinquency among all males in the DYS and the RYDS. The modified strain model is also estimated with the total male sample to determine the impact of family involvement on the traditional strain model. Independent examination of traditional and modified models allows for a comparison of their overall explanatory value and model fit. The Chi-square of the traditional and modified models will be compared to determine whether family involvement contributes substantively to the traditional model, and whether the inclusion of cultural influences results in greater explanatory power.

STRUCTURAL EQUATION MODELING WITH LISREL

Estimates provided by structural equation modeling are based on covariance matrices generated in PRELIS. Separate models are estimated using SIMPLIS for each of the five outcome variables, in an attempt to evaluate traditional strain theory in explaining general delinquency, alcohol use, drug use, property crime, and violent crime. According to criteria set by Bollen (1989), the models estimated in the current analysis are identified. All structural equation models are recursive, that is, all causal paths are in the same direction, and no ill conditioned matrices are utilized in estimating models (Kelloway, 1998).

The traditional strain model is first assessed using various tests of absolute fit, including a Chi-square significance test, the standardized root mean squared residual (RMR), and the goodness of fit index (GFI). Each of these tests demonstrates the ability of the model to reproduce the covariance matrix (Kelloway, 1998). The GFI is comparable to the R^2 in a regression equation, and indicates the amount of observed variance and covariance accounted for by a model (Hoyle & Panter, 1995). A GFI statistic greater than .9 indicates a good fit of the model to the data. As another gauge of a good fit, a *non*-significant Chi-square "implies that there is no significant discrepancy between the covariance matrix implied by the model and the population covariance matrix" (Kelloway, 1998:25). One problem commonly cited with the Chi-square test statistic is its link with sample size (Hu & Bentler, 1995; Kelloway, 1998). Researchers have cited potential problems with utilizing a Chi-square significance test as an accurate estimate of model fit with small and large samples. With a small sample, the test statistic (T) may not be Chi-square distributed, and therefore, may not be appropriate in evaluating model fit (Hu & Bentler, 1995:78). On the other hand, the increased statistical power provided by large samples makes it difficult to achieve a non-significant Chi-square. Models estimated with large samples are likely to produce a statistically significant statistic; in such cases, other fit indices are utilized to avoid a premature rejection of the specified model (Hu & Bentler, 1995). The final indicator of absolute fit to be reported is the RMR, which is based on an analysis of residuals and is cited as the simplest fit index. The RMR is the square root of the mean of the squared discrepancies between the covariance matrix implied by the model and the observed covariance matrix (Kelloway, 1998). The standardized RMR is utilized since it ranges from 0 to 1 and is simple to interpret (values less than .05 are indicative of a good fit).

In addition to tests of absolute fit which compare the model to the data, the comparative fit index (CFI) is also provided which indicates the fit of the model relative to a baseline model. The CFI is one of several incremental fit indices which measures the proportionate improvement in fit between the estimated model and a more restricted baseline (Hu & Bentler, 1995). Typically, the null model is used as the comparison, which assumes that all variables are unrelated. As an indicator of good fit, a CFI statistic of .9 suggests that the estimated model provides a ninety percent improvement over the null model.

SIMPLIS also provides coefficients of pathways specified by the model. Unstandardized coefficients are reported in the following sections, since standardized coefficients are inappropriate for interpreting product terms contained in the models (Aiken & West, 1991). The multiplicative product term in the latter half of the model is comprised of two mean-centered variables (delinquent values and access to drugs). Standardized coefficients produced by centered variables alter the metric of the measures and confound their interpretation (Aiken & West, 1991). Also included in SIMPLIS output is an indicator of the variance explained by each equation in the model (R^2). Since this study is focused on the utility of traditional strain theory in predicting delinquent behavior, the R^2 of each estimation is presented along with goodness of fit statistics described thus far (see Table 6a).

As an initial step in the multivariate test of strain theory, a traditional strain theory model is examined using the total male sample within the DYS and the RYDS. This approach provides a baseline from which to compare the modified strain model and allows the results to be compared with existing literature

Traditional and modified strain models are first examined utilizing identical measures across sites, which will allow for the replication of findings across the DYS and the RYDS. Once they are compared, strain theory is then examined using site specific measures. Analysis of site specific measures will determine whether differences in strain theory measures impact the overall model. Previous research has suggested that the degree of support for strain theory is linked to the measures used to test the model (Burton & Cullen, 1992; Burton et al., 1994; Farnworth & Leiber, 1989; Hoffman & Ireland, 1995). To examine the extent to which this is true, site specific items are included in the analysis. In most instances, site specific items represent more comprehensive operationalizations of strain concepts.

TABLE 6A. TRADITIONAL STRAIN THEORY MODEL BY DELINQUENCY, ALL MALES[a]

	GENERAL		ALCOHOL		DRUG USE		PROPERTY		VIOLENCE	
	DYS	RYDS	DYS	RYDS	DYS	RYDS	DYS	RYDS	DYS	RYDS
UNSTANDARDIZED COEFFICIENTS										
PUBLIC ASSISTANCE —> STRAIN/EXTERNALIZATION	.18*	.14*								
PUBLIC ASSISTANCE —> STRAIN/INTERNALIZATION	-.03	.09*								
STRAIN/EXTERNALIZATION —> CHALLENGE LEGITIMACY	-.05	-.04								
STRAIN/INTERNALIZATION —> CHALLENGE LEGITIMACY	-.09*	-.15*								
CHALLENGE LEGITIMACY —> DELINQUENT VALUES	.37*	.27*								
DELINQUENT PEERS —> DELINQUENT VALUES	.34*	.33*								
DELINQUENT PEERS —> DELINQUENCY	.50*	.96*	.20	.55*	.35*	.76*	.23*	.18*	.24*	.33*
DELINQUENT VALUES —> DELINQUENCY	.25	.57*	.62*	.88*	.38*	.56*	.08	.12*	.09	.19*
ACCESS TO DRUGS —> DELINQUENCY	.46*	.26*	.44*	.24*	.25*	.20*	.16*	.02	.12*	.09*
DEL. VALUES*DRUG ACCESS —> DELINQUENCY	-.00	.22	.21	.09	.22*	.23	.10	-.01	.15*	.13*

[a]Common coefficients are listed under the General Delinquency column, and relationships that vary with each outcome are in bold.
* p<.05 (one-tail test)

TABLE 6A. TRADITIONAL STRAIN THEORY MODEL BY DELINQUENCY, ALL MALES[a]

	GENERAL		ALCOHOL USE		DRUG USE		PROPERTY		VIOLENCE	
	DYS	RYDS	DYS	RYDS	DYS	RYDS	DYS	RYDS	DYS	RYDS
ERROR TERMS										
STRAIN/EXTERNALIZATION	.46*	.65*								
STRAIN/INTERNALIZATION	.71*	.89*								
CHALLENGE LEGITIMACY	.16*	.24*								
DELINQUENT VALUES	.21*	.15*								
DELINQUENCY	1.99*	2.43*	2.56*	2.16*	1.66*	1.99*	.72*	.32*	.40*	.44*
COVARIANCE OF ERROR TERMS										
STRAIN/EXTERNALIZATION <—> STRAIN/INTERNALIZATION	-.21*	-.36*								
FIT INDICES										
EXPLAINED VARIANCE IN DELINQUENCY	.24	.19	.18	.17	.17	.16	.12	.05	.19	.13
GOODNESS OF FIT INDEX (GFI)	.96	.94	.96	.94	.97	.93	.97	.94	.97	.94
STANDARDIZED ROOT MEAN SQUARED RESIDUAL (RMR)	.06	.08	.05	.08	.05	.09	.05	.08	.05	.08
COMPARATIVE FIT INDEX (CFI)	.90	.83	.90	.81	.92	.80	.91	.80	.92	.82
CHI-SQUARE	57.51	162.75	54.74	175.32	48.30	191.11	49.64	173.06	47.87	159.16
DEGREES OF FREEDOM	19	19	19	19	19	19	19	19	19	19

[a]Common coefficients are listed under the General Delinquency column, and relationships that vary with each outcome are in bold.

* $p < .05$ (one-tail test)

ESTIMATING THE TRADITIONAL STRAIN MODEL

Estimates of the traditional strain model are based on covariance matrices generated in PRELIS for the total male sample within each site (number of cases, DYS=323, RYDS=573). The traditional strain theory model is estimated as it is offered by Cloward and Ohlin (see Chapter 2), with the inclusion of an additional parameter. Given the nature of the strain interaction terms, it is necessary to include an error covariance between the two measures. Specifying the correlation between the two error terms acknowledges the overlap that exists in interaction terms. Five separate estimates of the traditional strain model are conducted within each site to examine the theory's ability to predict general delinquency, alcohol use, drug use, property crime, and violence. It should be noted that the various delinquency outcomes produce very similar results in terms of model fit and pathway coefficients; only pathways to delinquency vary from estimation to estimation (see Table 6a & Appendix I). Therefore, results of the general delinquency model will be described in detail; any variation from that basic model will be highlighted.[1]

Across all males in the DYS and RYDS samples, the majority of traditional strain theory relationships are supported by findings (Appendix I). At the front end of the model, class status (receipt of public assistance) significantly predicts strain. In the DYS, class status predicts one of the two strain measures, and in the RYDS, class influences both strain interaction terms. Receipt of public assistance significantly increases strain *and* externalization of blame in the DYS, but does not impact strain among those who internalize. In the RYDS, the positive influence is consistent across both strain interaction terms, as previously hypothesized. The RYDS social class coefficients indicate that receipt of public assistance increases strain, regardless of whether one internalizes or externalizes blame. The magnitude of the class influence, however, suggests a stronger impact on the strain/externalization interaction (.14) compared to strain and internalization of blame (.09). This finding may be indicative of a class influence on the externalization process, over and above its contribution to strain itself. This finding is consistent with Cloward and Ohlin's suggestion that the lower class adolescent is likely to experience feelings of unjust deprivation, given the "democratizing [of] the criteria of evaluation [for success] without at the same time increasing the opportunities available" (1960:120). Significant findings between class and strain/externalization in both sites support the theorists' hypothesis that structural disadvantage may produce feelings of unjust deprivation and lead to externalizing behavior. Generally, findings related to public assistance support the influence of class on strain, and at the same time, suggest an increased influence when strain is coupled with the externalization of blame.

In predicting the challenge to legitimacy, the findings observed across sites are similar. One strain interaction term is negatively related to the challenge to legitimacy, which, at first glance, seems contrary to expectations. A positive and significant impact of the strain/externalization interaction was expected to comport with Cloward and Ohlin's proposition that those who experience strain and externalize blame are likely to challenge the legitimacy of conventional norms. Further, no significant relationship was anticipated between strain/internalization and challenge. In testing the traditional model with all males combined, there appears to be no relationship between strain and externalization; however, a negative relationship between the strain and internalization interaction and challenge was found in both sites. The relationship is significant and suggests that as an adolescent male experiences strain and blames himself for failure to achieve the economic success goal, he is *less* likely to challenge the legitimacy of conventional means.

Despite its apparent conflict with hypotheses, this finding is consistent with the work of Cloward and Ohlin. In depicting the internalization process, they suggest that "attributing failure to one's own faults reveals an attitude supporting the legitimacy of the existing norms" (1960:112). In the current analysis, the legitimacy of norms appears to be strengthened among those who experience strain and internalize blame. Those who externalize blame, on the other hand, do not experience a similar affirmation of traditional values. Although it does not provide direct evidence of challenge as originally anticipated, the non-significant coefficient found in the DYS and the RYDS suggests that externalizers do not share the same propensity of internalizers to have traditional beliefs strengthened; this is consistent with strain theory assertions.

In the next phase of the model, support for traditional strain theory is found in both the DYS and RYDS samples. The influences of withdrawal and delinquent peers on delinquent values are positive and statistically significant. As one withdraws legitimacy (indicated by weakened conventional values), delinquent values are strengthened. In addition, association with delinquent peers significantly contributes to the development of a delinquent belief system. Taken together, the two variables explain 27 and 23 percent of the variance in delinquent values in the DYS and the RYDS, respectively.

To predict delinquent outcomes, the impact of delinquent peers and the interaction between delinquent values and illegitimate opportunity (as measured by access to drugs) is estimated.. Across sites, each estimation of delinquent behavior reveals a significant effect of peer delinquency on delinquent behavior. The positive relationship suggests that as an adolescent male associates with delinquent peers, delinquent behavior increases. Although the influence is consistent across all types of delinquent behavior, the magnitude of the peer impact varies (see Appendix I). For example, the impact of peers is the strongest in predicting general delinquency and weakest in predicting property crime (which is consistent across sites). In the DYS, there is no direct influence of peer delinquency on alcohol use.

When estimating the interaction between delinquent values and illegitimate opportunity in the last part of the strain theory model, main effects of delinquent values and drug access are controlled to determine whether the influence of the product term is due to the true interaction between measures, or is driven by the either of the main effects. Theoretically, neither a direct influence of delinquent values nor illegitimate opportunity is expected. The coefficient of the product term demonstrates the moderating influence of illegitimate opportunity on the relationship between delinquent values and delinquency (Aiken & West, 1991). The moderating influence was hypothesized by Cloward and Ohlin who asserted that delinquent values should produce criminal adaptations when criminal opportunities are present. Therefore, the product term should exert a positive influence on delinquent outcomes: as access to criminal activities increase, the relationship between delinquent values and delinquency is strengthened. One exception to this hypothesis is violent behavior; Cloward and Ohlin argue that violence emerges when neither legitimate nor illegitimate opportunities are present. As such, a negative relationship is expected between the product term and violence, indicating that as illegitimate opportunities diminish, a delinquent value system significantly increases violent behavior.

The interaction between delinquent values and illegitimate opportunity receives little support in the analysis. In the DYS, the product term is significant in predicting drug use and violence, and in the RYDS the interaction significantly predicts violence only. In the majority of equations estimated, the interaction between delinquent values and illegitimate opportunity is not supported. With few exceptions, findings suggest the absence of a moderating effect of illegitimate opportunity on the relationship between delinquent values and delinquency. It should also be noted that the impact on violence is not in the expected direction. Coefficients indicate that as illegitimate opportunities *increase*, the influence of delinquent values on violence also increases. This finding is a departure from the relationship hypothesized by Cloward and Ohlin, and may explained, in part, by a change in violent behavior over time. In 1960, Cloward and Ohlin describe violence as a mechanism of status attainment; when both legitimate and illegitimate opportunities are denied youth, they seek status through *expressive* violence. With the growth of the illegal drug market, violence in contemporary American society may be more *instrumental* in sustaining illegitimate business. Therefore, an increase in illegitimate opportunity could arguably lead to greater violence, as a means of protecting those illegal channels to success.

In spite of the relative insignificance of the product term, direct effects of delinquent values and access to drugs are found. The effects of the lower order terms are to be interpreted as 'conditional.' Aiken and West describe the coefficients as the effect on the dependent variable under the condition in which the other predictor equals a specified value (1991:37). Since the variables are centered, the specified value represents the mean; that is, each predictor represents the impact of that variable on delinquency, at the mean of the other predictor. For example, the delinquent values coefficient represents the impact of delinquent values on delinquent behavior at the mean of illegitimate opportunity. In turn, the drug access coefficient illustrates the impact of illegitimate opportunity on delinquency at the mean of delinquent values.

The conditional effect of delinquent values is not consistent across sites; in the DYS the measure is significantly predicts alcohol and drug use, and in the RYDS, delinquent values impacts all delinquent outcomes. In predicting general delinquency in the RYDS, males with an average level of access to illegitimate opportunity experience increased general delinquency as delinquent values increase.[2] While delinquent values is significant in all RYDS equations, the strength of its influence varies across delinquent behaviors (see Table 6a).

The impact of illegitimate opportunity is relatively consistent across sites; in the DYS, a lower order effect of access to drugs is observed on all varieties of delinquent behavior. Findings indicate that at the mean of delinquent values, access to drugs significantly increases all delinquent behavior. Although a similar effect of illegitimate opportunity is found in the RYDS, that influence is not significant in predicting property crime. It must be reiterated that the impact of delinquent values and illegitimate opportunity is interpreted as conditional (and not a main effect), given the centered nature of the measures.[3] Taken together, delinquent peers, delinquent values, illegitimate opportunity, and the product term account for 5 to 24 percent of the variance in delinquency outcomes across sites. In both samples the greatest amount of variance is explained in general delinquency, and the least amount of explained variance is found in the model predicting property crime.

At first glance, it appears that the traditional strain model provides a good fit to the DYS and RYDS data by absolute fit indices (listed in Table 6a). The primary indicator of an acceptable fit of is the GFI, which surpasses the threshold of model fit in all DYS and RYDS equations; in each of the equations the model accounts for 93 to 97 percent of the observed variance and covariance. Other fit indices are consistent with the GFI, but vary to some extent across sites. For example, the standardized RMR meets the threshold for goodness of fit (.05) in four of the five models in the DYS, but does not meet the threshold in RYDS (ranges from .08 to .09). At the same time, the CFI scores of the DYS fall within acceptable limits and indicate that the traditional strain model provides a 90 to 92 percent improvement over the null model. In the RYDS, the CFI ranges between .80 and .83 and does not meet the acceptable limits outlined by researchers (Hu & Bentler, 1995). In both sites, a statistically significant model Chi-square does not support a good fit, and indicates a statistically significant difference between the estimated model covariance matrix and the true population matrix. It is recognized, however, that a non-significant Chi-square is difficult to achieve with large sample sizes; it is not surprising in this instance that the statistic is significant.

Taken together, these goodness of fit indices suggest that the traditional strain model provides a reasonably good fit to the data for all males. In addition, indicators demonstrate a superior fit of the traditional model to DYS data when compared with the fit of the RYDS model.

Since one of the primary goals of this investigation is to compare the culturally modified strain model to the traditional model, a more appropriate test of fit lies in the comparison of the two models, as opposed to some external criteria of fit. This approach to comparative model fit is supported by Kelloway who suggests that, "the focus of assessing model fit almost invariably should be on comparing the fit of competing and theoretically plausible models" (1998:39). Although the absolute fit of the traditional strain model has been assessed, its comparative fit with the modified strain model is also evaluated.

ESTIMATING THE MODIFIED STRAIN MODEL

As a second step in the LISREL analysis, an estimate of the modified strain model is conducted with the total male sample within each site to determine whether the modified model provides a substantial improvement over the traditional model. The modified strain model introduces family involvement into traditional strain theory (see Table 6b and Appendix I). Family involvement is expected to reduce the adoption of delinquent values and association with delinquent peers:

Hypothesis #4b: Traditional cultural values, as transmitted by involvement with family, are likely to decrease the likelihood of adopting a delinquent value system. A negative relationship between family involvement and delinquent values is anticipated for all ethnic groups.

Hypothesis #6a: Involvement in family activity is expected to decrease the likelihood of developing delinquent peer associations. A negative relationship between family involvement and delinquent peers is anticipated for all ethnic groups.

To evaluate the utility of the modified model, several factors are examined. First, the influence of the family on delinquent values and involvement with delinquent peers is assessed. Second, the overall model fit is evaluated to determine whether inclusion of family involvement provides a substantial improvement. Finally, the impact of family involvement on the amount of explained variance in the strain model is assessed.

TABLE 6B. MODIFIED STRAIN THEORY MODEL BY DELINQUENCY, ALL MALES

	GENERAL		ALCOHOL USE		DRUG USE		PROPERTY		VIOLENCE	
	DYS	RYDS	DYS	RYDS	DYS	RYDS	DYS	RYDS	DYS	RYDS
UNSTANDARDIZED COEFFICIENTS										
PUBLIC ASSISTANCE —>	.18*	.14*								
PUBLIC ASSISTANCE —>	-.03	.09*								
STRAIN/EXTERNALIZATION —> CHALLENGE	-.05	-.04								
STRAIN/INTERNALIZATION —> CHALLENGE	-.09*	-.15*								
CHALLENGE LEGITIMACY —> DELINQUENT	.37*	.27*								
DELINQUENT PEERS —> DELINQUENT VALUES	.32*	.33*								
FAMILY INVOLVEMENT —> DELINQUENT PEERS	-.09*	-.10*								
FAMILY INVOLVEMENT —> DELINQUENT VALUES	-.06*	-.00								
DELINQUENT PEERS —> DELINQUENCY	.50*	.96*	.20	.55*	.35*	.76*	.23*	.18*	.24*	.33*
DELINQUENT VALUES —> DELINQUENCY	.25	.57*	.62*	.88*	.38*	.56*	.08	.12*	.09	.19*
ACCESS TO DRUGS —> DELINQUENCY	.46*	.26*	.44*	.24*	.25*	.20*	.16*	.02	.12*	.09*
DEL. VALUES*DRUG ACCESS —> DELINQUENCY	-.00	.22	.21	.09	.22*	.23	.10	-.01	.15*	.13*

[a] Note: Common coefficients are listed under the General Delinquency column, and paths added to the modified model are in bold.

[b] Note: Fit indices in this table cannot be compared with those in Table 6a. For model comparison, see nested estimates (Table 6c).

* p<.05 (one-tail test)

TABLE 6B. MODIFIED STRAIN THEORY MODEL BY DELINQUENCY, ALL MALES (CONT.)

	GENERAL		ALCOHOL USE		DRUG USE		PROPERTY		VIOLENCE	
	DYS	RYDS	DYS	RYDS	DYS	RYDS	DYS	RYDS	DYS	RYDS
ERROR TERMS										
STRAIN/EXTERNALIZATION	.46*	.65*								
STRAIN/INTERNALIZATION	.71*	.89*								
CHALLENGE LEGITIMACY	.16*	.24*								
DELINQUENT VALUES	.21*	.15*								
DELINQUENCY	1.99*	2.43*	2.56*	2.16*	1.66*	1.99*	.72*	.32*	.40*	.44*
COVARIANCE OF ERROR TERMS										
STRAIN/EXTERNALIZATION <—> STRAIN/INTERNALIZATION	-.21*	-.36*								
FIT INDICES [b]										
EXPLAINED VARIANCE IN DELINQUENCY	.18	.16	.14	.15	.12	.14	.09	.05	.14	.11
GOODNESS OF FIT INDEX (GFI)	.91	.91	.91	.91	.91	.90	.91	.91	.91	.91
STANDARDIZED ROOT MEAN SQUARED RESIDUAL (RMR)	.11	.10	.10	.10	.10	.10	.10	.10	.10	.09
COMPARATIVE FIT INDEX (CFI)	.65	.71	.64	.69	.63	.68	.62	.67	.65	.70
CHI-SQUARE	159.15	285.73	156.45	299.68	156.54	313.98	152.32	295.63	150.62	281.18
DEGREES OF FREEDOM	26	26	26	26	26	26	26	26	26	26

[a] Note: Common coefficients are listed under the General Delinquency column, and paths added to the modified model are in bold.
[b] Note: Fit indices in this table cannot be compared with those in Table 6a. For model comparison, see nested estimates (Table 6c).
* p<.05 (one-tail test)

To compare the modified and traditional strain models, a Chi-square difference test is conducted. This comparison is properly achieved when one model is nested within the other (Kelloway, 1998). In this case, the traditional model is completely contained within the modified model, and the two are estimated in nested sequence for comparison purposes. In SIMPLIS, the modified model is first estimated, which includes paths from family involvement to delinquent values and delinquent peers. Next, the two paths from family involvement are constrained to zero to approximate the traditional strain model. Note that the nested traditional strain model produces *different* estimates than those presented in Table 6a. To properly compare the modified and traditional models, they must be estimated with the same covariance matrix; in this case, the matrix includes family involvement. Fit indices of the modified model are then compared with those of the nested traditional model to determine whether constraining the relationships to zero adversely affects the model fit.

Incorporating family involvement and estimating additional parameters has a modest impact the traditional strain model coefficients. The inclusion of family involvement produces two significant paths in the DYS and one significant path in the RYDS. In the DYS, both paths are statistically significant, and in the expected direction. For all adolescent males in the DYS, increased family involvement significantly reduces delinquent values and involvement with delinquent peers. In the RYDS, only Hypothesis #6a is supported; family involvement reduces association with delinquent peers, yet has no influence on delinquent values. Significant paths from family involvement emerge in the modified model, however, other relationships are virtually unchanged.

In comparing the fit of the nested models (see Table 6c for Chi-square difference test), a statistically significant Chi-square difference was found across all delinquency outcomes in both sites. The findings suggest that the modified model, which specifies family influences, provides a significantly better fit than the model which assumes those relationships are zero. Other fit indices suggest an improved fit of the modified model, but are not as conclusive as the Chi-square difference test. On the whole, the GFI, standardized RMR, and CFI between the nested models are minor, but suggest a slightly improved fit of the modified strain model.[4] The percentage of explained variance was also compared across nested models, and the addition of family involvement does not ultimately increase the percentage of explained variance in delinquency. In fact, the family measure explains only two to three percent of the variance in delinquent peer association, and has a minor impact on delinquent values in the DYS only (the modified model explains only one percent more compared to the nested traditional model).

Nested comparisons between the traditional and modified models were also conducted within each ethnic group to determine whether setting family parameters to zero affects the model fit for Latinos, Whites, or Blacks. As hypothesized, an increased family influence was expected among minority groups when compared to Whites:

> **Hypothesis #10a:** Compared to the majority, African American and Latino families might serve as a source of strength in response to discrimination, and may ultimately serve as a protective factor against delinquent adaptations to strain. In the current analysis, the influence of the family in reducing delinquent values is expected to be stronger among minority groups compared to Whites.

In addition, the strongest family influence was expected among Latinos:

> **Hypothesis #4c:** The influence of family on delinquent value adoption is expected to be stronger for Latinos than Whites.
> **Hypothesis #6b:** The influence of family involvement on delinquent peer associations is expected to be stronger for Latinos than Whites.
> **Hypothesis #10b:** Based on previous empirical findings, the influence of the family on delinquent values and delinquent peer associations is expected to be strongest for Latinos. The Latino family may be less likely to reinforce mainstream ideals, and instead, provide other avenues of success for adolescents which are based on traditional values.

As anticipated, differences emerge between ethnic groups. Among White males, there is no significant family influence in either the DYS or the RYDS. Among Latinos in the DYS, both paths are statistically significant; an increase in Latino family involvement significantly reduces delinquent values and association with delinquent peers. Only one of the findings holds true for Latinos in the RYDS, however, as family involvement significantly reduces delinquent peer association. Within the African American group in the DYS, the family is negatively related to delinquent values, which is the only significant family influence observed for Blacks across sites. Taken together, these coefficients suggest partial support for hypotheses, since no family influence is found among White males, and the strongest evidence of a family effect is found among Latinos.

As an additional method of comparison, the Chi-square difference test was employed within each ethnic group (Table 6d). Nested comparisons between the traditional and modified strain models are somewhat consistent across ethnic groups. Among Latinos in the DYS and African Americans in both sites, constraining the paths to zero provides a significantly worse fit than the modified model (see Table 6d). The Chi-square difference between modified and traditional models for Latinos and Whites in the RYDS is marginally significant. The comparison cannot be replicated with White males in the DYS since there are too few to allow for LISREL model estimation. These findings demonstrate relative consistency in the impact of family involvement across ethnic groups. The significance of estimating additional parameters is most clearly demonstrated for African American males in each site.

Generally, comparisons between the traditional and modified models suggest an improved fit of the modified strain model. Absolute and comparative fit indices suggest a slight difference between models, and Chi-square difference tests in each site suggest that it is best to estimate additional parameters than to constrain them to zero. In the case of nested comparisons by ethnicity, the difference in Chi-square is statistically significant for Latinos in the DYS and African Americans in both sites, and is marginally significant for Latinos and Whites in the RYDS. For the purpose of the current analysis, it is important to elaborate upon the nature of the nested model comparison. As mentioned previously, a common matrix is necessary in the nested sequence and the traditional model is estimated with the same matrix as the modified model. The Chi-square of the 'pure' traditional model (Table 6a) cannot be directly compared with that of the modified model; to conduct an appropriate nested comparison it is necessary to estimate an 'intermediate' model which includes family involvement in the covariance matrix, but assumes its relationship with other variables is zero. Therefore, it is necessary to incorporate an additional source of variance in the matrix, namely family involvement, which is not a part of the traditional strain model (and is not considered in the initial model estimation presented in Table 6a).

The findings of nested estimations do not provide conclusive evidence that the modified model represents a substantial improvement to the pure traditional strain model. The difference between the nested models is statistically significant among the total male samples and certain ethnic groups. However, other fit indices demonstrate a minimal improvement of the modified model in overall model fit. In addition, the substantive contribution of family involvement is minimal; the amount of explained variance is similar between the model which incorporates family involvement and the model which assumes relationships between family involvement and other strain measures to be zero. Based on those findings and in the interest of parsimony and purity, the traditional strain model is employed in the remainder of the analyses. The traditional strain model constitutes a baseline model for estimating site specific measures below and for comparing differences between ethnic groups in the next chapter.

Table 6c. Comparing Fit of Nested Traditional and Modified Strain Models - All Males, DYS and RYDS

	Modified Strain				Traditional Strain (nested)				Chi-Square Difference			
	DYS		RYDS		DYS		RYDS		DYS		RYDS	
	x^2	df	x^2	df	x^2	df	x^2	df	x^2	df	x^2	df
General Delinquency	159.15	26	285.73	26	178.22	28	304.70	28	19.07*	2	18.97*	2
Alcohol Use	156.45	26	299.68	26	175.46	28	318.60	28	19.01*	2	18.92*	2
Drug Use	156.54	26	313.98	26	174.98	28	332.94	28	18.44*	2	18.96*	2
Property Crime	152.32	26	295.63	26	171.12	28	314.60	28	18.80*	2	18.97*	2
Violence	150.62	26	281.18	26	169.57	28	300.17	28	18.95*	2	18.99*	2

* $p < .05$

Table 6d. Comparing Fit of Nested Traditional and Modified Strain Models by Ethnicity

Latino Males

| | Modified Strain | | | | Traditional Strain (nested) | | | | Chi-Square Difference | | | |
| | DYS | | RYDS | | DYS | | RYDS | | DYS | | RYDS | |
	x^2	df	x^2	df	x^2	df	x^2	df	x^2	df	x^2	df
General Delinquency	102.12	26	150.62	26	112.79	28	156.11	28	10.67*	2	5.49	2
Alcohol Use	97.65	26	157.91	26	108.23	28	163.20	28	10.58*	2	5.29	2
Drug Use	108.71	26	159.13	26	118.94	28	164.62	28	10.23*	2	5.49	2
Property Crime	98.53	26	158.03	26	109.13	28	163.52	28	10.60*	2	5.49	2
Violence	98.32	26	148.75	26	108.88	28	154.18	28	10.56*	2	5.43	2

* $p < .05$

Table 6d. Comparing Fit of Nested Traditional and Modified Strain Models by Ethnicity (cont.)

White Males

	Modified Strain				Traditional Strain (nested)				Chi-Square Difference			
	DYS		**RYDS**		**DYS**		**RYDS**		**DYS**		**RYDS**	
	x^2	df	x^2	df	x^2	df	x^2	df	x^2	df	x^2	df
General	33.67	26	288.67	26	33.72	28	294.15	28	.05	2	5.48	2
Alcohol Use	39.61	26	292.11	26	39.62	28	297.35	28	.01	2	5.24	2
Drug Use	39.01	26	295.25	26	39.06	28	300.72	28	.05	2	5.47	2
Property Crime	39.34	26	284.92	26	39.37	28	290.17	28	.03	2	5.25	2
Violence	46.77	26	280.16	26	46.82	28	285.58	28	.05	2	5.42	2

* p<.05

Table 6d. Comparing Fit of Nested Traditional and Modified Strain Models by Ethnicity (cont.)

African American Males

	Modified Strain				Traditional Strain (nested)				Chi-Square Difference			
	DYS		RYDS		DYS		RYDS		DYS		RYDS	
	x^2	df	x^2	df	x^2	df	x^2	df	x^2	df	x^2	df
General	88.56	26	215.65	26	96.83	28	225.10	28	8.27*	2	9.45*	2
Alcohol Use	95.14	26	232.52	26	103.60	28	241.98	28	8.46*	2	9.46*	2
Drug Use	86.19	26	226.42	26	94.53	28	235.88	28	8.34*	2	9.46*	2
Property Crime	91.88	26	225.63	26	99.50	28	235.09	28	7.62*	2	9.46*	2
Violence	82.05	26	218.70	26	90.33	28	228.18	28	8.28*	2	9.48*	2

* $p<.05$

ANALYSIS OF SITE SPECIFIC MEASURES

The final analysis of the full samples involves an examination of site specific measures. Unique measures are employed in each site to get a closer look at the influence of varying operationalizations on relationships within the strain theory model. In the DYS, an index of blocked opportunity is examined as an alternative measure of strain. As described in Chapter 4, two interaction terms were constructed to capture the interaction between blocked opportunity and the externalization of blame. The new measures are substituted for the strain disjunction terms in site specific analyses. More comprehensive measures of withdrawal from conventional beliefs and delinquent values are also included, along with a product term which multiplies the site specific delinquent values variable with illegitimate opportunity (both are centered at the mean).

Structural equation estimations of DYS site specific measures produce similar results when compared to analyses of identical measures (Appendix I). The primary difference in models stems from the inclusion of the blocked opportunity and externalization interaction terms. The impact of class on blocked opportunity is similar to the impact of class on strain disjunction terms. Receipt of public assistance significantly increases perceptions of blocked opportunity and externalization, but does not exert the same influence on strain and internalization. This finding is consistent across both operationalizations of strain (blocked opportunity and strain disjunction). At the same time, however, the influence of identical and site specific strain measures on the withdrawal of legitimacy is not consistent. A negative influence of strain/internalization on withdrawal was found in previous analysis, which indicated that the presence of strain and internalization of blame reduces the likelihood of withdrawal. When blocked opportunity terms are substituted for the disjunction measures, neither interaction measure exerts a significant impact on the model.

Inclusion of the identical strain disjunction measure indicates strengthened conventional beliefs among those who experience strain and internalize blame. When the interaction between blocked opportunity and internalization is examined, that relationship does not persist. The difference in results produced by strain terms may, in part, reflect measurement variation. The strain disjunction measure incorporates both aspirations and expectations, where strain is produced by the combination of high aspirations and low legitimate opportunity (grades). In this instance, aspirations are more closely tied to the disjunction measure than in the blocked opportunity index. Commitment to the economic success goal at Time 1 might be somewhat predictive of the strength of one's conventional beliefs at a later date. Although strain indicates a disparity between the goal and the means of achieving it, those who internalize blame are not likely to abandon the success goal. Instead, they may reaffirm their commitment to conventional modes of attainment (as Cloward and Ohlin have suggested). Unlike the disjunction measure, the blocked opportunity index includes multiple items which gauge one's perceived access to legitimate opportunity. This measure may not support the strain hypothesis because it provides a more subjective assessment of legitimate opportunity than academic performance and is not directly tied to aspirations.

All other DYS site specific measures produce nearly identical results to the measures used across sites. For example, inclusion of more comprehensive delinquent values index produces similar path coefficients as the identical delinquent values measure. In addition, the site specific product term (combining delinquent values and illegitimate opportunity) and withdrawal measures produce similar results to identical measures. In assessing the fit indices of the site specific measurement model, an acceptable fit is determined (site specific, x^2=52.94, GFI=.96, CFI=.96).

In the RYDS, an elaborate social class measure was employed in place of the public assistance measure which is found in both sites. The variable incorporates receipt of public assistance, principle wage earner employment status and household income in determining class status, and provides a more comprehensive measure of socioeconomic disadvantage than the receipt of public assistance alone. Inclusion of the comprehensive class measure in the RYDS modestly affects model estimates. Path coefficients are nearly identical to those generated by the public assistance measure of class; class is positively related to both strain interaction terms, suggesting a consistent influence of class on strain, as predicted by the theory. Model fit indices indicate the site specific measure provides a good fit to the data (x^2=115.41, GFI=.96, CFI=.88).

Given the similarity across models using identical and site specific measures, it appears that the inclusion of more detailed measures across sites does not necessarily ensure a better model and/or estimates. Additionally, since the primary goal of the analysis is to compare ethnic groups and replicate findings across sites, consistent measures are vital.

Therefore, in the remainder of analyses, the discussion will be restricted to models with identical measures.

Initial tests of the traditional strain theory model across the total male sample in the DYS and the RYDS provide a great deal of support for the theory. In both sites, relationships specified by strain theory are statistically significant; structural equation models reveal a positive impact of public assistance on strain and externalization of blame. Support for other strain relationships are revealed across sites, including the impact of challenge to legitimacy on delinquent values, and the impact of peers on delinquent values and delinquent behavior. An unanticipated inverse relationship between the strain and internalization interaction term and challenge to legitimacy also emerged in both sites. The finding suggests that those who experience strain and internalize blame are less likely to withdraw legitimacy from conventional norms. Initially, this result seemed inconsistent with strain theory, however, upon further examination, the relationship appears to provide support for the theory. Differences between the sites emerge only in the interaction between delinquent values and illegitimate opportunity. The term is significant in predicting drug use the DYS and violent crime in both sites.

Goodness of fit indices demonstrate a good fit of the traditional strain model in both sites, however, DYS statistics are more robust (see Table 6a). Across all outcomes, traditional strain theory explains more than ten percent of the variance in delinquent behavior (with the exception of property crime in the RYDS). At the same time, a greater proportion of variance in delinquency is explained in the DYS. Overall, strain theory provides a reasonable explanation of general delinquency, alcohol and substance use, property crime, and violent crime.

When site specific measures are included they provide similar estimates as the identical measures. In the DYS, the inclusion of blocked opportunity measures fails to generate a link to the withdrawal of legitimacy, which may in part, reflect operationalization issues. Given the fact that findings are largely consistent using identical measures across sites, traditional strain variables and relationships appear to provide a useful model for understanding delinquency across males in the Denver and Rochester studies.

Testing Strain Theory by Ethnicity

This chapter describes structural equation analyses of the traditional strain theory model by ethnicity. In Chapter 6, family involvement was incorporated into the traditional strain theory model, but did not provide a marked improvement. Therefore, this chapter focuses on separate analyses of the traditional model by ethnicity. All structural equation models are estimated using the Maximum Likelihood method in the SIMPLIS program of LISREL 8.30, where models for ethnic groups can be stacked for simultaneous estimation. Stacking provides several advantages to the current study, since it allows for the estimation of models that are likely to contain multiple interactions between the grouping variable (ethnicity in this case) and other variables in the model. The method provides a test of differences in model parameters between ethnic groups. By stacking the model potential interactions between ethnicity and strain variables are captured. Stacking also allows some coefficients to be constrained to be equal for the ethnic groups and some to be allowed to vary; thus allowing for a test of slope differences as hypothesized in Chapter 3.[1]

The purpose of this study is to determine whether traditional strain theory applies equally across ethnic groups. As described in Chapter 3, factors related to ethnicity (for example, discrimination and culture) might impact relationships within the strain model. Predictions were made about potential differences in slopes between Latinos, Whites, and African Americans; the purpose of this chapter is to examine those hypothesized differences and to determine whether the traditional strain model has a differential application across ethnic groups. To achieve that end, path coefficients from stacked LISREL models are compared, and the utility of the model in explaining delinquent outcomes is assessed. Specifically, the traditional strain model is estimated to predict general delinquency, alcohol use, drug use, property crime, and violent crime. Findings from models predicting general delinquency are described in detail, primarily for the sake of simplicity; any divergence from those findings for the other outcomes will be noted in the text.

ESTIMATING STACKED MODELS IN LISREL

To determine whether differences in strain relationships exist across groups, the traditional model is estimated using stacked models. To produce separate estimates for each ethnic group, covariance matrices were computed using PRELIS for Latinos (n=161) and Blacks (n=132) in the DYS and Latinos (n=91), Whites (n=172), and Blacks (n=310) in the RYDS (see Appendix J for matrices used in analyses). Unfortunately, the number of White males in the Denver Youth Survey is too small for estimating structural equation models in LISREL (n=30).[2] Inclusion of White males in the LISREL analysis would produce unreliable results for the ethnic group, and estimates of other groups may also be adversely affected. As a result, the DYS stacked analyses are restricted to Latino and African American males only.

The strategy for assessing group differences in LISREL is adopted from Jaccard & Wan (1996), and involves the estimation of two models. The first model (referred to as Model 1 hereafter) estimates one set of parameters for the total sample and serves as a starting point which approximates the total male sample estimates found in Chapter 6. By setting equality constraints across groups, the assumption is made that no interactions exist by ethnicity. The model is expected to apply equally to all ethnic groups; as such, a common solution is derived. The second model, or Model 2, estimates separate paths for each ethnic group and calculates a model fit for the simultaneous estimation. Allowing certain paths to vary across groups tests for an interaction between ethnicity and strain theory concepts. Model 2 assumes that paths are not equal across groups and estimates unique coefficients for each. To determine whether an interaction effect is present, Model 2 is then compared to the first model which sets equality constraints across the groups. A Chi-square difference test is employed, where the fit index of the unconstrained model (Model 2) is subtracted from the Chi-square of the constrained model (Model 1).[3] If the difference between models is statistically significant, then an interaction effect is supported (Jaccard & Wan, 1996). In essence, a statistically significant difference in Chi-square indicates that allowing certain paths to vary (assuming an interaction) significantly improves the model fit. If the fit of Model 1 is improved by freeing hypothesized paths, then an interaction effect exists, and it is important to estimate separate paths for each group.

In the current analysis, the primarily goal is to determine whether freeing paths provides a better fit than constraining them, however, the study is also concerned with the relative impact of strain relationships across groups. Thus, when paths are allowed to vary in the stacked models, coefficient comparisons will be made between ethnic groups. In estimating stacked LISREL models, a sufficient comparison of group coefficients can be achieved by noting differences in magnitude and significance. Statistically, there is no appropriate test which can determine whether coefficients are significantly different (David McDowall, personal communication, 1999).

For the purpose of such a comparison, it is necessary to make a determination on the magnitude of coefficient differences. Unstandardized coefficients are utilized in the current analysis for two reasons: first, standardizing coefficients when models are stacked would produce a different metric for each ethnic group, and confuse any comparison that is made between them (Jaccard & Wan, 1996). Second, with the inclusion of a multiplicative interaction term in the model which is constructed from mean-centered variables, standardization would also serve to confuse interpretation of the coefficient (Aiken & West, 1991). Therefore, it is necessary to report unstandardized coefficients, which do not provide an objective rule of thumb to guide the determination of coefficient differences. In the absence of an objective standard, those coefficients which have a difference of .10 or greater will be considered an indicator of a moderate size difference. In paths that are of theoretical interest, coefficient differences of .05 will be highlighted, but interpretation of minor differences should be made with caution. Admittedly, this standard is somewhat arbitrary, but is helpful for describing group differences in a consistent fashion.[4]

STEP 1: CONSTRAINING ALL PATHS
Since strain theory is accepted as a general explanation of delinquent behavior; it is first estimated for its utility in explaining the delinquency

of all males within each site. In Model 1, equality constraints are set throughout the model and a common solution is generated for all ethnic groups (see Appendix K). Unstandardized path coefficients and model fit indices predicting general delinquency are presented, since they are relatively consistent across all delinquency outcomes (Table 7a). When paths are constrained across groups, findings are similar to those presented in Chapter 6, where all males are combined. The primary difference in analyses lies in the number of covariance matrices utilized for each analysis; in Chapter 6, one covariance matrix was generated for all males, and in the current estimation, separate matrices are included for each ethnic group. Since the models are stacked and all the group matrices are utilized, however, LISREL arrives at one solution for all ethnic groups. Model 1 generates a close approximation of the estimates for the total male samples described in Chapter 6 and provides strong support for traditional strain theory. The influence of class on the strain and externalization interaction term is significant in both sites, and indicates that those who receive public assistance are more likely to experience strain and externalize blame for failure to achieve economic success. In addition, the influence of strain/internalization on challenge to legitimacy is consistent across the DYS and the RYDS. The impact of weakened conventional beliefs and delinquent peers is also demonstrated in both sites, as is the causal relationship between delinquent peers and general delinquency. Males across the sites differ, however, in terms of the interaction between delinquent values and illegitimate opportunity; in the DYS illegitimate opportunity is significant in predicting general delinquency, while in the RYDS, the interaction and lower order effects are all statistically significant. The Goodness of Fit Index (GFI) indicates that the constrained model, or Model 1, provides a good fit to the data in the DYS only. The RYDS model approaches the threshold for goodness of fit, but does not meet it (GFI=.87). Likewise, the standardized Root Mean Squared Residual (RMR) indicates a good fit in the DYS only, while the Comparative Fit Index (CFI) does not support a good fit in either site.

TABLE 7A. CONSTRAINING ALL PATHS ACROSS ETHNIC GROUPS, PREDICTING GENERAL DELINQUENCY (MODEL 1)

	DENVER YOUTH SURVEY	ROCHESTER YOUTH DEVELOPMENT STUDY
UNSTANDARDIZED COEFFICIENTS		
PUBLIC ASSISTANCE —> STRAIN/EXTERNALIZATION	.17*	.17*
PUBLIC ASSISTANCE —> STRAIN/INTERNALIZATION	-.07	-.00
STRAIN/EXTERNALIZATION —>CHALLENGE LEGITIMACY	-.04	-.01
STRAIN/INTERNALIZATION —> CHALLENGE LEGITIMACY	-.08*	-.10*
CHALLENGE LEGITIMACY —> DELINQUENT VALUES	.34*	.22*
DELINQUENT PEERS —> DELINQUENT VALUES	.32*	.22*
DELINQUENT PEERS —> DELINQUENCY	.54*	.85*
DELINQUENT VALUES —> DELINQUENCY	.17	.51*
ACCESS TO DRUGS —> DELINQUENCY	.44*	.25*
DEL. VALUES*DRUG ACCESS —> DELINQUENCY	.00	.37*

* p<.05 (one-tail test)

TABLE 7A. CONSTRAINING ALL PATHS ACROSS ETHNIC GROUPS, PREDICTING GENERAL DELINQUENCY (CONT.)

	DENVER YOUTH SURVEY	ROCHESTER YOUTH
ERROR TERMS		
STRAIN/EXTERNALIZATION	.49*	.60*
STRAIN/INTERNALIZATION	.72*	.85*
CHALLENGE LEGITIMACY	.15*	.25*
DELINQUENT VALUES	.21*	.17*
DELINQUENCY	2.03*	2.33*
COVARIANCE OF ERROR TERMS		
STRAIN/EXTERNALIZATION <—> STRAIN/INTERNALIZATION	-.23*	-.31*
FIT INDICES		
GOODNESS OF FIT INDEX (GFI)	.92	.87
STANDARDIZED ROOT MEAN SQUARED RESIDUAL (RMR)	.09	.11
COMPARATIVE FIT INDEX (CFI)	.80	.51
CHI-SQUARE	126.00*	669.70*
DEGREES OF FREEDOM	54	89

* p<.05 (one-tail test)

STEP 2: FREEING PATHS ACROSS GROUPS

The second step in determining ethnic differences in the applicability of strain theory involves simultaneous, but independent, estimation of the traditional model across groups. This is achieved by stacking separate group estimates in one SIMPLIS command file (Model 2) and requesting a unique solution for each group. Simultaneous multi-group analysis produces estimates for each group separately and estimates goodness of fit indices for the model as a whole. In this case, unstandardized path coefficients are derived for Latinos and Blacks in the DYS and Latinos, Whites, and African Americans in the RYDS. In addition to estimating separate coefficients across groups, LISREL calculates goodness of fit indices which determine whether the model with separate estimates adequately reproduces the covariance matrices. The goodness of fit derived from the multi-group estimation is based on a "pooling of fit measures from each group separately" (Jaccard & Wan, 1996:24). Stacking models allows for an assessment of model fit when separate coefficients are estimated within each group.

In estimating Model 2, certain paths are allowed to vary across groups, and all others are constrained (Appendix K). Those paths related to hypotheses are allowed to vary by ethnicity. As described in Chapter 3, group differences are expected in the equations predicting challenge to conventional norms, delinquent values, and delinquent behavior. All other paths in the traditional strain model are expected to be consistent across groups, including the relationship between class and strain, and the impact of the interaction between delinquent values and illegitimate opportunity (as measured by the product term) on delinquent behavior.

In estimating the influence of strain on the challenge to legitimacy, it was expected that Latinos and African Americans, given their minority status in American society, would evidence a stronger relationship between strain and the challenge to legitimacy compared to whites:

Hypothesis #3: As discrimination influences the externalization of blame among Latinos, it impacts the relationship between externalization and the removal of legitimacy from conventional means. Therefore, a stronger relationship between the strain/externalization interaction term and challenge to legitimacy is expected for Latinos compared to whites.

Hypothesis #9b: Based Cloward and Ohlin's assertion that the visibility of barriers to legitimate opportunity leads to externalization and challenge to legitimacy of African Americans, a stronger impact of the strain/externalization interaction on the challenge to legitimacy is expected among both minority groups.

Cloward and Ohlin assert that African Americans may be more prone to externalize blame, since social structural barriers to their success are evident. Therefore, the paths predicting challenge to legitimacy were allowed to vary across groups.

To determine whether hypothesized differences bear out, data from the Rochester study are first examined, since they allow for a comparison of all three ethnic groups (Table 7b). Denver survey data are then examined to determine whether differences exist across minority groups. In estimating the relationship between the strain interaction terms and challenge, Latinos and Whites produce similar findings. As described in the analysis of the total male samples (Chapter 6), the interaction between strain and externalization is not positively related to challenge as traditional strain theory would suggest. Instead, the combination of strain and *internalization* of blame *reduces* challenge, which also provides support for strain theory.[5] It should be noted that the relationship between strain/internalization and challenge is a bit weaker among Latinos (-.17 compared to -.23 for Whites), which suggests that Latinos may be slightly less likely to have conventional beliefs reaffirmed. Therefore, in RYDS partial support is provided for the hypothesized difference between Latinos and Whites. Contrary to expectations, however, findings for minority groups are inconsistent; no relationship is found between either strain term for African Americans in the RYDS. In the DYS, differences also emerge between minority groups; the pattern among Latinos is similar to that observed in the RYDS with strain and internalization negatively related to challenge, however, among Blacks, strain and externalization is *negatively* related to challenge. This counterintuitive finding suggests that African Americans in the DYS who experience strain and externalize blame are *less* likely to withdraw legitimacy from conventional norms.

A differential impact of challenge on delinquent values was also anticipated across ethnic groups. It was hypothesized that challenge may not readily lead to delinquent values among Latinos, since the duality of the Latino experience may provide other options, including the involvement in traditional Latino culture, to the adolescent who has removed legitimacy from conventional norms (see Horowitz, 1983). Rather than adopt a delinquent value system, Latinos might have traditional values strengthened:

> **Hypothesis #4a:** The relationship between challenge to legitimacy and delinquent values is expected to be weaker for Latinos in the strain theory model, due to the influence of traditional cultural values

At the same time, a weaker peer influence was expected among minority groups (and Latinos, in particular), since other cultural influences may be most salient. For example, studies have demonstrated the impact of the family on Latino delinquency (supported in the literature and in the current analysis, see Chapter 6), and argue that involvement with family serves as a protective factor in the development of delinquent behavior. In Chapter 3, the following hypotheses were proposed:

> **Hypothesis #6c:** The influence of delinquent peers on *delinquent values* is expected to be weaker for Latinos than whites, due to the relative impact of the family.
>
> **Hypothesis #11a:** Between minority groups, Latinos are expected to evidence a weaker influence of peers on *delinquent values*, given the anticipated impact of the family.

Although family involvement is not included in the model, its affect may be demonstrated through differences in path coefficients across groups. At the same time, other cultural differences might contribute to slope differences across groups (for example, religiosity). Regardless of the source, a difference in the relationship between delinquent peers and the adoption of delinquent values is expected by ethnicity.

The impact of challenge on delinquent values is significant across all groups in both sites. The magnitude of the relationship is similar across Latinos, African Americans, and Whites. Therefore, support is not provided for Hypothesis #4a, since the challenge to legitimacy is similarly related to delinquent value adoption among Whites and Latinos.

Table 7b. Allowing Hypothesized Paths to Vary by Ethnicity[a], Predicting General Delinquency (Model 2)

UNSTANDARDIZED COEFFICIENTS	DENVER YOUTH SURVEY		ROCHESTER YOUTH DEVELOPMENT STUDY		
	LATINO	BLACK	LATINO	BLACK	WHITE
PUBLIC ASSISTANCE —> STRAIN/EXTERNALIZATION	.17*	.17*	.17*	.17*	.17*
PUBLIC ASSISTANCE —> STRAIN/INTERNALIZATION	-.07	-.07	-.00	-.00	-.00
STRAIN/EXTERNALIZATION —> CHALLENGE	.01	-.13*	-.05	-.00	-.01
STRAIN/INTERNALIZATION —> CHALLENGE	-.11*	-.05	-.17*	-.04	-.23*
CHALLENGE LEGITIMACY —> DELINQUENT VALUES	.34*	.32*	.23*	.19*	.27*
DELINQUENT PEERS —> DELINQUENT VALUES	.27*	.41*	.13*	.23*	.39*
DELINQUENT PEERS —> DELINQUENCY	.40*	.85*	.38*	1.09*	1.26*
DELINQUENT VALUES —> DELINQUENCY	.13	.13	.50*	.50*	.50*
ACCESS TO DRUGS —> DELINQUENCY	.44*	.44*	.20*	.20*	.20*
DEL. VALUES*DRUG ACCESS —> DELINQUENCY	.01	.01	.24	.24	.24
EXPLAINED VARIANCE IN DELINQUENCY (R^2)	.20	.29	.07	.18	.18

* $p < .05$ (one-tail test)

Table 7b. Allowing Hypothesized Paths to Vary by Ethnicity[a], Predicting General Delinquency (cont.)

	DENVER YOUTH SURVEY	ROCHESTER YOUTH DEVELOPMENT STUDY
ERROR TERMS		
STRAIN/EXTERNALIZATION	.49*	.60*
STRAIN/INTERNALIZATION	.72*	.85*
CHALLENGE LEGITIMACY	.15*	.24*
DELINQUENT VALUES	.21*	.16*
DELINQUENCY	2.01*	2.29*
COVARIANCE OF ERROR TERMS		
STRAIN/EXTERNALIZATION <—> STRAIN/INTERNALIZATION	-.23*	-.31*
FIT INDICES		
GOODNESS OF FIT INDEX (GFI)	.93	.88
STANDARDIZED ROOT MEAN SQUARED RESIDUAL (RMR)	.08	.11
COMPARATIVE FIT INDEX (CFI)	.82	.52
CHI-SQUARE	113.26*	619.20*
DEGREES OF FREEDOM	49	79

* $p < .05$ (one-tail test)

The influence of peers on the adoption of a delinquent value system is also estimated across groups. In the RYDS, support is provided for Hypotheses 6c and 11a. Compared to Whites, minority groups in the RYDS demonstrate a weaker peer influence on delinquent value adoption. As expected, Latinos have the smallest path coefficient from peers to delinquent values (.13 compared to .23 for Blacks and .39 for Whites). In the DYS, minority group differences are consistent; Latinos demonstrate a weaker peer influence on delinquent values than Blacks (.27 and .41, respectively).

In predicting delinquent outcomes, additional differences were anticipated in peer influences across groups. Specifically, the peer effect on delinquency is expected to be weaker among Latinos:

> **Hypothesis #6d:** The influence of delinquent peers on *delinquent behavior* is also expected to be weaker for Latinos than whites.
>
> **Hypothesis #11b:** Between minority groups, Latinos are expected to evidence a weaker influence of peers on *delinquent behavior*, given the anticipated impact of the family.

When estimating the peer influence on delinquency, a pattern similar to that obtained in predicting delinquent values is revealed. Minority groups differ from their non-minority counterparts in the RYDS: Latinos and Blacks have smaller unstandardized coefficients (.38 and 1.09, respectively), while Whites evidence the strongest peer effect on delinquency (1.26). In the DYS, the difference among minority groups is replicated; Latinos have a smaller coefficient (.40 compared to .85 for African Americans), indicating a weaker peer effect in explaining delinquency. Peer differences are consistent across various delinquent outcomes; in RYDS, Latinos produce the smallest coefficients between delinquent peers and alcohol use, drug use, property crime, and violence. In the DYS, Latinos have the weaker relationship in all models except that predicting property crime (where the peer influence is stronger for Latinos than Blacks).

EVALUATING MODEL FIT

In evaluating the fit of Model 2, the explained variance (R^2), the model Chi-square, and the goodness of fit index (GFI) are examined. In terms of the variance in general delinquency, Model 2 explains 18 percent of the variance among Whites and African Americans in the RYDS. In comparison, only seven percent of the variance in Latino delinquency is explained (see Table 7c). In the DYS, minority group differences persist; 29 percent of the variance in general delinquency is explained among Blacks in the DYS, and 20 percent of Latino delinquency is explained. It is interesting to note that a greater amount of variance is explained among Latinos of Mexican descent in the DYS than Latinos in the RYDS, who are primarily of Puerto Rican descent. Across all RYDS estimations predicting various outcomes, and in four of the five models in the DYS, less variance is explained in all varieties of delinquency for Latinos (see Table 7c). Therefore, the ability of the traditional strain model in explaining Latino delinquency is weaker than its ability to predict delinquency among Whites and African Americans. In predicting drug use and property crime, Whites in the RYDS generate the largest R^2, and in explaining alcohol use and violence, Blacks have the largest R^2. With the exception of property crime in the DYS, African American delinquency is better explained by traditional strain theory than Latino delinquency.

Table 7c. Percent of Variance Explained in Delinquency by Ethnicity (Model 2)

	General	Alcohol Use	Drug Use	Property	Violence
DYS					
Latino	20	10	13	15	14
African American	29	31	21	8	24
RYDS					
Latino	7	8	8	4	5
African American	18	19	13	6	18
White	18	17	29	15	8

* p<.05 (one-tail test)

Across the two sites, the Goodness of Fit Index demonstrates a better model fit in the DYS; a GFI of .93 is derived from Model 2 (predicting general delinquency) and indicates a good fit, while a GFI of .88 in the RYDS indicates an acceptable, but not outstanding fit. The standardized RMR and Comparative Fit Index are not consistent with the GFI, and do not indicate that Model 2 provides a good fit to the data in either site (standardized RMR=.08 DYS, .11, RYDS; CFI=.82 DYS, .52 RYDS). Of the two sites, the DYS model more closely approaches acceptable limits.

COMPARING MODELS

When comparing coefficients generated in Model 1 to those generated separately in Model 2, it appears that group differences are masked when estimates are pooled and a common solution is derived. For example, when paths are constrained across groups in Model 1 of the DYS, the coefficient of the path between delinquent peers and delinquency is .54. This estimate represents a combination of the unique group coefficients of .40 and .85 for Latinos and African Americans in Model 2. The same pattern emerges in the RYDS; when estimated separately, the path between delinquent peers and general delinquency varies across groups (.38 for Latino, 1.26 for White, and 1.09 for Black males). Once equality constraints are imposed, LISREL generates a common solution of .85. Although the relationship is statistically significant for each ethnic group, the common solution masks the variation in slope magnitude.

To compare the fit of Models 1 and 2, a Chi-Square difference test is conducted. Table 7d presents the x^2 for both models and calculates their difference. Across four of the five delinquency outcomes, a significant Chi-square difference is found. When certain paths are allowed to vary, the fit of the constrained model (Model 1) is significantly improved. It appears that the traditional strain model is best estimated separately by ethnic group, when hypothesized paths are allowed to vary. Findings suggest an interaction effect exists; the model which frees theoretically relevant parameters (Model 2) provides a better fit to the data. Judging from the magnitude in slope differences, the primary difference between ethnic groups appears to lie in the influence of delinquent peers. In addition, the influence of strain on challenge to legitimacy is not consistent across ethnic groups; African Americans appear the most different in terms of the strain effect on the challenge to legitimacy.

Table 7d. Chi-Square Difference Test, Model 1 (constrains all paths) and Model 2 (allows hypothesized paths to vary)

Denver Youth Survey

	Model 1 (all constrained)		Model 2 (partially free parameters)		Chi-Square Difference (Model 1- Model 2)	
	x^2	df	x^2	df	x^2	df
General	126.00	54	113.26	49	12.74*	5
Alcohol Use	129.58	54	112.19	49	17.39*	5
Drug Use	119.49	54	106.35	49	13.14*	5
Property	110.57	54	99.96	49	10.61	5
Violence	115.50	54	101.84	49	13.66*	5

Rochester Youth Development Study

	Model 1 (all constrained)		Model 2 (partially free parameters)		Chi-Square Difference (Model 1-Model 2)	
	x^2	df	x^2	df	x^2	df
General	669.70	89	619.20	79	50.50*	10
Alcohol Use	711.59	89	656.62	79	54.97*	10
Drug Use	698.99	89	632.11	79	66.88*	10
Property	733.32	89	662.50	79	70.82*	10
Violence	683.59	89	622.48	79	61.11*	10

*p<.05

PAIRWISE COMPARISONS

Results thus far indicate an interaction effect in the traditional strain model. Differences exist across groups on previously specified relationships. In addition, Chi-square difference tests indicate a better model fit when groups are allowed to vary on theoretically designated paths. To identify the specific differences across the three ethnic groups in the RYDS, nested Chi-square difference tests are conducted between all pairs of groups. Equality constraints are imposed across two groups at a time, and the Chi-square of each model is compared to that of the model where all groups are allowed to vary (Model 2). To determine whether paths vary between Latinos and Whites, equality constrains are imposed between the two groups and coefficients for Blacks are allowed to vary. The Chi-square generated by the estimation is compared to Model 2 to determine whether paths between Latinos and Whites should be allowed to vary (indicating an interaction exists), or whether they should be constrained to be equal. A significant x^2 difference indicates that the fit of the model is significantly improved by freeing paths, and an interaction between the two groups exists. Pairwise comparisons are also made between Latinos and Blacks, by setting constraints across the two groups and comparing the Chi-square to Model 2. Finally, differences between African Americans and Whites are explored.

Table 7e lists the model Chi-square derived from each pairwise estimation and compares it with that produced by Model 2. It is evident from the results that imposing constraints between any two groups provides a significantly worse fit compared to the model which allows paths to vary. Findings indicate the superiority of Model 2, which allows separate estimates to be generated by ethnicity. Pairwise comparisons suggest that each group varies from the others. Therefore, it is best to estimate separate coefficients across groups when examining traditional strain theory.

Table 7e. Pairwise Comparisons By Ethnicity, RYDS

Allowing Hypothesized Paths to Vary (Model 2)

	Model 2 (partially free)		Latino & White		Chi-Square Difference		Latino & Black		Chi-Square Difference		Black & White		Chi-Square Difference	
	x^2	df	x^2	df	x^2	df	x^2	df	x^2	df	x^2	df	x^2	df
General	619.20	79	645.86	84	26.66*	5	643.42	84	24.22*	5	641.50	84	22.30*	5
Alcohol Use	656.62	79	680.42	84	23.80*	5	687.19	84	30.57*	5	678.85	84	22.23*	5
Drug Use	632.11	79	679.35	84	47.24*	5	648.03	84	15.92*	5	673.30	84	41.19*	5
Property	662.50	79	710.69	84	48.19*	5	689.34	84	26.84*	5	694.88	84	32.38*	5
Violence	622.48	79	645.51	84	23.03*	5	661.94	84	39.46*	5	643.19	84	20.71*	5

*p<.05

OTHER INTERACTIONS IN STRAIN THEORY

As indicated in Chapter 3, there may be other differences in strain relationships across groups beside those posited by hypotheses. To explore this possibility, stacked models were estimated which allow all strain relationships to vary across groups (Model 3). Although differences in the class effect on strain were not previously hypothesized, the paths between public assistance and both strain interaction terms were allowed to vary (Appendix K). In Chapter 5, group differences were observed in the bivariate relationships between class and strain. Allowing those parameters to be estimated separately within each group provides the opportunity to uncover those potential differences in LISREL. At the same time, separate paths are estimated between delinquent values, illegitimate opportunity, and their product term. Although no differences were previously specified, the possibility of an interaction effect is explored.

When all paths are allowed to vary, several unanticipated differences between ethnic groups emerge. First, the impact of class on strain is not constant; in the RYDS, class significantly predicts strain for Blacks and Whites, but has no relationship to strain for Latinos (see Table 7f). Specifically, a positive relationship between class and the strain/internalization term is found for Whites, but not for the strain/externalization measure. Among African Americans in the RYDS, class is positively related to strain and externalization, but is negatively related to strain and internalization. This finding suggests that class impacts the likelihood of externalizing blame; African Americans who receive public assistance are less likely to experience strain and internalize blame; instead, they are more likely to externalize blame. Whites, on the other hand, are more likely to internalize blame for failure to achieve the economic success goal. In the DYS, findings among minority groups are similar to Blacks in the RYDS. For example, public assistance has a positive relationship with strain/externalization among Latinos and African Americans, and no relationship with strain/internalization.

In estimating the influence of the delinquent values and illegitimate opportunity product term in the DYS, relationships are consistent across the two minority groups. A lower order effect of illegitimate opportunity emerges, but the product term does not achieve statistical significance. In the RYDS, similarities are observed between African Americans and Whites; delinquent values exhibits the only significant effect of the three measures on general delinquency. The magnitude of the delinquent values impact is larger among Whites (1.09 compared to .41 for Blacks). Diverging from both African Americans and Whites in the RYDS, a conditional effect of access to drugs is revealed among Latinos, along with a positive (and statistically significant) product term coefficient. These findings suggest that illegitimate opportunity is an important consideration in explaining Latino delinquency, since a similar effect is not observed in either of the other ethnic groups.[6] In addition, the coefficient between illegitimate opportunity and delinquency derived when paths are constrained (Model 1) reflects the sole impact of illegitimate opportunities among Latinos. This finding suggests that paths should be allowed to vary across groups when estimating strain theory.

To determine whether the fully free model (Model 3) provides a superior fit above and beyond the model of theoretically driven path differences (Model 2), a Chi-square difference test is conducted between Model 2 and Model 3 (Table 7g). The inclusion of additional parameters does not significantly improve the fit of Model 2 in the DYS, regardless of the delinquency outcome examined. In the RYDS, however, the additional parameters are best estimated in all varieties of delinquency, with the exception of drug use. Freeing all parameters in the RYDS provides a significantly better fit than Model 2, where only certain paths are allowed to vary. This finding might be explained by the role of illegitimate opportunity across ethnic groups. In the DYS, the product term and main effects of delinquent values and illegitimate opportunity are consistent across Latinos and African Americans. In the RYDS, however, a significant impact of illegitimate opportunity is revealed for Latino males, but not for their African American or White counterparts.[7] In addition, the influence of delinquent values is not significant for Latinos as it is for the other ethnic groups.

Within the RYDS, a series of pairwise comparisons were also conducted, which determine that significant differences exist between all groups (Table 7h). The model which allows all paths to vary (Model 3) provides a significantly better fit than those which constrain any two groups to be equal. Therefore, findings in the RYDS reveal unanticipated differences between all ethnic groups and suggest that allowing *all* paths to vary provides a superior fit to the model based on hypothesized differences. In contrast, estimating additional parameters in the DYS does not significantly improve the model fit.

Table 7f. Allowing All Paths to Vary by Ethnicity, Predicting General Delinquency (Model 3)

	DENVER YOUTH		ROCHESTER YOUTH DEVELOPMENT		
UNSTANDARDIZED COEFFICIENTS	LATINO	BLACK	LATINO	BLACK	WHITE
PUBLIC ASSISTANCE —> STRAIN/EXTERNALIZATION	.18*	.15*	.04	.27*	.04
PUBLIC ASSISTANCE —> STRAIN/INTERNALIZATION	-.18*	.06	-.13	-.11*	.26*
STRAIN/EXTERNALIZATION —> CHALLENGE	.01	-.13*	-.05	-.00	-.01
STRAIN/INTERNALIZATION —> CHALLENGE LEGITIMACY	-.11*	-.05	-.17*	-.04	-.23*
CHALLENGE LEGITIMACY —> DELINQUENT VALUES	.34*	.32*	.23*	.19*	.27*
DELINQUENT PEERS —> DELINQUENT VALUES	.27*	.41*	.13*	.23*	.39*
DELINQUENT PEERS —> DELINQUENCY	.40*	.89*	.69*	1.17*	.98*
DELINQUENT VALUES —> DELINQUENCY	.29	.03	.05	.41*	1.09*
ACCESS TO DRUGS —> DELINQUENCY	.45*	.41*	.35*	.12	.18
DEL. VALUES*DRUG ACCESS —> DELINQUENCY	-.27	.27	.91*	-.10	.60*
EXPLAINED VARIANCE IN DELINQUENCY (R^2)	.22	.29	.15	.18	.23

* $p < .05$ (one-tail test)

Table 7f. Allowing <u>All</u> Paths to Vary by Ethnicity, Predicting General Delinquency (Cont.)

	DENVER YOUTH SURVEY		ROCHESTER YOUTH DEVELOPMENT STUDY		
	<u>LATINO</u>	<u>BLACK</u>	<u>LATINO</u>	<u>BLACK</u>	<u>WHITE</u>
ERROR TERMS					
STRAIN/EXTERNALIZATION		.49*		.59*	
STRAIN/INTERNALIZATION		.71*		.82*	
CHALLENGE LEGITIMACY		.15*		.24*	
DELINQUENT VALUES		.21*		.16*	
DELINQUENCY		1.98*		2.25*	
COVARIANCE OF ERROR TERMS					
STRAIN/EXTERNALIZATION <—> STRAIN/INTERNALIZATION		-.23*		-.29*	
FIT INDICES					
GOODNESS OF FIT INDEX (GFI)		.94		.89	
STANDARDIZED ROOT MEAN SQUARED RESIDUAL		.08		.11	
COMPARATIVE FIT INDEX (CFI)		.83		.54	
CHI-SQUARE		103.89*		587.44*	
DEGREES OF FREEDOM		44		69	

* $p < .05$ (one-tail test)

Table 7g. Chi-Square Difference Test, Model 2 and Model 3

Denver Youth Survey

	Model 2 (partially free)		Model 3 (all free)		Difference (Model 2-Model 3)	
	x^2	df	x^2	df	x^2	df
General	113.26	49	103.89	44	9.37	5
Alcohol Use	112.19	49	102.17	44	10.02	5
Drug Use	106.35	49	98.59	44	7.76	5
Property	99.96	49	93.80	44	6.16	5
Violence	101.84	49	94.56	44	7.28	5

Rochester Youth Development Study

	Model 2 (partially free)		Model 3 (all free)		Difference (Model 2 -Model 3)	
	x^2	df	x^2	df	x^2	df
General	619.20	79	587.44	69	31.76*	10
Alcohol Use	656.62	79	611.20	69	45.42*	10
Drug Use	632.11	79	618.21	69	13.90	10
Property	662.50	79	637.38	69	25.12*	10
Violence	622.48	79	600.40	69	22.08*	10

* $p<.05$

Table 7h. Pairwise Comparisons By Ethnicity, RYDS

Allowing All Paths to Vary (Model 3)

	Model 3 (all free)		Latino & White		Chi-Square Difference		Latino & Black		Chi-Square Difference		Black & White		Chi-Square Difference	
	x^2	df	x^2	df	x^2	df	x^2	df	x^2	df	x^2	df	x^2	df
General	587.44	69	622.24	79	34.80*	10	627.10	79	39.66*	10	628.98	79	41.54*	10
Alcohol Use	611.20	69	642.45	79	31.25*	10	673.09	79	61.89*	10	651.06	79	39.86*	10
Drug Use	618.21	69	664.41	79	46.20*	10	638.94	79	20.73*	10	670.44	79	52.23*	10
Property	637.38	69	685.45	79	48.07*	10	679.32	79	41.94*	10	684.95	79	47.57*	10
Violence	600.40	69	624.84	79	24.44*	10	650.24	79	49.84*	10	634.56	79	34.16*	10

* $p < .05$

Overall, support for strain theory is found across all groups; the paths estimated in the traditional strain model are significant and in the expected direction (with the exception of strain/externalization on challenge to legitimacy). However, path coefficients in the strain model also illustrate differences in the magnitude of strain relationships between ethnicity. For example, although the influence of delinquent peers is positive and significant for all ethnic groups, its effect is smaller among Latinos compared to other ethnic groups (as anticipated). In addition, the amount of variance in delinquency that is explained by the traditional strain model is inconsistent; traditional strain theory is least able to explain delinquency among Latino males compared to their White and African American counterparts.

The examination of models in this chapter illustrates a better fit to the data when separate parameters are estimated for each ethnic group. Forcing equality constraints across groups provides a significantly worse fit than the model which allows paths to vary. Findings in this chapter also reveal sources of variation between ethnic groups that were not previously expected (the impact of illegitimate opportunity, for example). Taken together, these findings reveal variation in traditional strain theory across groups. Although basic relationships in strain theory are supported across groups, the magnitude of those relationships is not constant. Future analyses should explore the potential sources of ethnic group variation in more detail.

CHAPTER 8
Discussion and Conclusion

This study has evaluated the utility of traditional strain theory in explaining the delinquency of various ethnic groups. The traditional strain model was examined with Latino, White, and African American males from the Denver Youth Survey and the Rochester Youth Development Study. The theory, as offered by Merton (1938) and expanded by Cloward and Ohlin (1960), has been regarded as a general explanatory model, and as such, is thought to apply equally to adolescent males regardless of ethnic background. Merton's description of strain theory asserted, at least implicitly, that those who are similarly situated within the social structure should react in similar ways. In their elaboration of Merton's work, Cloward and Ohlin discuss the influence of race on several elements of opportunity theory, but do not empirically examine those relationships. In addition, Cloward and Ohlin's comments on race have not been extended to the Latino population.

Given the lack of information on Latinos in the criminological literature, this study focused on the ability of strain theory to predict Latino delinquency. As a growing segment of the United States population and of the criminal justice system, it is becoming increasingly important to consider the etiology of Latino delinquency. From a theoretical standpoint, it is also important to determine whether explanations of crime and delinquency are applicable to various groups in society. Researchers have cautioned against applying traditional perspectives to Latinos, since those theories were originally generated to explain the delinquency of White, European immigrants (Blea, 1988; Mirandé, 1987). Along with other Chicano sociologists, Mirandé calls for the consideration of the history of Latinos in the United States, and the development of new theoretical frameworks which can accurately depict the Chicano experience.[1] Research on Latino delinquency suggests that historical and cultural characteristics are likely to influence traditional theoretical relationships (Rodriguez & Weisburd, 1991).

Potential sources of ethnic variation within traditional strain theory were explored. In previous studies, researchers have suggested that socio-cultural factors might account for empirical differences between ethnic groups in tests of strain theory (Jessor et al., 1968; Perez y Gonzalez, 1993; Rodriguez & Recio, 1992; Rodriguez & Weisburd, 1991; Short, 1964; Short & Strodtbeck, 1965; Simons & Gray, 1989). Ethnic variation has been found on separate strain theory dimensions, including the perception of blocked opportunity, levels of strain experienced, externalization of blame, and adaptations to strain. Given such findings, there may be reason to believe that certain elements of the Latino experience may interact with traditional strain theory concepts and influence relationships within the model.

To explore the generality of strain theory, several tasks were identified. The primary goal of the study was to test the assumption that strain theory is generalizable to all ethnic groups. Across the sites, the traditional strain theory model was examined across the total male sample and separately by ethnicity to determine whether the theory consistently explains delinquency across groups. The inclusion of multiple ethnic groups allowed for a comparison of models across Latino, White, and African American males. In addition, the inclusion of Latinos of primarily Mexican descent in the DYS and Puerto Ricans in the RYDS also provided the opportunity to observe within group variation by country of origin.

A second aim of the study was to provide a theoretical foundation for inter-group differences. Studies which explore Latino delinquency have been criticized for their atheoretical approach (Rebach, 1992). To address this concern, the literature on Latinos in the United States was utilized in generating hypotheses. Potential interactions between ethnicity and strain theory constructs were explored to identify the ways in which historical and/or cultural factors can influence strain theory. In Chapter 3, a theoretical framework was developed which identified potential differences and highlighted elements of the Latino experience that might affect strain theory relationships. For instance, differences were expected across ethnic groups in the exposure to strain, and cultural factors were expected to influence group adaptations to the strain experience. In a modified strain theory model, family involvement was incorporated as an indicator of Latino culture, and was hypothesized to vary across ethnic groups (based upon previous findings by Rodriguez & Weisburd, 1991; Smith, 1990; Smith & Krohn, 1995; Sommers et al., 1994; Vazsonyi & Flannery, 1997; Weber et al.,1995). In addition, other socio-cultural factors were discussed as potential influences on traditional strain theory relationships, including acculturation, language, religiosity, and a history of marginality and discrimination.

The traditional and modified strain models were examined empirically; males were first examined collectively in each site to determine the amount of support generated for strain as a general explanatory approach. Structural equation models were then estimated simultaneously for each ethnic group via a stacked modeling technique. Stacking allowed for simultaneous estimation across groups, and provided the opportunity to constrain or free paths across groups. Through a process of constraining paths across groups and subsequently allowing paths to vary, interaction effects were explored between ethnicity and strain theory concepts.

EXPOSURE TO STRAIN BY ETHNICITY

In evaluating the traditional strain model in the Denver Youth Survey and the Rochester Youth Development Study, mean differences between groups were anticipated: first, it was expected that minority groups experience greater structural disadvantage compared to White males, and as a result, would exhibit increased strain levels. Aside from class differences, the minority status of Latinos and African Americans was also expected to increase exposure to strain. Specifically, legitimate opportunities for economic success are likely to be restricted among minority groups, therefore leading to higher levels of strain.

Support for these hypotheses was provided by mean difference tests in both the DYS and the RYDS. First, Latino and African American males were more likely to receive public aid than their White counterparts. In addition, they were more likely to experience blocked opportunity, as indicated by academic performance, and as a result, have higher levels of strain. Latino and African American males did not differ from each other, however, on any of the measures related to the strain experience. Once social class was introduced, strain values were compared across class and race categories. Among those receiving public aid, there was no difference in either academic performance or strain level between ethnic groups. This finding lends support to traditional strain theory, indicating that individuals who are economically disadvantaged experience blocked opportunity and strain similarly, regardless of ethnic background. Merton and Cloward & Ohlin assert that class is the primary determinant of strain, and this finding demonstrates that the economically disadvantaged experience strain similarly.

Among those *not* receiving public aid, however, minority groups differed from Whites; Latinos and African Americans demonstrated significantly lower grades and higher strain than their White counterparts. Ethnic group differences in blocked opportunity and strain among those in only one of the class categories pointed to an interaction between class and ethnicity in the production of strain. This finding identified an additional source of strain not previously emphasized by traditional strain theorists, namely minority group status. The specific mechanism by which non-disadvantaged minorities experience strain cannot be determined by the current analysis, however, it is likely that an element of minority status, namely discrimination, strengthens Latino and African American perceptions of blocked opportunity and leads to strain. Cloward and Ohlin identified class as the primary source of strain, however, the current findings suggest that other social conditions are also likely to contribute to the strain experience.

With regard to mean differences, it was hypothesized that Latinos and African Americans would be more likely, on the average, to externalize blame when compared to White males. This assertion is consistent with the work of Cloward and Ohlin (1960), who suggest that a consequence of discrimination is the externalization of blame, vis a vis the perception of blocked opportunity. They suggest that barriers to success are more visible for African Americans and that argument is extended to include Latinos. In a comparison of group mean values, this hypothesis was not supported; minority groups in both the DYS and the RYDS are no more likely to externalize blame than are Whites.

In light of this finding, it is necessary to review the externalization measure included in the model. A dichotomous externalization of blame variable was derived in the DYS from questions pertaining to the perceived difficulty in achieving economic success. In the RYDS students were asked about potential impediments to economic advancement. The measures included in the analysis do not reflect an ideal operationalization of externalization for two reasons. First, the measures do not fully capture externalization as Cloward and Ohlin describe it. The theorists describe externalization as the "attribution of the cause of failure to the social order rather than to oneself" (1960:111), and in doing so, paint a more global picture of externalization than is captured by the current measure. Although responses were identified as external to the individual (for example, family or peer related reasons), the measure does not contain items related to the larger social order. This may be particularly problematic in estimating ethnic differences across groups. Latinos and African Americans may be more likely to blame the system more than Whites; since the measure does not capture global attitudes toward the social system, it is unclear whether that is the case. Second, the dichotomous nature of the measure does not capture varying levels of externalization; it seems plausible that placing blame for failure to achieve economic success can vary along a continuum of externalization. Unfortunately, the two category variable included in the current analysis does not allow for varying gradations of blame.

TRADITIONAL STRAIN THEORY
The first step in assessing traditional strain theory involved structural equation modeling of traditional strain across the entire male sample within each site. Males were combined in an effort to estimate the model as it has been in the past and to provide a baseline for group comparisons. Overall, support for strain theory is provided by both the DYS and the RYDS. LISREL goodness of fit indices suggest that the traditional strain model of all males provided a reasonably good fit to the data.

A superior fit of the traditional model in the DYS was revealed when compared with the fit of the RYDS model. This finding could be explained, in part, by the ethnic composition across sites. In the DYS, White males are excluded from structural equation analyses due to an insufficient sample size. Since fit indices in each model are derived for all groups included in the analysis, a better fit in the DYS is likely to be produced because the fit is derived from minority groups who may share more similarities than the three groups included in the RYDS. Findings described in Chapter 7 indicate significant differences between Whites and their minority group counterparts; therefore, it is likely that the inclusion of White males in the RYDS impacts common fit indices.

In estimating the strain model, the relationship between class status and strain was demonstrated; in both sites public assistance significantly predicted the strain and externalization interaction, and in the RYDS, class was also related to strain and internalization. This finding is consistent with the work of Cloward and Ohlin, who suggest that lower class males are more likely to experience strain and externalize blame. In estimating the subsequent influence of the strain and externalization interaction terms on the challenge of legitimacy, additional support for the theory was found. The influence of strain and externalization was revealed in an unexpected way; instead of a direct influence of strain/externalization, the strain and internalization interaction term was found to significantly and negatively impact the challenge to legitimacy. This finding indicated that those who experience strain and blame themselves for failure to achieve goals were significantly less likely to withdraw legitimacy. Since this outcome was not observed among those who externalize, it provides indirect support for the original strain theory proposition.

The influence of challenge to legitimacy and delinquent peer association on the adoption of a delinquent value system was strong in both sites. At the same time, the relationship between delinquent peers and delinquent behavior was supported. The influence was consistent across all types of delinquent behavior, however, the magnitude of the peer impact varied. For example, the peer influence was strongest in predicting general delinquency and weakest in predicting property crime in both sites.

In determining delinquent outcomes, the interaction between delinquent values and illegitimate opportunity received little support in the analysis. Access to illegitimate opportunity was expected to mediate the relationship between delinquent values and delinquency, such that those who have greater access to drugs and strong delinquent values would be most likely to become involved in delinquent activity. In the majority of equations estimated, the interaction between delinquent values and illegitimate opportunity was not supported. In the DYS, the interaction term was significant in predicting drug use and violence, and in the RYDS the interaction significantly predicted violence only. These findings provided weak support for a moderating effect of illegitimate opportunity on the relationship between delinquent values and delinquency.[2]

It is interesting to note the significant influence of the interaction term on violence in both the DYS and the RYDS. Additionally, the direction of the influence was not as anticipated; as access to drugs increases, the relationship between delinquent values and violence *increases*. While Cloward and Ohlin (1960) asserted that the absence of illegitimate opportunity would lead to violence, this study revealed that the presence of illegitimate opportunity (access to drugs) along with a delinquent value system serves to produce violent outcomes. These findings may be explained by changes in the conceptualization of violence over time. Violence in contemporary criminological literature has been described as having both expressive and an instrumental components. Cloward and Ohlin's depiction of violence is consistent with the expressive component. They depict violence as it arises out of a frustration over the inaccessibility of both legitimate and illegitimate opportunities and as an attempt to gain status. In today's society, evidence of instrumental violence has been cited which may be used to protect illegitimate opportunities, such as an illegal drug market. In the current analysis, an interactive effect between access to illegitimate opportunity and delinquent values is found, which appears to capture both the expressive and instrumental components of violence.

MODIFIED STRAIN THEORY
Although the traditional strain model provided a reasonably good fit, it was compared to the modified strain model. To perform the comparison, it was necessary that both models were estimated in a nested sequence in LISREL, using the same covariance matrix. To assess the contribution of family involvement to traditional strain, two unique paths in the model were examined. After comparing the two models, it appears that family involvement does not substantively contribute to the traditional strain model; in the DYS, increased family involvement significantly reduced delinquent values and involvement with delinquent peers, and in the RYDS, family involvement only reduced association with delinquent peers. Family involvement added little to the explained variance in either delinquent values or delinquent peer association, and did not affect other paths in the model. Although the Chi-square difference test indicated a significantly improved fit of the modified model, other fit indices did not provide the same support.

To get another look at the difference between traditional and modified strain, nested models were estimated across ethnic groups and revealed that family involvement had a differential influence across Latino, White and African American males. The variable did not impact either delinquent values or association with delinquent peers among RYDS White males, had a minor impact on Blacks in the DYS, and influenced Latinos in both sites. Given the inconsistencies across groups and minor substantive contribution to the traditional strain model, it was concluded that the modified model did not provide significant improvement over the traditional strain theory. The variation in findings by ethnicity suggested, however, that this theoretical concept might be further explored in the future. The impact of family involvement within the Latino population is consistent with existing literature (Pabon, 1998; Smith, 1990; Smith & Krohn, 1995), and suggests that Latinos who spend time with family are less likely to adopt delinquent values and associate with delinquent peers.

SITE SPECIFIC MEASURES

To allow for replication across sites, the majority of analyses was conducted with identical measures. Each site contained a public assistance measure which was used to assess the impact of class on strain. Strain in both sites was operationalized by a traditional disjunction measure; the difference between an individual's aspirations and expectations was calculated to derive a strain score. In addition, the DYS and the RYDS included identical measures of challenge to the legitimacy of norms, delinquent values, involvement with delinquent peers, access to drugs, and delinquency.[3]

Each site also contained unique measures which were used as alternatives to identical variables. Specifically, the DYS included a blocked opportunity index, which was compared to the strain disjunction measure. In past estimations of traditional strain theory, a variety of strain measures have produced varying levels of support for the theory (Burton & Cullen, 1992; Burton et al., 1994; Farnworth & Leiber, 1989; Hoffman & Ireland, 1995). To determine whether the blocked opportunity index produces greater support for the theory, the measure was employed in site specific analysis. At the same time, more comprehensive measures of challenge to legitimacy and delinquent values were included for comparison with identical measures.

Analysis of site specific measures indicated that additional items in both challenge to legitimacy and delinquent values indices did not serve as an improvement over identical measures. Relationships in the traditional strain model were consistent with those generated by identical measures across sites. Differences were observed, however, across strain measures. Although class appeared to influence blocked opportunity and the strain disjunction measures similarly, their subsequent impact on challenge varied. When blocked opportunity and externalization interaction terms were included in place of those generated with the strain disjunction, no link was found between either interaction term and challenge to legitimacy. Blocked opportunity, when coupled with either externalization or internalization of blame did *not* result in the challenge to legitimacy of conventional values. It was concluded, therefore, that the traditional strain disjunction term is most appropriate for producing support for the theory. It comports with Merton's and Cloward and Ohlin's conceptions of strain, and gauges the difference between economic aspirations and educational expectations. Although blocked opportunity taps into individual perceptions, it is not as closely linked with aspirations, as is the disjunction measure. Perhaps the combination of both aspirations and expectations (as traditional strain theorists define it) is the key for understanding the impact of strain on delinquency. Future operationalizations of strain might strive to incorporate aspirations with more subjective perceptions of blocked opportunity.

Academic performance may not be the ideal indicator of blocked opportunity to use in the creation of a strain disjunction term. School grades may not accurately reflect one's perception of the likelihood for future success. For example, one may have less than average grades but retain hope of achieving future economic success. Support for the measure has been provided by previous research (Menard, 1995), and in the current study self-reported grades served as the best alternative to an inflated educational expectations measure. Academic achievement can generally indicate where one is standing in relation to the economic success goal. As mentioned previously, however, it may not represent the same in the Latino population. Latinos have experienced limited educational success in the past and may not consider grades a predictor of success. Since the indicator may not be ideal for measuring strain across a multi-ethnic sample, future examinations of the theory should include alternative measures of blocked opportunity.

In the RYDS, a more elaborate class measure provided an alternative to public assistance and was included in site specific analysis to determine whether multiple sources of structural disadvantage are more strongly related to strain than the receipt of public assistance alone. Families were ranked according to principle wage earner employment status, family income, and receipt of public aid. The more inclusive class measure produced findings consistent with those obtained using public assistance alone.

An acculturation proxy variable, language of the parent interview, was also examined in the RYDS and its impact on aspirations was assessed. Those Latinos who are more acculturated were expected to be more likely to internalize the economic success goal; however, analyses revealed that males of Spanish and English speaking parents do not vary in aspiration levels. When class status was introduced, less acculturated Latinos in receipt of public assistance had higher aspirations than their English speaking counterparts. Among Latinos not receiving aid, no differences in aspirations were found. This finding may be indicative of the goals of recent immigrants; economic success may have served as a motivating factor in the decision to move to the United States. As such, it is likely to be reflected by structurally disadvantaged and newly arrived Latinos as a priority in their lives. This finding is inconsistent with the hypothesis that increased levels of acculturation produce a greater likelihood of internalizing the mainstream economic success goal.

To sum up findings on measurement issues, the identical measures utilized in the current analysis were adequate for testing a model of traditional strain theory. None of the unique measures in either site outperformed identical measures. In particular, a strong argument can be made for the continued use of the economic disjunction measure in future tests of strain theory.

ESTIMATING MODELS BY ETHNICITY

Having estimated the traditional strain model across the full male sample in each site, the analysis focused on the applicability of strain across ethnic groups. Since the primary aim of the study was to determine the consistency of strain theory across Latinos, Whites, and African Americans, stacked models were estimated in LISREL. First, a common solution was derived for all ethnic groups in each site, and then certain paths were allowed to vary, based on hypotheses presented in Chapter 3.

By allowing unique coefficients to be calculated for each group, anticipated differences in strain relationships were tested.

Overall, the consistency of findings across groups was noted, and strain theory was largely supported among Latinos, Whites, and African Americans. Primary strain relationships were significant within each group, thus supporting the notion that the theory is indeed a general explanatory model. In estimating separate paths for each group, however, one primary difference emerged. The source of ethnic variation was the role of delinquent peers in the internalization of a delinquent value system and production of delinquent behavior. Based in part on previous literature which highlights the relative importance of family compared to peers in the Latino culture, peers were expected to exert less of an influence on Latinos. In the LISREL estimation by ethnicity, Latinos evidenced the weakest peer influence on delinquent values in both the DYS and the RYDS. In addition, peers had the least influence on several delinquent behaviors; in the DYS, the Latino peer influence was weakest in predicting general delinquency, alcohol use, drug use, and violence, and in the RYDS, the peer influence was weakest for all delinquency outcomes except general delinquency. These findings are consistent with hypotheses and other literature which has documented a reduced peer influence on Latinos when compared to Whites (Rodriguez & Weisburd, 1991). Delinquent peers in both the DYS and the RYDS were less likely to strengthen Latino delinquent values or reinforce their delinquent behavior when compared to their White and African American counterparts. Although the current investigation cannot determine the source of the difference between minority groups, it is suggested that the duality of the Latino culture may provide an alternative source of values for Latino youth.

At the same time, variation between groups was observed in the explanatory power of traditional strain theory in predicting delinquent behavior. Specifically, less variance is explained in general delinquency, alcohol use, drug use, property crime, and violent crime for Latinos in the RYDS compared to other ethnic groups. The least amount of variance in the DYS was explained across all varieties of Latino delinquency, except property crime. Therefore, the ability of the traditional strain model to explain Latino delinquency was generally weaker than its ability to predict delinquency among Whites and African Americans.

To determine whether interaction effects of ethnicity were significant, a Chi-square difference test was conducted. The test was designed to determine whether the fit of the partially freed model (with separate estimates by ethnicity) provided a superior fit to the fully constrained model (one solution estimated for all groups). A comparison of both models revealed a statistically significant difference, indicating that it is best to allow certain paths to vary across groups. When paths were allowed to vary and interactions were hypothesized, the model provided a better fit to the data. A similar test was conducted across pairs in the RYDS, to determine specific ethnic group differences. Pairwise comparisons revealed that each ethnic group varied from the others, suggesting that it is best to estimate separate coefficients across groups when examining traditional strain theory.

As a final step, all paths of the traditional strain model were allowed to vary across groups, to capture differences not previously specified. The inclusion of additional parameters did not significantly improve the fit of the partially free model in the DYS, regardless of the delinquency outcome examined. In the RYDS, however, the additional parameters were best estimated in all varieties of delinquency, with the exception of drug use. When all paths were freed in the RYDS the influence of class on strain is was found to be inconsistent across groups. Class significantly predicted strain for Blacks and Whites in the RYDS, but had no relationship to strain for Latinos. Among Whites, public assistance significantly predicted the strain/internalization term only, and suggested that lower income whites were more likely to experience strain and internalize blame. On the other hand, African American males who receive public aid were more likely to more likely to externalize, and less likely to internalize blame, which Cloward and Ohlin have described (1960:121).

These findings depict variation in the influence of public assistance receipt by ethnicity. Perhaps the meaning of relying on public aid varies across groups, and has a differential influence on the strain experience. To determine whether the public assistance measure is unique, the RYDS comprehensive class measure was examined and appeared to influence strain for Whites and African Americans only, as with the public assistance variable. Among Latinos findings differ from those generated by public assistance; specifically, the comprehensive class measure significantly predicts both strain interaction terms. Therefore, there appears to be a differential impact of social class measures among Latinos. Aside from public assistance, indicators such as family income and principle wage earner employment status are more likely to produce strain. Since public assistance is unrelated to Latino strain, future research might better identify the meaning of receiving public aid within the ethnic group to understand its influence on various outcomes.

When paths from delinquent values, illegitimate opportunity, and their interaction term were freed, the importance of illegitimate opportunity in predicting delinquency among Latinos was discovered in the RYDS. The interaction term was significant and suggested that access to illegitimate opportunity mediated the relationship between delinquent values and delinquency. A conditional effect of drug access was also revealed for members of the ethnic group. Since a similar effect was not observed in either of the other ethnic groups, and the amount of explained variance in delinquency was doubled when paths were allowed to vary, illegitimate opportunity was found to be an important consideration in explaining Latino delinquency. The relative importance of illegitimate opportunity among the ethnic group might stem from the lack of legitimate opportunities for achieving success. As mentioned previously, Latinos in the RYDS are most deprived of legitimate opportunity compared to other ethnic groups. The lack of institutionalized opportunities for success might encourage the use of illegitimate opportunities for achieving the economic success goal.

The role of delinquent values also varied across ethnic groups; a lower order effect was found among Blacks and Whites, but was not revealed for Latinos. This finding might relate to the previous discussion of the Latino culture; if one accepts the notion of a dual emphasis on mainstream and traditional values within the Latino community, the diminished influence of delinquent values may stem from the internalization of traditional Latino values.

Findings of the fully free model suggested that the most proximal causes of strain and delinquency in the strain theory model vary by ethnicity. Only partial support was provided for class status as a precursor to strain; in the DYS, support was found for the traditional strain relationship among Latinos, while in the RYDS, the receipt of public assistance was unrelated to strain. In addition, the impact of delinquent peers and delinquent values was evident for African Americans and Whites only. Within the Latino population, however, access to illegitimate opportunities had a greater influence in determining delinquent outcomes. At the same time, the model which allowed all paths to vary provided a significantly better fit than that which constrained any two groups to be equal. It is concluded then, that allowing *all* paths to vary in the RYDS provided a superior fit to the model based only on hypothesized differences. In contrast, estimating additional parameters in the DYS did not significantly improve the model fit.

THEORETICAL IMPLICATIONS

This study provided support for traditional strain theory, as originated by Merton (1938) and developed by Cloward and Ohlin (1960). When all males were examined collectively in each site, significant relationships emerged and the progression was traced from class status to strain, and ultimately, to delinquency. In addition, the model provided a good fit to the data in both the DYS and the RYDS. Taken together, these findings suggest that strain theory is supported as a general explanation of adolescent male offending. The traditional strain model explained up to 24 percent of the variance in general delinquency, alcohol use, drug use, property crime, and violent crime.

At the same time, this investigation sought to assess the consistency in strain relationships across various ethnic groups. Mean difference tests were first conducted on strain theory concepts across Latinos, Whites, and African Americans which revealed higher values of public assistance, blocked opportunity, and strain among minority groups, as expected. Upon closer examination, an interaction was found between socioeconomic class and minority group status. Those who rely on government assistance similarly experience strain, as Cloward and Ohlin have argued. In that sense, ethnicity is relatively unimportant in exposing one to strain. Minority groups who do *not* receive public assistance were more vulnerable to strain than their White counterparts. This finding supported the hypothesis that minority groups are at increased risk for strain. Legitimate opportunities are likely to be blocked because of increased poverty, however, minority groups may also face barriers to legitimate opportunity which stem from discrimination and relegation to minority group status. Based on these findings, it appears that ethnicity does, in fact, interact with class to produce strain among Latinos and African Americans.

In estimating traditional strain across groups via structural equation modeling, differences were revealed between Latinos, Whites, and African Americans. For the most part, strain relationships were supported within each group, however, the magnitude of path coefficients differed. The weaker paths leading to delinquency among Latino males suggested that they are *less* likely to respond to strain with delinquency. The key difference between ethnic groups is in the influence of delinquent peers, which are less likely to reinforce delinquent values among Latinos. Moreover, the traditional strain model explained less of the variance in Latino delinquency compared to other ethnic groups. This finding indicates that the theory is least adequate in accounting for Latino delinquency.

When the traditional strain model was estimated separately by ethnicity and certain paths were allowed to vary, the model provided a significantly better fit than when a common solution was estimated for all three groups. This lent support to the hypothesis that ethnicity interacts with various strain concepts. Within the RYDS sample, it is ultimately best to allow *all* paths to vary.

Comparing Latino Groups

The current analysis provided the opportunity to examine precursors of Latino delinquency, a topic which has not received a great deal of attention in the criminological literature. The ethnic composition of the DYS and the RYDS also allowed for an intra-group comparison of Latinos by country of origin. Much of the findings in the study referred to Latinos generally, as the ethnic group compared with Whites and African Americans. Overall, the primary goal was to learn about Latino delinquency through an examination of the three primary ethnic groups. However, intragroup differences are also necessary to consider among Latinos (Marín & Marín, 1991).

Of all Latino groups, Mexican Americans and Puerto Ricans are most similar in terms of age structure, income, and educational attainment, and were expected to share similar patterns in offending. At the same time, however, it is important to compare Mexican Americans in the DYS with Puerto Ricans in the RYDS; differences in group history and demographic characteristics warrant such a comparison.

Overall consistencies were found between Latino groups. Support for the theory was found within each portion of the larger Latino population. A consistent influence of strain on challenge was found among Mexican Americans and Puerto Ricans. In addition, a weakened peer influence on delinquent values and delinquent behavior was observed across both groups; compared to their White and African American counterparts, Latinos in general, were less likely to be influenced by peers. This finding lent support to the similarity of Latino groups, and may indicate a cultural difference in developing adaptations to strain. It was suggested throughout this study that Latinos may have an opportunity to fall back on a traditional value system when faith in conventional goals is lost.

When all paths are allowed to vary, class was unrelated to strain among Puerto Ricans in the RYDS. This finding suggested that there may exist other barriers to legitimate opportunity among Latinos in Rochester, aside from class status. Moreover, a stronger impact of illegitimate opportunity was revealed among the same group when compared to their Mexican American counterparts in the DYS. Such findings may indicate the uniqueness of the legitimate and illegitimate opportunity structures in Rochester, New York. Future research might include a neighborhood level analysis to determine sources of strain among Puerto Ricans and their illegitimate opportunities.

The findings of this study provided support for traditional strain theory in the Denver Youth Survey and Rochester Youth Development Study. The theory has been accepted as a general explanatory model, and for the most part, it provided an adequate explanation of delinquency when all males were examined as a whole. The basic structure of the model was consistent across Latino, White, and African American Males, however, findings were not identical across groups. When ethnic groups were analyzed separately, the magnitude of certain slopes varied by ethnicity. Independent model estimation in LISREL identified a weakened delinquent peer influence within the Latino population. In addition, the adequacy of traditional strain theory in explaining Latino delinquency is relatively weak. Results are consistent across sites, which reveals systematic differences across ethnic groups. Overall, the findings reveal support for group similarities and at the same time, point to specific differences.

Future investigations of strain theory might examine the theory across multiple ethnic groups to clarify the need for a culturally specific model. Studies might improve upon several problematic measures in the current analysis, such as the externalization of blame and blocked opportunity.[4]

In addition, future studies should attempt to identify the specific mechanism(s) by which differences exist in the traditional strain model for Latinos. The current analysis examined the influence of family involvement on traditional strain theory, however, its contribution to the traditional strain theory model is limited. Compared to other ethnic groups, the family variable had the greatest impact among Latinos. Within the DYS, an increase in Latino family involvement significantly reduced delinquent values and association with delinquent peers. In the RYDS, family involvement significantly reduced delinquent peer association. A family involvement effect was not found among White males in the RYDS, and a small impact was found among Blacks in both sites. While the impact of family involvement differed across groups, it was not sufficient in fully explaining the difference in delinquent value adoption across groups.

Given the findings of this study, it is clear that future tests of the traditional strain model should be conducted separately by ethnicity. When a common solution is derived for all groups, differences between them are masked. Additionally, this study revealed interactions between ethnicity and traditional strain concepts; future estimates of the model should incorporate those interactions. Most importantly, the source of ethnic variation in strain theory relationships needs to be explored. Future research should include cultural elements other than family involvement to more fully explore group exposure and adaptation to strain. An elaboration of the traditional strain model might ultimately increase the ability of the theory to explain Latino delinquency.

Notes

CHAPTER ONE THROUGH CHAPTER EIGHT

CHAPTER 1

1. Darnell F. Hawkins agrees that in this day and age, "there are grim reminders that race still matters in the United States and other parts of the postcolonial world" (1995:1). Traditionally divisions have been drawn down the color line, which is still evidenced in American society today. Hawkins also points out that interethnic conflict has also existed throughout history, but in recent years has become more widespread. Division based on ethnic differences may be as common in the twenty-first century as racial division has been in the twentieth century.

2. Increased awareness of Latinos in the United States, particularly in the years since Merton advanced his theory of anomie, occurred for several reasons; "the rapid growth of the population and a pronounced regional concentration which heightened the national visibility of Latinos as an ethnic group" (Bean & Tienda, 1987:56). Contributing to the rapid growth of the Latino population since 1960 are increased immigration and higher fertility rates among Latino women (Bean & Tienda, 1987).

3. Exceptions include tests of strain theory with multiethnic samples conducted by Jessor et al. (1968), Elliott & Voss (1974), and Simons & Gray (1989).

4. The term Hispanic is described as a government creation, offered by the Task Force on Racial/Ethnic Categories, and is used by government agencies such as the Census Bureau (del Pinal & Singer, 1997). Those who wish to avoid using a government-imposed label often prefer the term Latino.

5. During the 1990s, approximately 85% of Latinos lived in nine states, including California, Texas, New York, Florida, Illinois, New Jersey, Arizona, New Mexico, and Colorado. In addition, approximately 90% of all Latinos live in metropolitan areas, compared to 76% non-Latinos (del Pinal & Singer, 1997).

6. As of the 1996 Current Population Survey, ten percent of Mexican American and Puerto Rican males were unemployed, as were ten and eleven percent of women (respectively).

7. Figures from the 1996 Current Population Survey indicate a high school completion rate of 86% for Whites, 75% for Blacks, and 53% for Latinos. Within the Latino population, 60% of Puerto Ricans graduated high school, compared to 47% of Mexican Americans (del Pinal & Singer, 1997).

CHAPTER 2

1. While society had previously been seen as a source of controlling deviant behavior, Merton pointed out that the social structure can also be considered a cause of deviance. See S. Freud's *Civilization and its Discontents* (1930).

Notes

2. Cloward and Ohlin's *Delinquency and Opportunity* (1960) builds upon the previous work of Richard Cloward (1959) in expanding Merton's theory of anomie.

3. Cloward and Ohlin (1960) discuss the propensity of African Americans to externalize rather than internalize blame for failure to achieve economic success, since barriers to goal achievement are highly visible for them. In an examination of strain theory by race and class, Simons & Gray (1989) also suggest that African Americans in lower-status positions may be more likely to blame the system for their failure. Lower class minorities, in general, "are more apt than persons of higher status to encounter situations in which opportunities are blocked based upon what are perceived to be unjust and arbitrary institutional arrangements" (p.92).

4. Menard argues for the inclusion of intervening variables between strain and delinquency, and focuses on the modes of adaptation and their influence on delinquent outcomes. While not identifying them as such, modes of adaptation (as Menard describes them) are strikingly similar to Cloward and Ohlin's notion of the withdrawal of legitimacy. Adaptations are described in terms of acceptance or rejection of goals and norms. Innovation and retreatism are both characteristic of a rejection of norms, however, innovators accept traditional culture goals, and retreatists reject both goals and norms. The rejection of institutionalized methods of goal attainment is representative of withdrawal of legitimacy and finds statistical support in Menard's study.

5. In an examination of various strain measures, Burton et al. cite relative deprivation as indicative of the "essence of the Merton-Cohen-Cloward and Ohlin perspective... that crime is prompted not by the strain of absolute deprivation brought on by blocked opportunities, but from being deprived of what others in society have the opportunity have the opportunity to obtain" (1994:216). The authors admit, however, that relative deprivation diverges from Merton's original conceptualization of strain.

6. This finding comports with previous commentary on relative deprivation measures. The fact that support was not found with a relative deprivation measure cannot lead to a rejection of strain theory. The strain perspective does not focus on relative blocked opportunity. The absolute disjunction measure is compatible with the strain perspective, and provides empirical support.

7. Greenberg also examines the strain/delinquency relationship while controlling for educational expectations, and finds a consistent influence of the discrepancy measure on delinquency across all levels of expectation. He concludes that support for strain is found even when controlling for main effects of educational aspirations or educational expectations.

8. In his analysis, Jensen (1995) finds significant direct effects of aspirations and expectations on delinquency, but does not find the interaction term to be significant. Greenberg explains Jensen's findings as support for strain.

9. Agnew creates absolute and relative measures of strain, and finds both to be unrelated to delinquent outcomes. In addition, he tests for non-linear relationships with a series of dummy variables, and fails to find support for strain. Finally, analysis is conducted among lower class youth only, which reveals weak support for the theory.

10. This represents one of several recent studies which examines strain as individual frustration/dissatisfaction/anger with economic achievement (Agnew, 1994; Burton & Dunaway, 1994).

11. Agnew et al. include the following six factors: a) high relative and absolute importance of monetary success; b) desire for large amounts of money; c) low importance attached to alternative goals; d) reduced legitimate opportunities for goal attainment; e) belief that monetary success will not be achieved through legitimate means; f) belief that individual is worse off monetarily than others in similar positions.

12. Agnew et al. do not define secondary economic aspirations and expectations measures as such, rather refer to them as the goal of making a lot of money (which is compared with other family and peer related goals), and low expectations for making a lot of money. These two measures are combined and examined along with other interaction terms. It is unfortunate that the authors do not examine the disjunction between general aspirations and expectations separately, instead of combining the measure with other interaction terms. A second (and more appropriate) examination of the traditional strain measure could have been conducted, assessing the impact of economic disjunction along with main effects of aspirations and expectations. Instead, the analysis of traditional measures was limited to those items which contain dollar amounts desired and expected.

13. Note that the externalization of blame measure is combined with other dissatisfaction items to create the strain measure, and is not ultimately treated as a conditioning factor, as it was originally intended. The utilization of cross-sectional data limits the extent to which conditioning factors can be examined as outcomes of strain and precursors of delinquency.

CHAPTER 3

1. Differences between the two groups are statistically significant (p<.0000). In both sites, parents report whether they receive food stamps, welfare, or AFDC. A more detailed description of the public assistance variable will be presented in Chapter 4.

2. Kornhauser argues that all members of society are likely to desire "more comfort, greater economic security, the esteem of their fellows, and greater control over their lives" (1978:169), and provides empirical evidence which suggests that achievement orientation does not differ by class. Contrary to strain

theory precepts, she asserts that the desire for financial security is not culturally based; instead, it is described as a basic human characteristic.

3. The measure employed to assess financial aspirations of youth appears to tap into disappointment in not achieving financial success, which Heller concludes is not the same as aspiration. In addition, she argues that Mexican American parents tend to prepare their children for failure more than White parents, and therefore, Chicano youth might rank lower overall on feelings of disappointment.

4. Although this study recognizes differences among Latinos by country of origin, the argument about the larger Latino population applies across Mexican Americans and Puerto Ricans, which are included in the DYS and the RYDS, respectively. Both are relatively recent immigrant groups (with primary immigration periods occurring in the early to mid 20th century); both are concentrated in urban areas (Mexican Americans are typically concentrated in Southwest cities and Puerto Ricans in New York); and both groups maintain close ties with their country of origin (Aguirre & Turner, 1995; Sowell, 1981).

5. According to Vigil, "there is considerable evidence that the amount of time one's family has been in the United States, especially with later generations of native-born Mexican Americans, determines the level and rate of adoption of Anglo-American patterns" (1988:38).

6. The interaction between race and socioeconomic status has previously been suggested by Simons and Gray (1989), who argue that lower-class Blacks are likely to experience discrimination in addition to class barriers to success, and are therefore most susceptible to strain.

7. Similarly, Padilla (1993) has described a restricted job market for Puerto Ricans in Chicago.

8. Not all intentions of the educational system are malicious. Mirandé describes internal diversity within the liberal model of education, with variations ranging from openly assimilationist positions that pay only token attention to bilingualism and biculturalism, to sincere but misguided efforts that seek to help Chicanos attain parity (1985:102). Such sincere efforts are misguided, however, because they offer a more concealed version of assimilationism, since they do not openly blame the school for Chicano failure.

9. Strain items included age, marital status, language spoken in the home, occupation, education, between-generation mobility, religion, and social participation.

10. Analysis is conducted with males only to keep consistent with Cloward and Ohlin's contention that female adolescents are less likely to be concerned with occupational opportunities than males (1960).

11. Note that mean differences do not achieve statistical significance.

12. The notion of familism as a coping mechanism among the lower class population has previously been cited. Valdez describes the work of Rodman (1963), who observed that lower class families combine mainstream and traditional values to develop a unique value system which enhances their well-

being. The lower class emulates the values of the larger society, including achievement, and at the same time, maintains elements of traditional culture.

13. Note that differences between the ethnic groups persist once socioeconomic status and generation is controlled for.

14. In predicting substance use among the same samples, Rodriguez and Recio (1992) apply the Integrated Social Control (ISC) model and find a similar family influence among Puerto Ricans when a comprehensive substance use measure is employed.

15. The direct influence of acculturation on delinquency does not appear to be consistent, however, but varies across types of delinquent behavior. A positive impact on general delinquency and violence is found, and a negative impact on drug use is observed. Sommers et al. (1993) attribute increased drug use among those *less* enmeshed in the mainstream to acculturation stress, whereby substance use serves as a coping mechanism.

16. Differences between generations are statistically significant. Compared to first or second generations, third generation Chicanos experience increased contact with family members. This finding remains significant even after controlling for the number of relatives living in close proximity. Contact among third generation is not merely a product of family size.

17. Adult ambivalence to youth crime is explained by several factors: personal ties to kids or their families, fear of youth, and distrust of the criminal justice system. Permissiveness, however, is dependent on the type of crime that is committed in the neighborhood. Sullivan reports more tolerance for theft than violent crime.

18. Minority groups have been defined as "people who, because of their physical or cultural characteristics, are singled out from others in the society in which they live for differential and unequal treatment and who therefore regard themselves as objects of collective discrimination" (Wirth, 1945:347, as cited in Aguirre & Turner, 1995).

19. Differences between minority and majority youth are anticipated beyond those which are due to varying class levels.

20. Although illegal immigration is not an issue among the Puerto Rican population, they also experience prejudice and social structural disadvantage when they move to the states (Aguirre & Turner, 1995).

21. As mentioned earlier in the chapter, the internalization of American success goals among Latinos has been questioned (Blea, 1988; Horowitz, 1983).

22. As a whole, Latinos represent an undereducated minority group, however, there are differences by country of origin. For example, Cuban Americans are more likely to complete high school than Latinos of Mexican or Puerto Rican descent (del Pinal & Singer, 1997).

23. Although a consistent influence of family attachment is demonstrated across minority groups, Brook et al. (1992) find that attachment is the most important family variable among Puerto Ricans.

CHAPTER 4

1. For a detailed description of the project funded by the Office of Juvenile Justice and Delinquency Prevention, see Huizinga et al. (1993a). The Pittsburgh Youth Study is also part of the Program of Research on the Causes and Correlates of Delinquency; since Pittsburgh does not have a sizeable Latino community, it is not included here.

2. The importance of operationalizing strain concepts has been illustrated by previous tests of the theory. Empirical investigations suggest that the level of support for strain is related to the manner in which strain concepts are operationalized (Burton and Cullen, 1992; Farnworth and Leiber,1989). As such, this study employs various measures of strain concepts to test the traditional and modified strain theory models.

3. In 1984, the city of Rochester reported a crime rate of 9,420 per 100,000 population, which was well above the national and New York state rates (5,031 and 5,577, respectively), and even surpassed that of New York City (8,375) (FBI statistics reported in Farnworth et al., 1991).

4. The proportion of males in the RYDS sample exceeds that of the DYS sample (82 versus 75 percent of total samples included in current analysis). This is partially explained by the exclusion of 'other' race categories in the DYS, which was not necessary in the RYDS. The unique selection criteria resulted in a four percent loss of cases in the DYS.

5. The lower retention rate among Puerto Ricans in the sample is explained by the frequency of Puerto Rican adolescents moving out of the parental home, compared to African Americans and Whites. For more detailed information on this analysis of retention rates, see Krohn and Thornberry (1999).

6. Note that some items are reverse coded, so that higher values consistently indicate an increase in blocked opportunity (see Appendix A).

7. Ten percent of all RYDS cases earn a score of zero on STRAIN2, while 22 percent receive the same score on the simple disjunction measure (STRAIN). The primary difference in the size of the zero category is the value of one in STRAIN2; individuals who report money as important and report a 'B' grade average are assigned a strain value, since they report money is important yet lack full access to legitimate opportunity. In the simple strain measure, each item has a value of three and once subtracted results in zero.

8. Note that the RYDS index includes a specific question about the use of crack, which is combined with other hard drugs to produce an identical measure across sites.

9. For each of the delinquent peer items, it was necessary to recode 'don't know' responses. The number of recoded cases varies by item; the majority of items involve recoding 30 or less cases, with a maximum of 42 'don't know' responses for peer truancy.

10. Centering delinquent values (CDELVAL) does not affect the measure as an endogenous variable. Although the mean of the centered measure changes, its distribution does not; therefore, there are no anticipated problems with incorporating the centered measure into the structural equation model in LISREL.

11. To ensure consistent delinquency indices across sites, the current analysis replicates recoding procedures of the RYDS on DYS measures. To avoid problems with outliers, extreme values were truncated according to the following procedures. First, the frequencies of all delinquency items were reviewed. Variables which contain a maximum value which exceeds the second highest value by 200 percent were identified for recoding (17 of 32 delinquency items were identified). Second, extreme values were truncated by taking the square root of the distance between the two highest values, multiplying that by two, and adding the value to the second highest variable score. This recoding scheme for DYS delinquency items best approximates the RYDS coding convention and is based on the distance between the outlier and the second highest value, such that relative distance between the two highest values is maintained across measures. Across all delinquency indices a value of one was added prior to taking the logarithmic transformation, to avoid calculating the natural log of zero values.

12. Since the DYS conducts annual interviews, separate questions are included to capture family involvement during the school year and during the summer. The mean of the two items is taken to create an estimate of involvement in family activity throughout the year.

13. This argument may not be as relevant in 1998 as it had been in 1960, however, given female independence and presence in the workforce. The current analysis would address this crucial gender issue, however, the number of females across both sites is too small to permit such an inquiry at this time.

14. The following DYS variables contain missing data: Public assistance (n=6); self-reported grades (n=5); externalization of blame (n=2); challenge to legitimacy of conventional beliefs (n=1); access to drugs (n=1); student evaluation of neighborhood crime (n=3).

15. Among RYDS measures assessed at Time 1, substitution is necessary for five cases. Missing data from the wave 5 economic aspirations measure have been replaced with wave 4 data. For academic performance, substitution required self-reported grades from wave 4 (n=1), and when not available, information on student grades is also taken from parent interviews during Time 1 (n=3). Grade substitution results in one missing case, which affects both the grades measure and strain interaction terms. Due to missing information at wave 7, data from wave 6 are utilized for measures of the externalization of blame (n=11), conventional beliefs (n=3), delinquent values (n=5), peer delinquency (n=5), peer conventional values (n=12), neighborhood drug use (n=3), and student access to drugs (n=3).

CHAPTER 5

1. Variables which have been transformed for use in the LISREL analysis are not included in the descriptives table. Univariate and bivariate results of transformed variables are not vital to the current analysis of group means; therefore, a discussion of those measures will resume in the next chapter.

2. The number of White males in the DYS is relatively small compared to the number of Latinos and African Americans in the sample. In spite of variation in group size, findings are fairly consistent with those found in the RYDS.

3. Unless otherwise stated, statistical significance is achieved at p is less than or equal to .05 using a one-tail test. A one-tailed test of significance is appropriate, given the hypothesized differences between groups.

4. An analysis of strain differences by class was also conducted using a more comprehensive measure of social class as found in the RYDS. Recall the dichotomous measure captures those in the study who meet any of the following criteria: a.) receive public assistance, b.) principle wage earner in household is unemployed, or c.) household income falls below the poverty level. Compared to findings utilizing public assistance, ethnic differences in strain are found within both categories of the comprehensive class measure. Minority groups in the RYDS, regardless of class, have significantly higher levels of strain than Whites. African Americans and Latinos, however, do not significantly differ from each other. In this case, minority status appears to have an independent effect on strain.

5. Utilizing a comprehensive measure of class (available only in the RYDS), results are fairly consistent. Minority groups who do not qualify as lower class differ from Whites in academic performance. At the same time, however, a significant difference is found between lower class minority groups and Whites. Unfortunately, this finding cannot be replicated with DYS data.

6. Note that the direct relationship with strain is examined in this instance, although Figure 4a illustrates a relationship between class and both STREXTA and STREXTB, which represent the interaction between strain and the externalization of blame. Strain interaction terms are intended for use in the LISREL analyses, where they can be examined simultaneously in predicting the challenge to legitimacy. In the current section, the relationship between class and strain is examined generally, and the influence of class on the strain interaction terms is expected to be consistent in LISREL; regardless of the eventual source of blame, class should predict strain.

7. Note that the coefficient among Whites in the DYS does not achieve statistical significance (p=.066), perhaps because of the small sample size. However, the correlation coefficient is much higher than that of either minority group in the DYS.

8. The path leading to challenge in the strain model is not discussed in the current section. The theory asserts that the interaction between strain and the externalization of blame weakens the legitimacy of conventional beliefs. Given

the inclusion of interaction terms at this point in the model, this relationship cannot be fully explored using bivariate analyses. Although it is possible to examine the direct relationships between strain and challenge and the externalization of blame and challenge to legitimacy, those associations do not provide an accurate portrayal of strain theory hypotheses. Main effects of strain and externalization are not modeled by traditional strain theory, as neither one is expected to directly relate to challenge on its own. Instead, the *interaction* between strain and the externalization of blame is most crucial to the theory; therefore, bivariate relationships are not explored, and those concepts will be examined in LISREL.

9. Although correlation coefficients in the DYS are significant across both minority groups, the RYDS reveals a statistically significant impact among African Americans only. Note that the correlation coefficient among Latinos in the RYDS approaches significance (p=.107, one-tail test). Comparatively speaking, the influence of family among minority groups is substantively significant; coefficients among White males are much smaller in comparison (see Table 5d.).

10. Support for Hypothesis #13b is found among two of six delinquency indices, where the Latino peer influence is weaker than that of African Americans (drug use and serious delinquency indices). On general delinquency, alcohol use, and property crime indices, the Latino peer influence is stronger than African Americans.

11. The traditional strain theory model, as depicted in Figure 4a, includes a multiplicative interaction term between delinquent values and a measure of illegitimate opportunity (access to drugs). Although the causal model includes direct arrows between the root measures and delinquency, they are included solely as control variables in the LISREL analysis. Theoretically, there is no expectation main effects of delinquent values nor illegitimate opportunity; the measures are included to satisfy statistical requirements, and to allow for a comprehensive examination of the interaction term in structural equation modeling. Therefore, correlation coefficients between delinquent values and strain and access to drugs and strain are not discussed in the current chapter. An examination of the product term using bivariate analyses is also inappropriate for the current section; the complex set of relationships between delinquent values, illegitimate opportunity and delinquent outcomes will be explored in the following chapter.

12. The use of academic performance as an indicator of blocked opportunity has previously been discussed (Chapter 4). Self reported grades are included in the current analysis to serve as a proxy for educational expectations, which is most common in other evaluations of traditional strain theory. Had educational expectations been used in place of grades, the inconsistencies across strain measures might not exist. However, one might argue that the inclusion of educational expectations would produce similar findings, as it is subject to the

same primary shortcoming of academic performance: it does not provide a subjective interpretation of educational achievement on future economic success.

13. Given the difference in measures of class, the public assistance variable is utilized for the remainder of the analyses, since it is available in both sites. Also, the comprehensive measure did not perform substantially better than public assistance.

CHAPTER 6

1. This approach will provide a more parsimonious explanation of results; all relevant output statistics will be provided for all models, and the variation from the general delinquency model is presented. However, a detailed description of each would be lengthy and unnecessary, since the models are virtually identical (with the exception of pathway coefficients predicting each outcome).

2. Specific interpretation of the unstandardized coefficient is difficult, given the fact that delinquent values and illegitimate opportunity measures are scaled; each represents the mean of multiple items which range between one and four. In addition, given the natural logarithmic transformation of the dependent variable, interpretation of the coefficients and identifying the specific increase in delinquency is complex. Therefore, causal relationships are generally described.

3. Conditional effects are described, although the product term is non-significant. The literature on interaction terms suggests two approaches to handling non-significant interaction terms. First, a researcher might decide to omit the interaction in the face of non-significance to reduce error in the model. On the other hand, if the theory requires the inclusion of the product term, a researcher might decide to leave the term in the model, even if it does not significantly contribute to the explanation of delinquency (Aiken & West, 1991). In the current analysis, the interaction term is left in the model, since it is theoretically relevant. In addition, the conditional effects of delinquent values and illegitimate opportunity are interpreted, although they were not originally included in traditional strain theory.

4. Differences in fit indices between Table 6a and Table 6b cannot be compared, since they represent models tested with different matrices. The fit indices of the nested models are examined, however (the results of nested traditional model are not presented here), and indicate a good fit of both models. Findings also indicate that the model which estimates the additional relationships provides a slightly better fit to the data.

CHAPTER 7

1. For a more complete description of LISREL estimations, see Hayduk (1987).

2. Although the number of Latino males in the RYDS is smaller than other ethnic groups, reliable estimates can be generated, given the relative number of parameters estimated in the model. Bentler & Chou (1987) suggest an acceptable ration of cases to parameters fall between 5:1 and 10:1. In the traditional strain model 18 parameters are estimated; therefore, the size of the Latino population in the RYDS fits within this range.

3. Jaccard & Wan (1996) comment that the model must fit well at step 1 – the Chi-square statistic should be non-significant – to proceed to step 2. However, given the previous discussion of Chi-square and its link to sample size, other indicators of fit are examined as well. In addition, the primarily concern is the difference between models which estimate differences and those which assume consistency across groups. Therefore, measures of absolute fit are less important than results of comparisons across theoretical models.

4. An alternative strategy was also explored, where the difference between coefficients was assessed and findings described in terms of a percentage. This approach was employed to identify differences of fifty percent or larger. In computing percent differences, the same conclusions can be drawn for differences of .10 or larger (the same paths were identified for discussion).

5. The negative relationship between strain/internalization and challenge is described in Chapter 6. The finding suggests that males who experience strain and internalize blame for failure to achieve goals are *less* likely to withdraw legitimacy from conventional beliefs. In essence, they may experience a strengthening of conventional values. Those who externalize blame, on the other hand, do not experience such a re-affirmation of beliefs. This supports traditional strain theory assertions.

6. When all paths are allowed to vary, 15% of the variance in general delinquency is explained. This improves upon the explanatory value of Model 1, where only certain paths are allowed to vary (R^2=.07). This finding suggests that when all paths vary, greater variance in delinquency is explained among Latinos.

7. This finding is consistent in models predicting general delinquency, alcohol use, and violence in the RYDS.

CHAPTER 8

1. While the argument was made about Chicanos, or Mexican Americans, it may be extended to other Latino groups. The inclusion of multiple Latino groups in the study provides the opportunity to determine whether the applicability of strain is limited only among Mexican Americans or is consistent across groups.

2. To determine whether the weak influence of the product term is due to the inclusion of lower order effects, models were estimated without delinquent values or illegitimate opportunity. In estimating the model with the interaction term only, findings are relatively consistent. The product term is significantly related to violence in the DYS only.

3. The only item included in the analysis of identical measures which is not exact across sites is the externalization of blame. The dichotomous variable in the DYS is derived from a series of items in which students identify the source(s) of blocked legitimate opportunity for making money. In the RYDS, however, students are asked about sources of limited educational opportunity.

4. Throughout the chapter, several shortcomings with the measures are identified. Future research might include a more global and continuous measure of the externalization of blame. In addition, blocked opportunity should be assessed with measures other than academic performance, since the meaning of grades might vary by ethnicity.

Appendix A
Strain Measures

ACCEPTANCE OF ECONOMIC SUCCESS GOAL

DENVER YOUTH SURVEY
How important is it to you to have a great deal of money? Would you say it's...
1 Not Important at All
2 Not Too Important
3 Somewhat Important
4 Pretty Important
5 Very Important

ROCHESTER YOUTH DEVELOPMENT STUDY
How important is it to you to have a great deal of money someday? Would you say it's...
1 Not Important at All
2 Not Very Important
3 Important
4 Very Important

PERCEPTION OF BLOCKED OPPORTUNITY

DENVER YOUTH SURVEY
Which of the following best describes the grades you are getting in school?
0 Mostly F's
1 Mostly D's
2 Mostly C's
3 Mostly B's
4 Mostly A's

ROCHESTER YOUTH DEVELOPMENT STUDY

Looking at all your grades last Spring, would you say you were closest to a...

    0 F student
    1 D Student
    2 C Student
    3 B Student
    4 Straight A Student

BLOCKED OPPORTUNITY INDEX

DENVER YOUTH SURVEY

The next questions ask about how you feel about your opportunities to get ahead...

1. You probably won't be able to do the kind of work that you want to do because you won't have enough education.
2. A person like you has a pretty good chance of going to college.*
3. Most people are better off than you are.
4. You'll never have as much opportunity to succeed as kids from other neighborhoods.
5. You are as well off as most people.*
6. The world is usually good to people like you.*
7. Unless your family can afford to move out of your neighborhood, you won't get ahead very fast.
8. You won't be able to finish high school because your family will want you to get a job.
9. There is a good chance that some of your friends will have lots of money.*
10. Your family can't give you the opportunities that most kids have.
11. You'll never have enough money to go to college.
12. There isn't much chance that a kid from your neighborhood will ever get ahead.
13. If a kid like you works hard (he/she) can get ahead.*
14. Most successful people probably used illegal means to become successful.
15. When things are going badly, you know they won't be bad all the time.*
16. All you see ahead are bad things not good things.
17. As you get older, things will be better.*
18. You never get what you want so it's dumb to want anything.
19. You will have more good times than bad times.*
    1 Strongly Disagree
    2 Disagree
    3 Neither Agree nor Disagree
    4 Agree
    5 Strongly Agree

* Item reverse coded for index

Externalization of Blame Measures

DENVER YOUTH SURVEY

REASONS FOR NOT MAKING A LOT OF MONEY
Why do you think you will not have a lot of money when you grow up?[a]
1 Personal Limitations
2 Formal Training Limitations*
3 Family Limitations*
4 Formal Education Limitations*
5 Societal Limitations*
6 Don't Need Money
7 Won't Get a Good Job*
8 Money-related, Hard to Save Money

REASONS WHY MAKING A LOT OF MONEY WILL BE HARD
Why do you think it will be hard for you to have a lot of money?[a]
1 Personal Limitations
2 Education Limitations*
3 Competition with Others
4 Have to Work Hard
5 Societal Limitations*
6 Formal Training Limitations*

[a] Question Paraphrased
* Identified as an external source of blocked opportunity

ROCHESTER YOUTH DEVELOPMENT STUDY

REASONS FOR SCHOOL DROPOUT
We are interested in why you are no longer in school. Did you leave because...
1. You got bad grades in school?
2. Your teachers didn't like you?*
3. You didn't like the courses at school?*
4. You didn't like the school you were assigned to?*
5. You didn't like the teachers, principal or counselors?*
6. You didn't like the other students?*
7. You thought that school was a waste of time?
8. Your friends dropped out?*
9. Your parents didn't care or encouraged you to drop out?*
10. You needed to make money or get a job?
11. You left to get married?
12. You left to have a baby or to take care of a baby?
13. You left to join the armed forces?
14. You got in trouble with the law?
15. You got expelled, suspended or kicked out?
    1 Yes
    2 No

REASONS FOR NOT GRADUATING HIGH SCHOOL
Do you think you won't graduate from high school because...
1. You got bad grades?
2. You don't like the courses?*
3. You don't like the teachers, principal or counselors?*
4. Your teachers, principal or counselors don't like you?*
5. You plan to get a GED?
6. Your family doesn't encourage you to continue?*
7. You plan to join the armed forces?
8. You plan to get married or move in with your girlfriend/boyfriend?
9. You need to care for your child?
10. You got in trouble with the law?
11. You're just not interested in continuing with school?
    1 Yes
    2 No

REASONS FOR NOT ATTENDING COLLEGE
Do you think you won't go to college because...
1. You got bad grades?
2. You won't get financial aid or a scholarship?*
3. Your family won't encourage you to go?*
4. Your family won't be able to support you financially?*
5. You have enough schooling?
6. You need to make money or get a job?
7. You plan to join the armed forces?
8. Your friends aren't going to college?*
9. You plan to get married or move in with your girlfriend/boyfriend?
10. You need to care for your child?
11. You're going for other training or schooling (e.g. police, trade school, etc.)?
12. You got in trouble with the law?
13. You're just not interested in going to college or you think college is a waste of time?
   1 Yes
   2 No

REASONS FOR NOT COMPLETING COLLEGE
Does [graduation from college] depend on...
1. Your grades?
2. Getting into a certain school or program?*
3. Getting financial aid or a scholarship?*
4. Your family's encouragement?*
5. Getting a job?
6. Joining the armed forces?
7. What your friends do or say?*
8. Staying out of trouble with the law?
   1 Yes
   2 No

* Identified as an external source of blocked opportunity

Challenge of Legitimacy Measures

CONVENTIONAL BELIEFS

DENVER YOUTH SURVEY
The last questions are about the things you value in life. How important do you think the following things are? How important is it to...
1. Have a good reputation in the community?
2. Study hard for good grades?
3. Work hard to get ahead?
4. Save money for the future?
5. Have a college education?
6. Own your own home?
7. Have a good paying job?
8. Have a happy life?
9. Plan ahead?
10. Have self-control?
11. Be careful what you spend?

    1 Not Important at All
    2 Not Too Important
    3 Somewhat Important
    4 Pretty Important
    5 Very Important

ROCHESTER YOUTH DEVELOPMENT STUDY
Now, I'd like to ask you about different goals you have. How important is it to you...
1. To have a good reputation in the community?
2. To study hard for good grades?
3. To work hard to get ahead?
4. To save money for the future?

    1 Not Important at All
    2 Not Very Important
    3 Important
    4 Very Important

Appendix D
Delinquent Values Measures

DELINQUENT VALUES SCALE

DENVER YOUTH SURVEY
Tell me how wrong you think it is for someone your age to do each of the following things. How wrong is it to...
1. Skip school without an excuse?
2. Steal something worth $50?
3. Steal something worth $100?
4. Use alcohol?
5. Use marijuana?
6. Use hard drugs such as heroin, cocaine, crack, or LSD?
7. Purposely damage or destroy property that did not belong to them?
8. Go joyriding, that is, take a motor vehicle such as a car or motorcycle for a ride or drive without the owner's permission?
9. Use a weapon, force, or strongarm methods to get money or things from people?
10. Hit someone with the idea of hurting them?
11. Attack someone with a weapon or with the idea of seriously hurting them?
12. Lie, disobey or talk back to adults such as parents, teachers or others?
13. Steal something worth less than $5?
14. Go into or try to go into a building to steal something?
15. Sell hard drugs such as heroin, cocaine, crack, or LSD?
16. Use tobacco?
17. Have sexual intercourse before marriage?
18. Get pregnant (outside of marriage)?
19. Get a girl pregnant (outside of marriage)?
20. Hit your boy/girlfriend?
21. Have sex outside of marriage?
22. Cheat on taxes?
23. Hit your spouse/partner?
    1 Not Wrong at All
    2 A Little Bit Wrong
    3 Wrong
    4 Very Wrong

223

ROCHESTER YOUTH DEVELOPMENT STUDY

Next I'm going to read a list of things some people do. How wrong do you think it is to...

1. Skip classes without an excuse?
2. Steal something worth $50?
3. Steal something worth $100?
4. Drink alcohol?
5. Use marijuana, reefer or pot?
6. Use hard drugs such as crack, heroin, cocaine, LSD, or acid?
7. Damage or destroy someone else's property on purpose?
8. Take a car or motorcycle for a ride without the owner's permission?
9. Use a weapon or force to get money or things from people?
10. Hit someone with the idea of hurting them?
11. Attack someone with a weapon or with the idea of seriously hurting them?

    1 Not Wrong at All
    2 A Little Bit Wrong
    3 Wrong
    4 Very Wrong

Appendix E
Measures of Delinquent Peers

INVOLVEMENT WITH DELINQUENT PEERS

DENVER YOUTH SURVEY
How many of your friends...
1. Skipped school without an excuse?
2. Stolen something worth more than $5 but less than $100?
3. Stolen something worth more than $100?
4. Used alcohol?
5. Used marijuana?
6. Used hard drugs such as heroin, cocaine, crack, or LSD?
7. Purposely damaged or destroyed property that did not belong to them?
8. Taken a motor vehicle such as a car or motorcycle for a ride or drive without the owner's permission?
9. Used a weapon, force, or strongarm methods to get money or things from people?
10. Hit someone with the idea of seriously hurting them?
11. Attacked someone with a weapon or with the idea of seriously hurting them?
   1 None of Them
   2 Few of Them
   3 Half of Them
   4 Most of Them
   5 All of Them

ROCHESTER YOUTH DEVELOPMENT STUDY
How many friends...
1. Skipped school without an excuse?
2. Stole something worth more than $5 but less than $50?
3. Steal something worth more than $100?
4. Drank alcohol?

225

5. Used marijuana, reefer or pot?
6. Used hard drugs such as heroin, cocaine, LSD, or acid?
7. Used crack?
8. Damaged or destroyed someone else's property on purpose?
9. Took a car or motorcycle for a ride or drive without the owner's permission?
10. Used a weapon or force to get money or things from people?
11. Hit someone with the idea of hurting them?
12. Attacked someone with a weapon or with the idea of seriously hurting them?
    1 None of Them
    2 A Few of Them
    3 Some of Them
    4 Most of Them

Illegitimate Opportunity

ACCESS TO ALCOHOL AND DRUGS

DENVER YOUTH SURVEY
How easy would it be for you to get _____ or have someone get it for you?
1. Alcohol
2. Marijuana
3. Illegal drugs
    1 Very Difficult
    2 Difficult
    3 Easy
    4 Very Easy

ROCHESTER YOUTH DEVELOPMENT STUDY
How easy would it be for you to buy _____ or to have someone buy it for you?
1. Alcohol
2. Marijuana, reefer or pot
3. Other illegal drugs
    1 Very Difficult
    2 Difficult
    3 Easy
    4 Very Easy

Self Reported Delinquency

DELINQUENCY INDICES

GENERAL DELINQUENCY

Have you...
1. Run away from home?
2. Skipped classes without an excuse?
3. Lied about your age to get into some place or to buy something?
4. Hitchhiked a ride with a stranger?
5. Carried a hidden weapon?
6. Been loud or rowdy in a public place where someone complained and you got in trouble?
7. Begged for money or things from strangers?
8. Been drunk in a public place?
9. Damaged, destroyed, marked up, or tagged somebody else's property on purpose?
10. Set fire on purpose or tried to set fire to a house, building, or car?
11. Avoided paying for things, like a movie, taking bus rides, using a computer, or anything else?
12. Gone into or tried to go into a building to steal or damage something?
13. Tried to steal or actually stolen money or things worth $5 or less?
14. Tried to steal or actually stolen money or things worth between $5-$50?
15. Tried to steal or actually stolen money or things worth between $50-$100?
16. Tried to steal or actually stolen money or things worth more than $100?
17. Tried to buy or sell things that were stolen?
18. Taken someone else's car or motorcycle for a ride without the owner's permission?
19. Stolen or tried to steal a car or other motor vehicle?
20. Forged a check or used fake money to pay for something?
21. Used or tried to use a credit card, bank card, or automatic teller card without permission?

22. Tried to cheat someone by selling them something that was not what you said it was or that was worthless?
23. Attacked someone with a weapon or with the idea of seriously hurting or killing them?
24. Hit someone with the idea of hurting them?
25. Been involved in gang or posse fights?
26. Thrown objects such as rocks or bottles at people?
27. Used a weapon or force to make someone give you money or things?
28. Made obscene phone calls?
29. Been paid for having sexual relations with someone?
30. Physically hurt or threatened to hurt someone to get them to have sex with you?
31. Sold marijuana, reefer or pot?
32. Sold hard drugs such as crack, heroin, cocaine, LSD, or acid?

ALCOHOL USE
Have you...
1. Drunk beer or wine without your parents permission?
2. Drunk hard liquor without your parents permission?

DRUG USE
Have you...
1. Used marijuana, reefer or pot?
2. Inhaled things, other than cigarettes, like glue to get high?
3. Tried LSD, acid, or cubes?
4. Tried cocaine, coke or snow, other than crack?
5. Tried crack?
6. Tried heroin or smack?
7. Tried angel dust or PCP?
8. Tried tranquilizers, ludes or Valium?
9. Tried downers, yellow jackets or red or blue devils?
10. Tried uppers, speed bennies or black beauties?

PROPERTY CRIME
Have you...
1. Avoided paying for things, like a movie, taking bus rides, using a computer, or anything else?
2. Gone into or tried to go into a building to steal or damage something?
3. Tried to steal or actually stolen money or things worth $5 or less?
4. Tried to steal or actually stolen money or things worth between $5-$50?
5. Tried to steal or actually stolen money or things worth between $50-$100?

6. Tried to steal or actually stolen money or things worth more than $100?
7. Tried to buy or sell things that were stolen?
8. Taken someone else's car or motorcycle for a ride without the owner's permission?
9. Stolen or tried to steal a car or other motor vehicle?
10. Forged a check or used fake money to pay for something?
11. Used or tried to use a credit card, bank card, or automatic teller card without permission?
12. Tried to cheat someone by selling them something that was not what you said it was or that was worthless?

VIOLENCE

Have you...
1. Attacked someone with a weapon or with the idea of seriously hurting or killing them?
2. Hit someone with the idea of hurting them?
3. Been involved in gang or posse fights?
4. Thrown objects such as rocks or bottles at people?
5. Used a weapon or force to make someone give you money or things?
6. Physically hurt or threatened to hurt someone to get them to have sex with you?

Correlation Matrices by Site and Ethnicity

Denver Youth Survey, Latino Males (n=161)

Time 1 & Time 2 Variables

	1	2	3	4	5	6	7	8	9	10	11	12	13	14	15	16	17
Demographics																	
1. Public Assistance	1.00																
Time 1																	
2. Aspirations	-.09	1.00															
3. Self-Reported Grades	-.06	.03	1.00														
4. Strain Disjunction	-.01	.47*	-.82*	1.00													
5. Blocked Opportunity	.26*	.03	-.27*	.21*	1.00												
Time 2																	
6. Externalize Blame	.16*	-.07	-.07	.05	.07	1.00											
7. Strain/Externalize	.19*	.16*	-.42*	.49*	.17*	.68*	1.00										
8. Strain/Internalize	-.18*	.36*	-.50*	.63*	.07	-.55*	-.37*	1.00									
9. Challenge Legitimacy	.07	-.31*	-.02	-.15*	.16*	.18*	.11	-.26*	1.00								
10.Challenge Legitimacy 2	.02	-.33	-.01	-.18	.15*	.17*	.08	-.26*	.92*	1.00							
11. Delinquent Values	.03	.10	-.12	.14*	.11	.12	.19*	-.01	.29*	.25*	1.00						
12. Delinquent Values 2	.04	.11	-.16*	.18*	.13	.11	.19*	.02	.27*	.25*	.95*	1.00					
13. Delinquent Peers	.10	.09	-.25*	.28*	.11	.07	.27*	.06	.01	-.01	.41*	.43*	1.00				
14. Access to Drugs	-.17*	.06	-.02	.08	-.13*	.00	.08	.01	-.04	-.06	.39*	.42*	.46*	1.00			
15. Del. Values/Access	.03	.03	-.09	.08	.07	.04	.05	.04	-.04	-.07	.28*	.27*	.23*	-.01	1.00		
16. Del. Values/Access	.05	.02	-.11	.10	.06	.05	.07	.05	-.04	-.07	.26*	.25*	.23*	-.01	.96*	1.00	
17. Family Involvement	.05	-.18*	.13	-.18*	-.15*	-.05	-.15*	-.06	-.02	-.01	-.25*	-.27*	-.22*	-.24*	-.11	-.07	1.00

*p < .05 (one-tail test)

Denver Youth Survey, Latino Males (n=161)

Time 2 & Time 3 Variables

	General Delinquency	Alcohol Use	Drug Use	Property Crime	Violent Crime
Time 2					
Externalization of Blame	.16*	.15*	.10	.05	.10
Strain/Externalization	.24*	.13*	.09	.07	.16*
Strain/Internalization	-.17*	-.13*	-.16*	-.13	-.13
Challenge Legitimacy of Norms	.11	.13*	.03	.07	.00
Challenge Legitimacy of Norms 2	.09	.15*	-.02	.06	.01
Delinquent Values	.24*	.29*	.22*	.23*	.23*
Delinquent Values 2	.19*	.25*	.17*	.18*	.18*
Delinquent Peers	.31*	.14*	.27*	.32*	.30
Access to Drugs	.42*	.30*	.30*	.27*	.28*
Delinquent Values/Drug Access	-.02	.06	.12	.10	.11
Delinquent Values/Drug Access 2	-.05	.03	.08	.08	.07
Family Involvement	-.09	-.13	.10	-.10	-.06
Time 3					
General Delinquency	1.00	.53*	.44*	.60*	.55*
Alcohol Use		1.00	.40*	.33*	.35*
Drug Use			1.00	.29*	.34*
Property Crime				1.00	.52*
Violent Crime					1.00

*p <.05 (one-tail test)

Denver Youth Survey, White Males (n=30)

Time 1 & Time 2 Variables

	1	2	3	4	5	6	7	8	9	10	11	12	13	14	15	16	17
Demographics																	
1. Public Assistance	1.00																
Time 1																	
2. Aspirations	.28	1.00															
3. Self-Reported Grades	-.28	-.32*	1.00														
4. Strain Disjunction	.37*	.64*	-.76*	1.00													
5. Blocked Opportunity	.33*	.11	-.28	.20	1.00												
Time 2																	
6. Externalize Blame	-.01	.10	-.35*	.22	.01	1.00											
7. Strain/Externalize	.24	.32*	-.34*	.46*	-.19	.75*	1.00										
8. Strain/Internalize	.23	.47*	-.57*	.75*	.35*	-.32*	-.24	1.00									
9. Challenge Legitimacy	-.14	-.31*	.03	-.09	-.27	-.00	.01	-.10	1.00								
10.Challenge Legitimacy 2	-.16	-.41*	-.03	-.11	-.12	-.01	-.10	-.05	.93	1.00							
11. Delinquent Values	-.16	-.22	-.16	.15	-.15	.16	.13	.07	.41*	.50*	1.00						
12. Delinquent Values 2	-.14	-.22	-.17	.17	-.18	.13	.13	.08	.42*	.50*	.97*	1.00					
13. Delinquent Peers	.04	-.24	-.11	-.05	-.14	.21	.24	-.12	.19	.30*	.68*	.73*	1.00				
14. Access to Drugs	.03	-.27	.07	-.23	-.32*	.03	.02	-.27	-.08	-.07	.18	.25	.50*	1.00			
15. Del.Values/Access	.03	.19	.10	.16	.10	.20	.31*	-.05	-.36	-.41	-.26	-.22	.06	-.04	1.00		
16. Del. Values/Access	.00	.25	.13	.13	.16	.19	.31*	-.10	-.43*	-.48*	-.25	-.25	.01	-.10	.96*	1.00	
17. Family Involvement	-.01	.14	.27	-.03	-.07	.02	.13	.13	-.07	-.19	-.08	-.10	-.12	.00	.48*	.46*	1.00

*p <.05 (one-tail test)

Denver Youth Survey, White Males (n=30)

Time 2 & Time 3 Variables

	General Delinquency	Alcohol Use	Drug Use	Property Crime	Violent Crime
Time 2					
Externalization of Blame	.24	-.00	.29	.08	.72*
Strain/Externalization	.15	.04	.10	.20	.68*
Strain/Internalization	-.15	-.08	-.17	-.26	.08
Challenge Legitimacy of Norms	.19	-.06	-.07	-.04	-.04
Challenge Legitimacy of Norms 2	.20	-.04	.04	.02	-.06
Delinquent Values	.45*	.37*	.47*	.38*	.39*
Delinquent Values 2	.50*	.45*	.52*	.44*	.38*
Delinquent Peers	.58*	.47*	.52*	.63*	.54*
Access to Drugs	.40*	.62*	.60*	.27	.38*
Delinquent Values/Drug Access	.06	.15	.27	.19	.06
Delinquent Values/Drug Access 2	-.04	.11	.21	.16	.03
Family Involvement	.03	-.06	.20	.20	.07
Time 3					
General Delinquency	1.00	.53*	.55*	.49*	.32*
Alcohol Use		1.00	.68*	.28	.23
Drug Use			1.00	.30*	.41
Property Crime				1.00	.28
Violent Crime					1.00

*p <.05 (one-tail test)

Denver Youth Survey, African American Males (n=132)

Time 1 & Time 2 Variables

	1	2	3	4	5	6	7	8	9	10	11	12	13	14	15	16	17
Demographics																	
1. Public Assistance	1.00	.19*	-.06	.19*	.21*	.07	.17*	.05	.09	.04	.05	.07	.08	-.05	.02	.02	.15*
Time 1																	
2. Aspirations		1.00	-.05	.58*	-.01	-.04	.16*	.44*	-.25	-.33*	.03	-.02	.10	.03	-.03	-.01	-.08
3. Self-Reported Grades			1.00	-.80*	-.14	-.15*	-.34*	-.51*	.13	.18*	-.12	-.15*	-.14*	-.15*	-.05	-.04	.06
4. Strain Disjunction				1.00	.18*	.12	.38*	.69*	-.18*	-.28*	.16*	.16*	.20*	.12	-.01	-.02	-.13
5. Blocked Opportunity					1.00	.24*	.27*	-.04	.04	.01	.26*	.30*	.20*	-.13	.20*	.17*	-.28*
Time 2																	
6. Externalize Blame						1.00	.80*	-.52*	-.12	-.05	.10	.12	.09	.10	-.15*	-.13	-.11
7. Strain/Externalize							1.00	-.42*	-.21*	-.17	.11	.08	.09	.06	-.15*	-.17*	-.12
8. Strain/Internalize								1.00	-.01	-.14	.07	.10	.13	.08	.10	.11	-.03
9. Challenge Legitimacy									1.00	.91*	.29*	.37*	.14	.11	-.06	-.06	-.07
10.Challenge Legitimacy 2										1.00	.26*	.32*	.13	.03	-.09	-.08	-.09
11. Delinquent Values											1.00	.95*	.52*	.29*	.17*	.10	-.22*
12. Delinquent Values 2												1.00	.54*	.31*	.09	.06	-.20*
13. Delinquent Peers													1.00	.51*	.18*	.19*	-.09
14. Access to Drugs														1.00	-.09	-.07	-.03
15. Del.Values/Access															1.00	.95*	-.06
16. Del. Values/Access																1.00	-.05
17. Family Involvement																	1.00

*p <.05 (one-tail test)

Denver Youth Survey, African American Males (n=132)

Time 2 & Time 3 Variables

	General Delinquency	Alcohol Use	Drug Use	Property Crime	Violent Crime
Time 2					
Externalization of Blame	.15*	.12	.03	.13	.05
Strain/Externalization	.16*	.02	.00	.05	.00
Strain/Internalization	-.01	-.03	.20*	.04	.10
Challenge Legitimacy of Norms	.11	-.05	-.04	.22*	.10
Challenge Legitimacy of Norms 2	.05	-.03	-.06	.21*	.04
Delinquent Values	.28*	.32*	.31*	.17*	.29*
Delinquent Values 2	.27*	.31*	.27*	.21*	.29*
Delinquent Peers	.53*	.55*	.46*	.28*	.50*
Access to Drugs	.47*	.44*	.32*	.31*	.36*
Delinquent Values/Drug Access	.15*	.16*	.16*	.09	.27*
Delinquent Values/Drug Access 2	.11	.17*	.16*	.07	.26*
Family Involvement	-.06	-.14*	-.08	-.17*	.02
Time 3					
General Delinquency	1.00	.60*	.44*	.48*	.60*
Alcohol Use		1.00	.58*	.19*	.46*
Drug Use			1.00	.11	.28*
Property Crime				1.00	.23*
Violent Crime					1.00

*p < .05 (one-tail test)

Rochester Youth Development Study, Latino Males (n=91)

Time 1 & Time 2 Variables

	1	2	3	4	5	6	7	8	9	10	11	12	13	14	15
Demographics															
1. Public Assistance	1.00														
2. Lower Class	.82*	1.00													
Time 1															
3. Aspirations	-.09	-.04	1.00												
4. Self-Reported Grades	-.12	-.17	-.06	1.00											
5. Strain Disjunction	.04	.14	.55*	-.84*	1.00										
Time 2															
6. Externalize Blame	.15	.22*	.12	-.37*	.38*	1.00									
7. Strain/Externalize	.05	.18*	.29*	-.58*	.66*	.83*	1.00								
8. Strain/Internalize	-.02	-.07	.26*	-.21*	.29*	-.63*	-.53*	1.00							
9. Challenge Legitimacy of Norms	.01	.02	-.30*	-.18*	.00	.12	.09	-.11	1.00						
10. Delinquent Values	.15	.16	-.11	-.13	.05	.27*	.20*	-.19*	.40*	1.00					
11. Delinquent Peers	.12	.16	-.01	-.11	.08	.20*	.13	-.07	.17	.49*	1.00				
12. Access to Drugs	-.13	-.15	.03	-.03	.03	.10	.05	-.04	.06	.32*	.26*	1.00			
13. Del.Values/Access Drugs	.43*	.45*	-.08	.02	-.04	.16	.01	-.05	-.09	.23*	.12	-.36*	1.00		
14. Family Involvement	-.19*	-.07	-.04	.19*	-.16	-.10	-.10	-.05	-.18*	-.13	-.11	-.03	-.09	1.00	
15. Parent Spanish Interview	.30*	.41*	-.05	-.05	.06	-.16	-.11	.20	-.05	.01	-.20*	.19*	-.10	-.10	1.00

*p <.05 (one-tail test)

Rochester Youth Development Study, Latino Males (n=91)

Time 2 and Time 3 Variables

	General Delinquency	Alcohol Use	Drug Use	Property Crime	Violent Crime
Time 2					
Externalization of Blame	.11	.20*	.33*	.15	.03
Strain/Externalization	.17	.26*	.41*	.25*	.04
Strain/Internalization	-.08	-.18*	-.19*	-.07	-.04
Challenge Legitimacy of Norms	.03	.01	.03	.09	-.00
Delinquent Values	.25*	.42*	.27*	.13	.25*
Delinquent Peers	.46*	.36*	.29*	.27*	.31*
Access to Drugs	.17*	.37*	.15	.19*	.19*
Delinquent Values/Drug Access	.10	.11	.06	-.08	.14
Family Involvement	-.05	.06	-.05	-.02	.00
Parent Completed Spanish Interview	.01	-.07	-.15	-.12	.14
Time 3					
General Delinquency	1.00	.53*	.47*	.66*	.64*
Alcohol Use		1.00	.54*	.37*	.43*
Drug Use			1.00	.56*	.39*
Property Crime				1.00	.41*
Violent Crime					1.00

*p < .05 (one-tail test)

Rochester Youth Development Study, White Males (n=172)

Time 1 & Time 2 Variables

	1	2	3	4	5	6	7	8	9	10	11	12	13	14
Demographics														
1. Public Assistance	1.00													
2. Lower Class	.79*	1.00												
Time 1														
3. Aspirations	.08	.05	1.00											
4. Self-Reported Grades	-.19*	-.07	-.06	1.00										
5. Strain Disjunction	.20*	.08	.62*	-.75*	1.00									
Time 2														
6. Externalize Blame	.16*	.05	.07	-.27*	.21	1.00								
7. Strain/Externalize	.02	-.04	.24*	-.50*	.56*	.73*	1.00							
8. Strain/Internalize	.20*	.14*	.46*	-.35*	.58*	-.48*	-.35*	1.00						
9. Challenge Legitimacy of Norms	-.12	-.12	-.30*	.01	-.22	.19*	.12	-.36*	1.00					
10. Delinquent Values	.05	-.07	.04	-.13*	.11	.34*	.33*	-.20*	.46*	1.00				
11. Delinquent Peers	-.10	-.05	-.02	-.22*	.17*	.29*	.42*	-.22*	.39*	.51*	1.00			
12. Access to Drugs	.07	-.06	-.05	-.20*	.14*	.23*	.26*	-.10	.18*	.33*	.40*	1.00		
13. Del.Values/Access Drugs	-.16*	-.08	.18*	.02	.10	.12	.16*	-.05	-.09	-.22*	-.05	-.23*	1.00	
14. Family Involvement	-.02	-.05	-.00	.08	-.11	-.02	-.06	-.06	-.08	-.08	-.18	-.09	.17*	1.00

*p < .05 (one-tail test)

Rochester Youth Development Study, White Males (n=172)

Time 2 and Time 3 Variables

	General Delinquency	Alcohol Use	Drug Use	Property Crime	Violent Crime
Time 2					
Externalization of Blame	.37*	.35*	.43*	.24*	.36*
Strain/Externalization	.42*	.31*	.52*	.47*	.37*
Strain/Internalization	-.22*	-.22*	-.26*	-.19*	-.16*
Challenge Legitimacy of Norms	.10	.14*	.19*	.18*	.10
Delinquent Values	.44*	.39*	.36*	.36*	.29*
Delinquent Peers	.46*	.37*	.53*	.51*	.36*
Access to Drugs	.28*	.20*	.32*	.23*	.18*
Delinquent Values/Drug Access	.04	.04	.05	.07	.02
Family Involvement	-.05	.16*	-.10	-.23*	-.04
Time 3					
General Delinquency	1.00	.47*	.59*	.50*	.58*
Alcohol Use		1.00	.56*	.32*	.26*
Drug Use			1.00	.51*	.42*
Property Crime				1.00	.31*
Violent Crime					1.00

*p < .05 (one-tail test)

Rochester Youth Development Study, African American Males (n=309)

Time 1 & Time 2 Variables

	1	2	3	4	5	6	7	8	9	10	11	12	13	14
Demographics														
1. Public Assistance	1.00													
2. Lower Class	.83*	1.00												
Time 1														
3. Aspirations	-.03	-.02	1.00											
4. Self-Reported Grades	-.08	-.09	.01	1.00										
5. Strain Disjunction	.05	.05	.60*	-.77*	1.00									
Time 2														
6. Externalize Blame	.22*	.20*	-.01	-.11*	.08	1.00								
7. Strain/Externalize	.20*	.17*	.09	-.23*	.24*	.88*	1.00							
8. Strain/Internalize	-.09*	-.07	.48*	-.54*	.73*	-.54*	-.48*	1.00						
9. Challenge Legitimacy of Norms	.08	.07	-.34*	-.03	-.18*	.07	.01	-.17*	1.00					
10. Delinquent Values	.12*	.05	-.16*	-.06	-.05	.14*	.10*	-.12*	.30*	1.00				
11. Delinquent Peers	-.04	-.09*	-.07	-.06	.02	-.03	.00	.01	.08	.36*	1.00			
12. Access to Drugs	-.15*	-.13*	-.03	-.08	.05	-.05	.01	.04	-.01	.22*	.32*	1.00		
13. Del.Values/Access Drugs	.16*	.12*	.03	.02	.00	.03	.05	-.03	.01	.22*	.09	-.40*	1.00	
14. Family Involvement	.02	.03	.09	.06	-.02	-.15*	-.17*	.11*	-.24*	-.13*	-.12*	-.09	.03	1.00

*p <.05 (one-tail test)

Rochester Youth Development Study, African American Males (n=309)

Time 2 and Time 3 Variables

	General Delinquency	Alcohol Use	Drug Use	Property Crime	Violent Crime
Time 2					
Externalization of Blame	.08	.12*	.10*	-.00	.01
Strain/Externalization	.05	.10*	.10*	-.00	-.01
Strain/Internalization	.04	.13*	.10*	.11*	.01
Challenge Legitimacy of Norms	.07	.09	.06	.06	.03
Delinquent Values	.29*	.32*	.29*	.17*	.27*
Delinquent Peers	.37*	.30*	.32*	.17*	.35*
Access to Drugs	.23*	.26*	.19*	.09*	.18*
Delinquent Values/Drug Access	.03	-.03	.06	.01	.07
Family Involvement	-.16*	-.09*	-.10*	.01	-.12*
Time 3					
General Delinquency	1.00	.50*	.46*	.45*	.63*
Alcohol Use		1.00	.69*	.23*	.38*
Drug Use			1.00	.20*	.35*
Property Crime				1.00	.40*
Violent Crime					1.00

*p <.05 (one-tail test)

Causal Models Estimated in LISREL With Total Male Samples

Estimating the Traditional Strain Model with the Total Male Samples

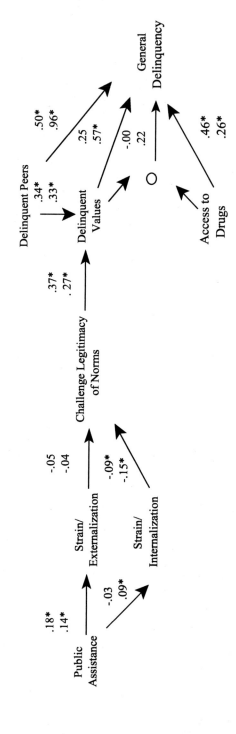

Note: DYS coefficients listed above RYDS estimate
*p<.05 (one-tail test)

Estimating the **Traditional Strain Model** with the Total Male Samples (cont.)

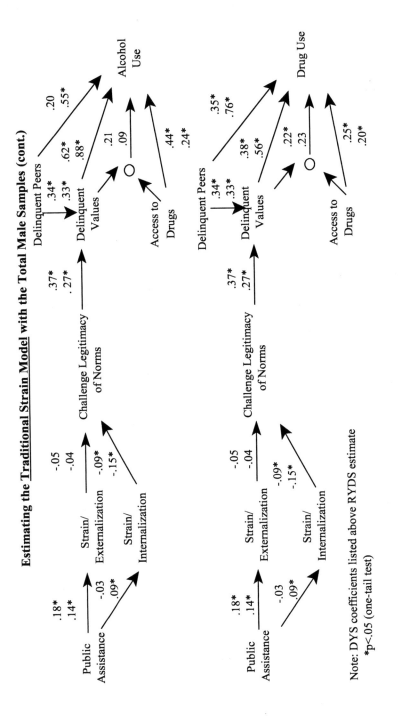

Note: DYS coefficients listed above RYDS estimate
*p<.05 (one-tail test)

Estimating the Traditional Strain Model with the Total Male Samples (cont.)

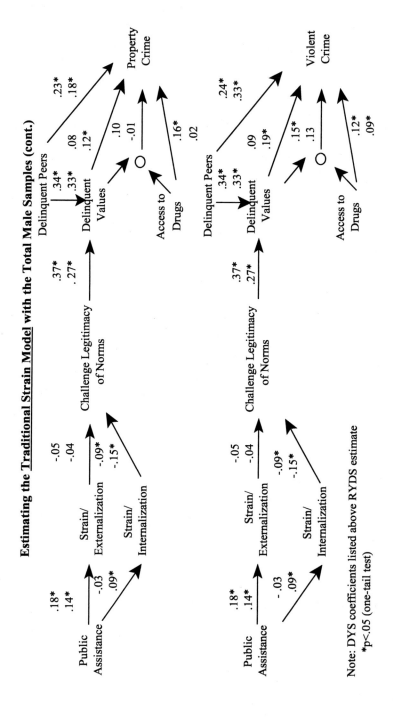

Note: DYS coefficients listed above RYDS estimate

*p<.05 (one-tail test)

Estimating the Modified Strain Model with the Total Male Samples

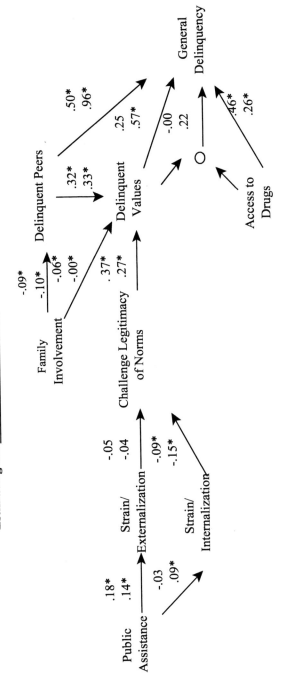

Note: DYS coefficients listed above RYDS estimate
  *p<.05 (one-tail test)

Estimating the Modified Strain Model with the Total Male Samples (cont.)

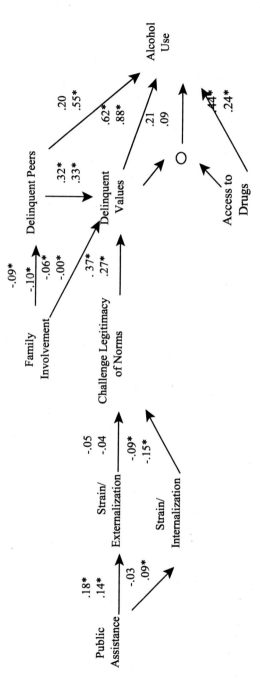

Note: DYS coefficients listed above RYDS estimate
*p<.05 (one-tail test)

Estimating the Modified Strain Model with the Total Male Samples (cont.)

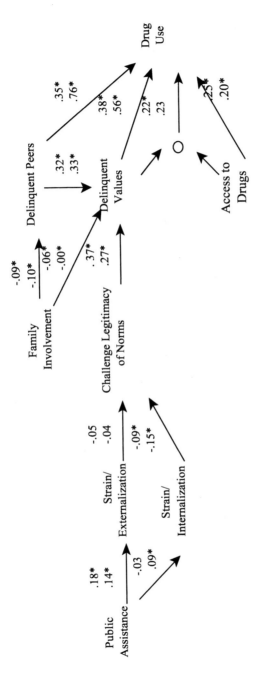

Note: DYS coefficients listed above RYDS estimate

*p<.05 (one-tail test)

Estimating the Modified Strain Model with the Total Male Samples (cont.)

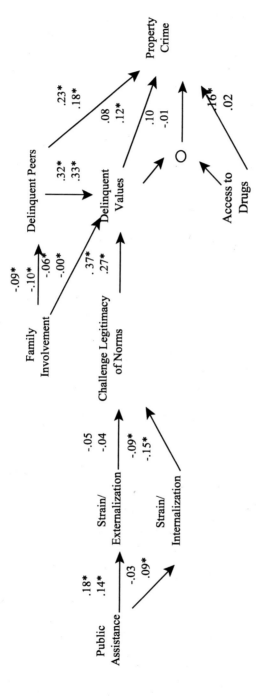

Note: DYS coefficients listed above RYDS estimate
*p<.05 (one-tail test)

Estimating the Modified Strain Model with the Total Male Samples (cont.)

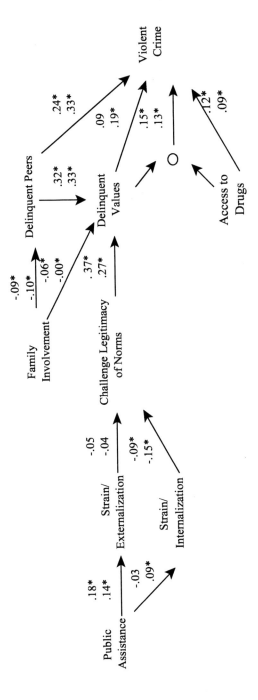

Note: DYS coefficients listed above RYDS estimate

*p<.05 (one-tail test)

Estimating the Traditional Strain Model with <u>Site-Specific Measures</u>, Total Male Sample

Denver Youth Survey

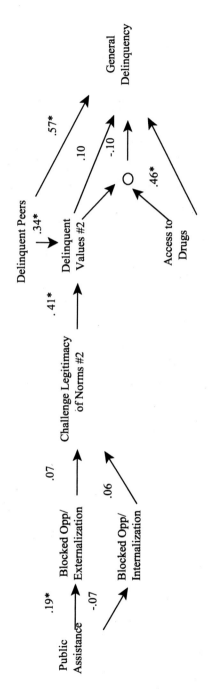

*p<.05 (one-tail test)

Estimating the Traditional Strain Model with <u>Site-Specific Measures</u>, Total Male Sample (cont.)

Rochester Youth Development Study

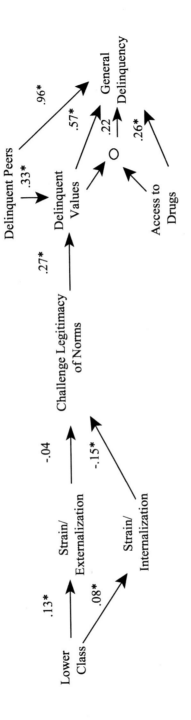

*p<.05 (one-tail test)

Covariance Matrices Used to Estimate Traditional Strain Theory

DENVER YOUTH SURVEY
TOTAL MALE SAMPLE (N=323)

	GENIL	ALCIL	DRUIL	PROIL2	PERIL
GENIL	2.628				
ALCIL	1.582	3.161			
DRUIL	1.007	1.244	2.009		
PROIL2	0.770	0.433	0.283	0.824	
PERIL	0.627	0.471	0.308	0.236	0.495
PUBASST	-0.045	-0.193	0.016	-0.024	0.048
STREXT	0.226	0.098	0.049	0.044	0.060
STRINT	-0.139	-0.134	-0.028	-0.036	-0.017
BKOPEXT	0.166	0.136	0.084	0.034	0.039
BKOPINT	-0.204	-0.129	-0.092	-0.012	-0.040
CHLEGIT	0.066	0.033	-0.001	0.037	0.008
CHLEGIT2	0.034	0.044	-0.010	0.029	0.003
CDELVAL	0.239	0.306	0.225	0.097	0.096
CDELVAL2	0.203	0.274	0.188	0.086	0.083
CDRUGACC	0.761	0.696	0.473	0.285	0.244
CDELXILL	0.043	0.111	0.121	0.055	0.073
CDL2XILL	0.008	0.090	0.095	0.037	0.058
PEERDELD	0.451	0.381	0.340	0.194	0.189
CFAMINV	-0.156	-0.285	0.064	-0.135	-0.021

	PUBASST	STREXT	STRINT	BKOPEXT	BKOPINT	CHLEGIT
PUBASST	1.000					
STREXT	0.179	0.492				
STRINT	-0.033	-0.221	0.708			
BKOPEXT	0.138	0.330	-0.254	0.414		
BKOPINT	0.052	-0.262	0.268	-0.301	0.502	
CHLEGIT	0.022	-0.005	-0.052	0.005	0.015	0.163
CHLEGIT2	-0.002	-0.008	-0.060	0.008	0.007	0.131
CDELVAL	0.003	0.054	0.006	0.036	-0.001	0.067
CDELVAL2	0.014	0.049	0.019	0.038	0.000	0.067
CDRUGACC	-0.108	0.052	0.038	0.011	-0.125	-0.004
CDELXILL	0.026	-0.005	0.034	-0.005	0.060	-0.018
CDL2XILL	0.027	-0.004	0.033	-0.002	0.049	-0.018
PEERDELD	0.088	0.099	0.048	0.044	-0.007	0.018
CFAMINV	0.131	-0.101	-0.051	-0.055	-0.036	-0.017

	CHLEGIT2	CDELVAL	CDELVAL2	CDRUGACC	CDELXILL	CDL2XILL
CHLEGIT2	0.124					
CDELVAL	0.055	0.296				
CDELVAL2	0.055	0.264	0.262			
CDRUGACC	-0.020	0.174	0.183	1.171		
CDELXILL	-0.022	0.053	0.039	-0.025	0.350	
CDL2XILL	-0.021	0.039	0.032	-0.024	0.314	0.311
PEERDELD	0.013	0.170	0.169	0.361	0.084	0.080
CFAMINV	-0.018	-0.146	-0.138	-0.182	-0.024	-0.009

	PEERDELD	CFAMINV
PEERDELD	0.485	
CFAMINV	-0.139	1.532

DENVER YOUTH SURVEY
LATINO MALES (N=161)

	GENIL	ALCIL	DRUIL	PROIL2	PERIL
ALCIL	1.712	3.315			
DRUIL	1.182	1.016	2.091		
PROIL2	0.975	0.677	0.414	0.954	
PERIL	0.727	0.481	0.395	0.391	0.587
PUBASST	0.009	-0.110	0.124	-0.040	0.007
STREXT	0.319	0.190	0.118	0.059	0.093
STRINT	-0.234	-0.187	-0.201	-0.096	-0.081
BKOPEXT	0.206	0.215	0.151	0.029	0.049
BKOPINT	-0.150	-0.115	-0.122	0.016	-0.067
CHLEGIT	0.077	0.097	0.028	0.034	0.001
CHLEGIT2	0.051	0.097	-0.008	0.028	0.002
CDELVAL	0.227	0.270	0.171	0.144	0.095
CDELVAL2	0.163	0.218	0.124	0.111	0.069
CDRUGACC	0.740	0.620	0.513	0.314	0.224
CDELXILL	-0.012	0.057	0.109	0.089	0.053
CDL2XILL	-0.048	0.019	0.070	0.064	0.031
PEERDELD	0.447	0.224	0.315	0.256	0.182
CFAMINV	-0.127	-0.259	0.159	-0.156	-0.046

	PUBASST	STREXT	STRINT	BKOPEXT	BKOPINT	CHLEGIT
PUBASST	1.000					
STREXT	0.185	0.585				
STRINT	-0.177	-0.248	0.706			
BKOPEXT	0.186	0.359	-0.286	0.453		
BKOPINT	-0.044	-0.309	0.314	-0.356	0.514	
CHLEGIT	0.023	0.036	-0.081	0.040	-0.003	0.175
CHLEGIT2	0.001	0.021	-0.067	0.029	0.002	0.150
CDELVAL	0.030	0.077	-0.012	0.041	-0.025	0.064
CDELVAL2	0.037	0.074	0.005	0.038	-0.020	0.055

	PUBASST	STREXT	STRINT	BKOPEXT	BKOPINT	CHLEGIT
CDRUGACC	-0.199	0.073	0.014	-0.007	-0.076	-0.018
CDELXILL	-0.010	0.011	0.028	0.006	0.012	-0.019
CDL2XILL	0.003	0.018	0.030	0.007	0.003	-0.018
PEERDELD	0.110	0.164	0.044	0.051	-0.017	0.018
CFAMINV	0.076	-0.122	-0.058	0.000	-0.044	0.004

	CHLEGIT2	CDELVAL	CDELVAL2	CDRUGACC	CDELXILL	CDL2XILL
CHLEGIT2	0.127					
CDELVAL	0.046	0.287				
CDELVAL2	0.041	0.252	0.247			
CDRUGACC	-0.026	0.224	0.224	1.150		
CDELXILL	-0.020	0.089	0.077	0.013	0.329	
CDL2XILL	-0.019	0.077	0.070	0.010	0.295	0.291
PEERDELD	0.007	0.172	0.171	0.410	0.113	0.107
CFAMINV	0.012	-0.152	-0.146	-0.305	-0.072	-0.043

	PEERDELD	CFAMINV
PEERDELD	0.612	
CFAMINV	-0.206	1.489

DENVER YOUTH SURVEY
AFRICAN AMERICAN MALES (N=132)

	GENIL	ALCIL	DRUIL	PROIL2	PERIL
GENIL	2.335				
ALCIL	1.613	3.118			
DRUIL	0.887	1.338	1.736		
PROIL2	0.600	0.244	0.123	0.737	
PERIL	0.629	0.573	0.267	0.104	0.477
PUBASST	-0.140	-0.297	-0.005	0.002	0.054
STREXT	0.164	0.001	-0.029	0.027	0.004
STRINT	-0.013	-0.036	0.240	0.030	0.059
BKOPEXT	0.136	0.104	-0.001	0.061	0.008
BKOPINT	-0.143	-0.120	-0.018	-0.010	0.013
CHLEGIT	0.062	-0.031	-0.014	0.074	0.026
CHLEGIT2	0.022	-0.017	-0.022	0.059	0.009
CDELVAL	0.231	0.301	0.213	0.061	0.107
CDELVAL2	0.211	0.273	0.181	0.070	0.104
CDRUGACC	0.777	0.834	0.451	0.252	0.269
CDELXILL	0.138	0.171	0.131	0.028	0.113
CDL2XILL	0.097	0.170	0.123	0.016	0.104
PEERDELD	0.518	0.612	0.379	0.115	0.223
CFAMINV	-0.121	-0.340	-0.162	-0.208	0.020

	PUBASST	STREXT	STRINT	BKOPEXT	BKOPINT	CHLEGIT
PUBASST	1.000					
STREXT	0.148	0.447				
STRINT	0.065	-0.237	0.749			
BKOPEXT	0.083	0.346	-0.267	0.406		
BKOPINT	0.110	-0.243	0.242	-0.275	0.499	
CHLEGIT	0.047	-0.049	-0.005	-0.025	0.037	0.135
CHLEGIT2	0.020	-0.036	-0.041	-0.011	0.010	0.110
CDELVAL	0.036	0.035	0.034	0.042	0.033	0.057
CDELVAL2	0.047	0.025	0.045	0.047	0.036	0.070
CDRUGACC	-0.079	0.037	0.073	0.039	-0.150	0.046
CDELXILL	0.014	-0.063	0.055	-0.056	0.134	-0.013
CDL2XILL	0.014	-0.066	0.057	-0.047	0.114	-0.013
PEERDELD	0.062	0.034	0.071	0.039	0.011	0.033
CFAMINV	0.244	-0.123	-0.028	-0.138	-0.042	-0.033

	CHLEGIT2	CDELVAL	CDELVAL2	CDRUGACC	CDELXILL	CDL2XILL
CHLEGIT2	0.109					
CDELVAL	0.046	0.283				
CDELVAL2	0.054	0.257	0.262			
CDRUGACC	0.012	0.165	0.173	1.179		
CDELXILL	-0.017	0.055	0.029	-0.061	0.373	
CDL2XILL	-0.015	0.029	0.019	-0.047	0.336	0.338
PEERDELD	0.027	0.174	0.174	0.350	0.071	0.072
CFAMINV	-0.036	-0.153	-0.138	-0.046	-0.049	-0.037

	PEERDELD	CFAMINV
PEERDELD	0.402	
CFAMINV	-0.081	1.669

ROCHESTER YOUTH DEVELOPMENT STUDY
TOTAL MALE SAMPLE (N=573)

	S89GENIL	S89ALCIL	S89DRUIL	S89PROL2	S89PERIL
S89GENIL	3.026				
S89ALCIL	1.405	2.636			
S89DRUIL	1.315	1.584	2.407		
S89PROL2	0.447	0.281	0.318	0.338	
S89PERIL	0.775	0.419	0.395	0.143	0.517
PUBASST	0.052	0.035	0.046	0.016	0.063
LOWERCL	-0.016	0.045	0.004	0.002	0.014
STREXT	0.225	0.274	0.356	0.093	0.038
STRINT	-0.010	-0.003	-0.054	-0.001	0.009
CHLEGIT	0.036	0.063	0.077	0.016	0.001
CDELVAL	0.246	0.264	0.217	0.046	0.085

	S89GENIL	S89ALCIL	S89DRUIL	S89PROL2	S89PERIL
CDRUGACC	0.429	0.396	0.336	0.065	0.140
CDELXILL	0.029	0.010	0.037	0.001	0.020
PEERDELD	0.352	0.269	0.287	0.064	0.122
CFAMINV	-0.136	-0.010	-0.115	-0.030	-0.034

	PUBASST	LOWERCL	STREXT	STRINT	CHLEGIT	CDELVAL
PUBASST	1.000					
LOWERCL	1.000	1.000				
STREXT	0.142	0.134	0.674			
STRINT	0.089	0.083	-0.350	0.896		
CHLEGIT	-0.080	-0.090	0.030	-0.126	0.255	
CDELVAL	0.111	0.028	0.072	-0.070	0.082	0.208
CDRUGACC	-0.062	-0.088	0.056	0.051	0.001	0.109
CDELXILL	0.159	0.147	0.026	-0.021	-0.005	0.023
PEERDELD	-0.039	-0.054	0.052	-0.026	0.043	0.097
CFAMINV	0.058	0.071	-0.076	0.049	-0.088	-0.044

	CDRUGACC	CDELXILL	PEERDELD	CFAMINV
CDRUGACC	0.942			
CDELXILL	-0.145	0.181		
PEERDELD	0.158	0.015	0.262	
CFAMINV	-0.037	0.011	-0.057	0.568

ROCHESTER YOUTH DEVELOPMENT STUDY
LATINO MALES (N=91)

	S89GENIL	S89ALCIL	S89DRUIL	S89PROL2	S89PERIL
S89GENIL	2.897				
S89ALCIL	1.521	2.964			
S89DRUIL	0.975	1.147	1.811		
S89PROL2	0.666	0.380	0.405	0.509	
S89PERIL	0.694	0.497	0.271	0.151	0.420
PUBASST	0.083	-0.098	0.292	-0.130	0.100
LOWERCL	0.168	0.151	0.365	-0.071	0.156
STREXT	0.334	0.528	0.617	0.248	0.045
STRINT	-0.051	-0.176	-0.258	0.022	0.067
CHLEGIT	-0.034	-0.080	0.052	-0.036	-0.074
CDELVAL	0.189	0.337	0.167	0.023	0.063
CDRUGACC	0.253	0.572	0.174	0.073	0.106
CDELXILL	0.138	0.200	-0.043	0.051	0.145
PEERDELD	0.268	0.126	0.267	-0.071	-0.061
CFAMINV	-0.046	0.094	-0.086	0.006	0.035

	PUBASST	LOWERCL	STREXT	STRINT	CHLEGIT	CDELVAL
PUBASST	1.000					
LOWERCL	1.000	1.000				
STREXT	0.043	0.198	1.287			
STRINT	-0.134	-0.206	-0.512	0.872		
CHLEGIT	0.188	0.212	0.027	-0.123	0.308	
CDELVAL	0.219	0.204	0.108	-0.085	0.096	0.242
CDRUGACC	-0.161	-0.200	0.055	-0.019	0.019	0.140
CDELXILL	0.138	0.091	0.034	0.108	-0.142	0.041
PEERDELD	0.373	0.405	0.032	-0.201	0.207	0.129
CFAMINV	-0.293	-0.181	-0.061	0.013	-0.092	-0.047

	CDRUGACC	CDELXILL	PEERDELD	CFAMINV
CDRUGACC	0.828			
CDELXILL	-0.140	0.392		
PEERDELD	0.114	-0.244	0.638	
CFAMINV	-0.018	0.031	-0.127	0.387

ROCHESTER YOUTH DEVELOPMENT STUDY
WHITE MALES (N=172)

	S89GENIL	S89ALCIL	S89DRUIL	S89PROL2	S89PERIL
S89GENIL	2.199				
S89ALCIL	1.046	2.286			
S89DRUIL	1.436	1.393	2.711		
S89PROL2	0.349	0.238	0.424	0.240	
S89PERIL	0.420	0.193	0.336	0.066	0.240
PUBASST	0.016	0.104	-0.048	-0.117	-0.152
LOWERCL	-0.062	0.024	-0.134	-0.204	-0.173
STREXT	0.488	0.370	0.660	0.180	0.140
STRINT	-0.253	-0.260	-0.331	-0.067	-0.061
CHLEGIT	0.075	0.105	0.154	0.041	0.024
CDELVAL	0.273	0.245	0.243	0.065	0.059
CDRUGACC	0.375	0.267	0.470	0.105	0.077
CDELXILL	0.021	0.022	0.027	0.018	0.004
PEERDELD	0.274	0.227	0.352	0.097	0.070
CFAMINV	-0.060	0.180	-0.129	-0.084	-0.016

	PUBASST	LOWERCL	STREXT	STRINT	CHLEGIT	CDELVAL
PUBASST	1.000					
LOWERCL	0.998	1.000				
STREXT	0.035	-0.060	0.603			
STREXT	0.260	0.175	-0.214	0.619		
CHLEGIT	-0.168	-0.162	0.043	-0.138	0.235	
CDELVAL	0.078	-0.091	0.106	-0.064	0.093	0.171

	PUBASST	LOWERCL	STREXT	STRINT	CHLEGIT	CDELVAL
CDRUGACC	0.102	-0.073	0.177	-0.067	0.078	0.120
CDELXILL	-0.224	-0.115	0.046	-0.016	-0.016	-0.033
PEERDELD	-0.149	-0.064	0.131	-0.069	0.075	0.084
CFAMINV	-0.030	-0.064	-0.037	-0.036	-0.027	-0.024

	CDRUGACC	CDELXILL	PEERDELD	CFAMINV
CDRUGACC	0.800			
CDELXILL	-0.075	0.131		
PEERDELD	0.145	-0.007	0.162	
CFAMINV	-0.063	0.045	-0.053	0.566

ROCHESTER YOUTH DEVELOPMENT STUDY
AFRICAN AMERICAN MALES (N=310)

	S89GENIL	S89ALCIL	S89DRUIL	S89PROL2	S89PERIL
S89GENIL	3.076				
S89ALCIL	1.341	2.674			
S89DRUIL	1.113	1.752	2.266		
S89PROL2	0.503	0.285	0.247	0.373	
S89PERIL	0.962	0.514	0.439	0.233	0.695
PUBASST	-0.081	0.015	0.042	0.057	-0.085
LOWERCL	-0.201	-0.015	0.007	0.038	-0.174
STREXT	0.033	0.127	0.102	-0.007	-0.021
STREXT	0.107	0.256	0.194	0.057	0.037
CHLEGIT	0.111	0.115	0.076	0.000	0.033
CDELVAL	0.176	0.223	0.179	0.042	0.085
CDRUGACC	0.364	0.405	0.256	0.039	0.144
CDELXILL	-0.023	-0.052	0.023	0.005	0.000
PEERDELD	0.333	0.305	0.243	0.064	0.147
CFAMINV	-0.151	-0.122	-0.132	-0.007	-0.075

	PUBASST	LOWERCL	STREXT	STRINT	CHLEGIT	CDELVAL
PUBASST	1.000					
LOWERCL	1.000	1.000				
STREXT	0.275	0.253	0.451			
STRINT	-0.112	-0.100	-0.296	0.969		
CHLEGIT	0.084	0.072	0.009	-0.036	0.253	
CDELVAL	0.113	0.042	0.027	-0.048	0.065	0.207
CDRUGACC	-0.210	-0.193	-0.010	0.074	-0.017	0.095
CDELXILL	0.213	0.185	0.023	-0.013	0.005	0.037
PEERDELD	-0.099	-0.157	0.019	0.066	0.078	0.070
CFAMINV	0.031	0.031	-0.100	0.096	-0.099	-0.048

	CDRUGACC	CDELXILL	PEERDELD	CFAMINV
CDRUGACC	1.033			
CDELXILL	-0.217	0.210		
PEERDELD	0.150	0.008	0.244	
CFAMINV	-0.075	0.013	-0.042	0.606

Causal Models Estimated in LISREL by Ethnicity

Traditional Strain Model by Ethnicity - Constraining All Paths to be Equal (Model 1)

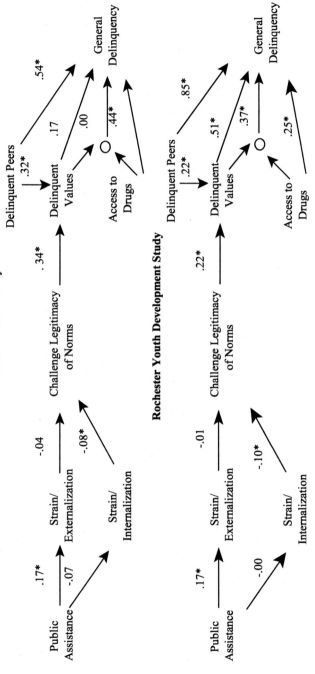

Denver Youth Survey

Rochester Youth Development Study

*p<.05 (one-tail test)

Traditional Strain Model by Ethnicity - Allowing Hypothesized Paths to Vary (Model 2)
Denver Youth Survey

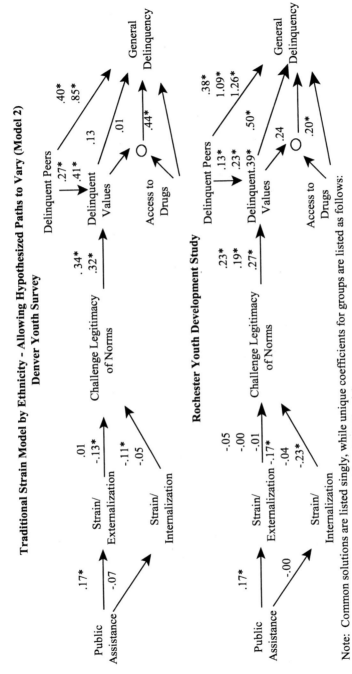

Rochester Youth Development Study

Note: Common solutions are listed singly, while unique coefficients for groups are listed as follows:
Latinos, African Americans, Whites (RYDS only)

*p<.05 (one-tail test)

Traditional Strain Model by Ethnicity - Allowing <u>All</u> Paths to Vary (Model 3)
Denver Youth Survey

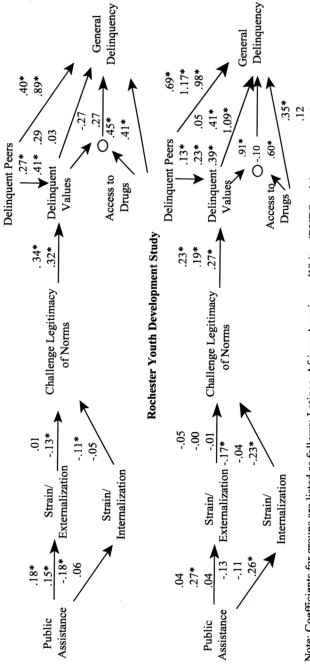

Note: Coefficients for groups are listed as follows: Latinos, African Americans, Whites (RYDS only)
*p<.05 (one-tail test)

References

Agnew, R. 1992. Foundation for a General Strain Theory of Crime and Delinquency. *Criminology*, 30:47-87.

Agnew, R. 1994. Delinquency and the desire for money. *Justice Quarterly*, 11:411-427.

Agnew, R., Cullen, F. T., Burton, V. S., Evans, T. D., & Dunaway, R. G. 1996. A new test of classic strain theory. *Justice Quarterly*, 13:681-704.

Aguirre, A., & Turner, J. H. 1995. *American Ethnicity: The Dynamics and Consequences of Discrimination.* New York: McGraw-Hill.

Aiken, L. S., & West S. G. 1991. *Multiple Regression: testing and interpreting interactions.* Newbury Park: Sage Publications.

Akers, R. L. 1994. *Criminological Theories: Introduction and Evaluation.* Los Angeles: Roxbury Publishing Company.

Amey, C.H., & Albrecht, S.L. 1998. Race and ethnic differences in adolescent drug use: the impact of family structure and the quantity and quality of parental interaction. *Journal of Drug Issues*, 28:283-298.

Bean, F. D., & Tienda, M. 1987. *The Hispanic Population of the United States.* New York: Russell Sage Foundation.

Bentler, P. M., & Chou, C. P.(1987). Practical issues in structural equation modeling. *Sociological Methods and Research,* 16:78-117.

Berger, P. L. 1963. *Invitation to Sociology: A Humanistic Perspective.* Garden City: Doubleday & Company, Inc.

Bernard, T. J. 1984. Control criticisms of strain theories: an assessment of theoretical and empirical adequacy. *Journal of Research in Crime and Delinquency*, 21:353-372.

Blea, I. I. 1988. *Toward a Chicano Social Science.* New York: Praeger Publishers.

Bollen, K. A. (1989). *Structural Equations with Latent Variables.* New York: John Wiley & Sons.

Brook, J. S., Whiteman, M., Balka, E. B., & Hamburg, B. A. 1992. African-American and Puerto Rican drug use: Personality, familial, and other environmental risk factors. *Genetic, Social, and General Psychology Monographs*, 118:417-438.

Bullington, B. 1977. *Heroin Use in the Barrio.* Lexington: Lexington Books.

Burton, V. S., & Cullen, F. T. 1992. The empirical status of strain theory. *Journal of Crime and Justice*, 15:1-30.

Burton, V. S., Cullen, F. T., Evans, D., & Dunaway, R. G. 1994. Reconsidering strain theory: Operationalization, rival theories and adult criminality. *Journal of Quantitative Criminology*, 10:213-239.

Chavez, L. 1991. *Out of the Barrio: Toward a New Politics of Hispanic Assimilation.* New York: Basic Books.

Clark, J. P.; & Wenniger, E. P. 1963. Goal orientations and illegal behavior among juveniles. *Social Forces,* 41:49-59

Cloward, R. A. 1959. Illegitimate means, anomie, and deviant behavior. *American Sociological Review*, 24:164-176.

Cloward, R. A., & Ohlin, L. E. 1960. *Delinquency and Opportunity.* New York: The Free Press.

Cohen, A. K. 1955. *Delinquent Boys: The Culture of the Gang.* New York: The Free Press.

Covey, H. C., Menard, S., & Franzese, R. J. 1992. *Juvenile Gangs.* Springfield: Charles C.Thomas Publisher.

Cullen, F.T. 1988. Were Cloward and Ohlin strain theorists? Delinquency and opportunity revisited. *Journal of Research in Crime and Delinquency,* 25:214-241.

Curry, G.D., & Spergel, I.A. 1992. Gang involvement and delinquency among Hispanic and African-American adolescent males. *Journal of Research in Crime and Delinquency,* 29:273-291.

Del Pinal, J., & Singer, A. 1997. *Generations of Diversity: Latinos in the United States.* Population Bulletin, Volume 52, Number 3. Washington, DC: Population Reference Bureau, Inc.

Elliott, D. S. 1962. Delinquency and perceived opportunity. *Sociological Inquiry,* 32:216-227.

Elliott, D. S., Huizinga, D., & Ageton, S. S. 1985. *Explaining Delinquency and Drug Use.* Beverly Hills: Sage Publications.

Elliott, D. S., & Voss, H. L. 1974. *Delinquency and Dropout.* Lexington: Lexington Books.

Esbensen, F. & Huizinga, D. 1991. Community Structure and Drug Use: from a social disorganization perspective. *Justice Quarterly,* 7:691-709.

Farnworth, M., & Leiber, M. J. 1989. Strain theory revisited: Economic goals, educational means, and delinquency. *American Sociological Review,* 54:263-274.

Farnworth, M., Thornberry, T. P., Lizotte, A. J., and Krohn, M. D. 1991. Sampling design and implementation. *Technical Report Number 1.* Albany: University at Albany.

Flowers, R. B. 1988. *Minorities and Criminality* (Contributions in Criminology and Penology, Vol. Number 21). Westport:Greenwood Press.

Freud, S. 1930. *Civilization and its Discontents.* New York: W. W. Norton & Company.

Gil, A.G., Vega, W.A., & Biafora, F. 1998. Temporal influences of family structure and family risk factors on drug use initiation in a multiethnic sample of adolescent boys. *Journal of Youth andAdolescence*, 27:373-393.

Greenberg, D. F. 1999. The weak strength of social control theory. *Crime & Delinquency*, 45:66-81.

Hawkins, D. F. 1995. *Ethnicity, Race, and Crime: Perspectives across time and place.* Albany: State University of New York Press.

Hayduk, L. A. (1987). *Structural Equation Modeling with LISREL.* Baltimore: Johns Hopkins University Press.

Heller, C. S. 1971. *New Converts to the American Dream? Mobility Aspirations of Young Mexican Americans.* New Haven: College & University Press Services, Inc.

Hirschi, T. 1969. *Causes of Delinquency.* Berkeley: University of California Press.

Hoffman, J. P., & Ireland, T. O. 1995. Cloward and Ohlin's strain theory reexamined: an elaborated theoretical model. In Adler, F. and Laufer, W. S. (Eds.) *The Legacy of Anomie Theory.* New Brunswick: Transaction Publishers.

Horowitz, R. 1983. *Honor and the American Dream: Culture and Identity in a Chicano Community.* New Brunswick: Rutgers University Press.

Hochschild, J. L. 1995. *Facing Up to the American Dream: Race, Class, and the Soul of the Nation.* Princeton: Princeton University Press.

Hoyle, R. H., & Panter, A. T. (1995). Writing about structural equation models. In Hoyle, R. H. (Ed.), *Structural Equation Modeling: Concepts, Issues, and Applications.* Newbury Park: Sage Publications.

Hu, L., & Bentler, P. M. (1995). Evaluating model fit. In Hoyle, R. H. (Ed.), *Structural Equation Modeling: Concepts, Issues, and Applications.* Newbury Park: Sage Publications.

Huizinga, D., Loeber, R., & Thornberry, T. P. 1993a. *Urban Delinquency and Substance Abuse: Technical Report.* Prepared for the Office of Juvenile Justice and Delinquency Prevention, U.S. Department of Justice.

Huizinga, D., Loeber, R., & Thornberry, T. P. 1993b. Longitudinal study of delinquency, drug use, sexual activity, and pregnancy among children and youth in three cities. *Public Health Reports,* 108:90-96.

Huizinga, D., Loeber, R., & Thornberry, T. P. 1994. *Urban Delinquency and Substance Abuse: Initial findings.* Prepared for the Office of Juvenile Justice and Delinquency Prevention, U.S. Department of Justice.

Ireland, T. O. 1996. *Elaborated Strain Theory: Building and Testing an Individual-level Theory of Delinquent Behavior.* Unpublished Ph.D. Dissertation, University at Albany.

Jaccard, J., Turrisi, R. & Wan, C. K. 1990. *Interaction Effects in Multiple Regression.* Newbury Park: Sage Publications.

Jaccard, J., & Wan, C. K. (1996). *LISREL approaches to interaction effects in multiple regression*. (Sage University Paper series on Quantitative Applications in the Social Sciences, 07-114). Thousand Oaks: Sage Publications.

Jensen, G. F. 1995. Salvaging structure through strain: a theoretical and empirical critique. In Adler, F. and Laufer, W. S. (Eds.) *The Legacy of Anomie Theory*. New Brunswick: Transaction Publishers.

Jessor, R., Graves, T. D., Hanson, R. C., & Jessor, S. J. 1968. *Society, Personality, and Deviant Behavior: A Study of a Tri-ethnic Community*. New York: Holt, Rinehart and Winston, Inc.

Kelloway, E. K. (1998). *Using LISREL for Structural Equation Modeling*. Newbury Park: Sage Publications.

Kornhauser, R. R. 1978. *Social Sources of Delinquency: An appraisal of analytic models*. Chicago: University of Chicago Press.

Krohn, M. D., & Thornberry, T. P. 1993. Network Theory: A model for understanding drug abuse among African-American and Hispanic youth. Pp. 102-128 in M. R. De La Rosa & Juan-L. Recio Adrados (Eds.), *Drug Abuse Among Minority Youth: Advances in Research and Methodology*, NIDA Research Monograph 130, U.S. Department of Heath and Human Services.

Krohn, M. D., & Thornberry, T. P. 1999. Retention of Minority Populations in Panel Studies of Drug Use. *Drugs & Society*, 14:185-207.

Liska, A. E. 1971. Aspirations, expectations, and delinquency: Stress and additive models. *Sociological Quarterly,* 12:99-107.

Mann, C. R. 1995. The contribution of institutionalized racism to minority crime. In Hawkins, D. F. (Ed.), *Ethnicity, Race, and Crime: Perspectives Across Time and Place*. Albany: State University of New York Press.

Marín, G., & Marín, B. V. (1991). *Research with Hispanic Populations*. Newbury Park: Sage Publications.

McMillen, M. M. & Kaufman, P. 1997. *Dropout Rates in the United States: 1996.* Washington, DC: National Center for Education Statistics.

Menard, S. 1995. A developmental test of Mertonian anomie theory. *Journal of Research in Crime and Delinquency,* 32:136-174.

Merton, R. K. 1938. Social Structure and Anomie. *American Sociological Review,* 3:672-682.

Merton, R. K. 1957. *Social Theory and Social Structure.* New York: The Free Press.

Merton, R. K. 1968. *Social Theory and Social Structure.* New York: The Free Press.

Mirandé, A. 1985. *The Chicano Experience: An Alternative Perspective.* Notre Dame: University of Notre Dame Press.

Mirandé, A. 1987. *Gringo Justice.* Notre Dame: University of Notre Dame Press.

Moore, J. W. 1978. *Homeboys: Gangs, Drugs and Prison in the Barrios of Los Angeles.* Philadelphia: Temple University Press.

Moore, J.W. 1991. *Going Down to the Barrio: Homeboys and Homegirls in Change.* Philadelphia: Temple University Press.

Moore, J. W., & Pachon, H. 1985. *Hispanics in the United States.* Englewood Cliffs: Prentice-Hall, Inc.

Murguia, E., Chen, Z., & Kaplan, H.B. 1998. A comparison of causal factors in drug use among Mexican Americans and Non-Hispanic Whites. *Social Science Quarterly,* 79:341-360.

Nettler, G. 1974. *Explaining Crime.* New York: McGraw-Hill Book Company.

Oboler, S. 1995. *Ethnic Labels, Latino Lives: Identity and the Politics of (re) Presentation in the United States.* Minneapolis: University of Minnesota Press

Pabon, E. 1998. Hispanic adolescent delinquency and the family: a discussion of sociocultural influences. *Adolescence,* 33:941-955.

Padilla, F. M. 1993. The quest for community: Puerto Ricans in Chicago. In Moore, J. W. & Pinderhughes, R. (Eds.) *In the Barrios: Latinos and the Underclass Debate.* New York: Russell Sage Foundation.

Perez y Gonzalez, M. E. 1993. *The Relationship Between Acculturation and Juvenile Delinquency Among Puerto Rican Male Adolescents in the South Bronx, New York City.* Unpublished Ph.D. Dissertation, Fordham University.

Peterson, G.E., & Harrell, A. V. 1992. Introduction: Inner-city isolation and opportunity. In Harrell, A. V. & Peterson, G. E. (Eds.) *Drugs, Crime, and Social Isolation: Barriers to Urban Opportunity.* Washington, D.C.: The Urban Institute Press.

Quicker, J. C. 1974. The effect of goal discrepancy on delinquency. *Social Problems,* 22:76-86.

Rebach, H. 1992. Alcohol Use Among American Minorities. In J. S. Trimble, C. S. Bolek, & S. J. Niemcryk (Eds.), *Ethnic and Multicultural Drug Abuse: Perspectives on Current Research.* New York: The Haworth Press, Inc.

Reddy, M. A. (Ed.). 1993. *Statistical Record of Hispanic Americans.* Detroit: Gale Research, Inc.

Rodriguez, O., & Recio, Juan-L. 1992. The Applicability of the Integrated Social Control Model to Puerto Rican Drug Use. *Journal of Crime and Justice,* 15:1-32.

Rodriguez, O., & Weisburd, D. 1991. The Integrated Social Control Model and Ethnicity: The Case of Puerto Rican American Delinquency. *Criminal Justice and Behavior*, 18:464-479.

Rodriguez, O., & Zayas, L. H. 1990. Hispanic adolescents and antisocial behavior: Sociocultural factors and treatment implications. In Stiffman, A. R., & Davis, L. E. (Eds.) *Ethnic Issues in Adolescent Mental Health*. Newbury Park: Sage Publications.

Romero, L. M.., & Stelzner, L. G. 1985. Hispanics and the Criminal Justice System. In Cafferty, P. S. & McCready, W. C. (Eds.) *Hispanics in the United States: A New Social Agenda*. New Brunswick: Transaction Books.

Rowe, D. C., Vazsonyi, A. T., & Flannery, D. J. 1994. No more than skin deep: Ethnic and racial similarity in developmental process. *Psychological Review*, 101:396-413.

Short, J. F. 1964. Gang delinquency and anomie. In Clinard, M.B. (Ed.) *Anomie and Deviant Behavior*. New York: The Free Press.

Short, J. F., & Strodtbeck, F. L. 1965. *Group Process and Gang Delinquency*. Chicago: The University of Chicago Press.

Simons, R. L., & Gray, P. A. 1989. Perceived Blocked Opportunity as an Explanation of Delinquency among Lower-Class Black Males: A Research Note. *Journal of Research in Crime and Delinquency*, 26:90-101.

Smith, C. A. 1990. *Delinquency and Family Life: The Role of Ethnicity and Environment*. Unpublished Ph.D. Dissertation, State University of New York.

Smith, C. A., & Krohn, M. D. 1995. Delinquency and family life among male adolescents: The role of ethnicity. *Journal of Youth and Adolescence*, 24:69-93.

Sommers, I., Fagan, J., & Baskin, D. 1993. Sociocultural Influences on the Explanation of Delinquency for Puerto Rican Youths. *Hispanic Journal of Behavioral Sciences*, 15:36-62.

Sommers, I., Fagan, J., Baskin, D. 1994. The influence of acculturation and familism on Puerto Rican delinquency. *Justice Quarterly*, 11:207-228.

Sowell, T. 1981. *Ethnic America: A History*. New York: Basic Books, Inc.

Stinchcombe, A. L. 1964. *Rebellion in a High School*. Chicago: Quadrangle Books.

Sullivan, M. L. 1989. *Getting Paid: Youth Crime and Work in the Inner City*. Ithaca: Cornell University Press.

Sutherland, E. H. 1947. *Principles of Criminology* 4th ed. Philadelphia: Lippincott.

Valdez, E.O. 1996. Chicano families and urban poverty: Familial strategies of cultural retention. In Roberto M. De Anda (Ed.) *Chicanas and Chicanos in Contemporary Society*. Boston: Allyn & Bacon.

Valenzuela, A., & Dornbusch, S. M. 1996. Familism and assimilation among Mexican-origin and Anglo high school students. In De Anda, R. M. (Ed.), *Chicanas and Chicanos in Contemporary Society*. Boston: Allyn and Bacon.

Vazsonyi, A. T., & Flannery, D. J. 1997. Early adolescent delinquent behaviors: associations with family and school domains. *Journal of Early Adolescence*, 17: 271-293.

Vigil, J. D. 1988. *Barrio Gangs: Street Life and Identity in Southern California*. Austin: University of Texas Press.

Walker, S., Spohn, C., & DeLone, M. 1996. *The Color of Justice: Race, Ethnicity, and Crime in America*. Belmont: Wadsworth Publishing Company.

Weber, L. R., Miracle, A., & Skehan, T. 1995. Family bonding and delinquency: racial and ethnic influences among U.S. youth. *Human Organization*, 54:363-372.

West, C. 1993. *Race Matters*. New York: Vintage Books.

West, S. G., Aiken, L. S., & Krull, J. L. 1996. Experimental personality designs: analyzing categorical by continuous variable interactions. *Journal of Personality*, 64:1-48.

Williams, N. 1990. *The Mexican American Family: Tradition and Change*. New York: General Hall, Inc.

Wilson, W. J. 1984. The Urban Underclass. In L. W. Dunbar (Ed.) *Minority Report: What has happened to blacks, Hispanics, American Indians, and Other Minorities in the Eighties*. New York: Pantheon Books.

Wirth, L. 1945. The problem of minority groups. In Linton, R. (Ed.) *The Science of Man in the World Crisis*. New York: Columbia University Press.

Index